THE SLEAZE MERCHANTS

Other Books by John McCarty

Nonfiction

Hollywood Gangland: The Movies' Love Affair with the Mob

Movie Psychos and Madmen: Film Psychopaths from Jekyll and Hyde to Hannibal Lecter

Thrillers: Seven Decades of Classic Film Suspense

The Modern Horror Film: 50 Contemporary Classics

The Complete Films of John Huston

John McCarty's Official Splatter Movie Guide, Vols. I and II

Splatter Movies: Breaking the Last Taboo of the Screen

Alfred Hitchcock Presents (with Brian Kelleher)

The Little Shop of Horrors Book (with Mark Thomas McGee)

The Amazing Herschell Gordon Lewis and His World of Exploitation Film (with Daniel Krogh)

You're on Open Line: Inside the Wacky World of Late-Night Talk Radio

Fiction

Deadly Resurrection

Anthologies

The Fearmakers: The Screen's Directorial Masters of Suspense and Terror

THE SLEAZE MERCHANTS

ADVENTURES IN EXPLOITATION FILMMAKING

EDITED BY

John McCarty

ST. MARTIN'S GRIFFIN NEW YORK

THE SLEAZE MERCHANTS: ADVENTURES IN EXPLOITATION FILMMAKING. Copyright © 1995 by John McCarty.

Design by Jaye Zimet
Layout by MM Design 2000, Inc.

Library of Congress Cataloging-in-Publication Data

McCarty, John.
    The sleaze merchants: adventures in exploitation filmmaking/
John McCarty.
        p.   cm.
    ISBN 0-312-11893-7
    1. Motion picture directors and producers—United States.
2. Sensationalism in motion pictures.   3. Low-budget motion pictures.   I. Title.
PN1998.2.M42   1995
791.43'0233'092273—dc20   94-41159
                                                                CIP

First St. Martin's Griffin Edition: March 1995
10 9 8 7 6 5 4 3 2 1

Contents

Acknowledgments

n behalf of myself and my contributors, I would like to thank the following individuals and organizations for their respective courtesies and help in providing this glimpse into the offbeat, always strapped for cash, alternately desperate and howlingly funny, and sometimes inspiring world of the exploitation filmmaker: Eric J. Caidin; David DeCoteau; David F. Friedman; Walter L. Gay; Bruce G. Hallenbeck; Ken Hanke; Herschell Gordon Lewis; William Lustig; Bret McCormick; Ted V. Mikels; Brett Piper; Fred Olen Ray; Jim Wynorski; Hollywood Book & Poster; Linda Rauh of Film Favorites; Mike Accomando of Dreadful Pleasures; Matthew R. Bradley; Bill George; Trevor Paul; and Gordon Van Gelder of St. Martin's Press. And a word of special thanks to Dan Krogh for the use of some of his material in the Herschell Gordon Lewis chapter.

Introduction

In 1949, the major studios were forced by law to divest themselves of their theater chains, thus ending their long-standing monopoly over every aspect of the motion-picture business from production through distribution and exhibition. The nation's movie screens suddenly became fair game.

Now on their own most exhibitors continued to prefer major studio product over foreign and independently made films, but the growing popularity of a new medium—*free* television—prompted the major studios to cut back severely on the number of films they produced each year. In one of the fastest maturation periods in entertainment history, the infant medium of television grew up almost overnight—at least in terms of audience size—and by the mid-1950s had killed off the staple Hollywood B movie, thus sounding the death knell for the traditional double feature as well. Very soon there just weren't enough films available to fill the nation's indoor and growing number of outdoor movie theaters, especially since it was the custom back then to change marquees not every couple of weeks (as is typically the case today), but often *three times a week*.

And so, a new breed of movie mogul—albeit not a new breed of *moviemaker*—stepped in to plug the gap: the exploiteers, or as one of their own, David F. Friedman, has dubbed them: "The circulating salesmen of cinema sleaze." It's a description I like and have altered slightly for the title of this book because I feel it captures in amusing and noncondemnatory fashion what these folks and their films were—and are—all about.

It's easy—but not at all fair in some instances—just to dismiss the work of the sleaze merchants as "trash" aimed at the "lowest common denominator" of the moviegoing public, and therefore not worth preserving, let alone writing about. But that approach, I believe, misses what is, perhaps, the single most important point about these filmmakers, and the most valuable lesson to be learned from their exploits: They *loved* making movies, having discovered that the real fun of moviemaking, the *exhilaration* of it, lay not in the deal or the dough, nor even in the quality of what is achieved, but in the simple acting of *doing*.

In this sense, the sleaze merchants remind us of the pioneers who picked up the movie business by its bootstraps during the early years of this century. Their shoot-from-the-hip style recalls for us that long-ago era when the movies were still young. This may explain why, today, there is such interest in exploitation films and filmmakers among younger moviegoers—and, especially, among young moviemaking hopefuls, who perhaps see in the do-it-yourself, never-say-die sagas of the sleaze merchants a reason to take heart: "Hey, maybe I'll never achieve the success of a Steven Spielberg, but maybe I could be a Herschell Gordon Lewis, and I might have a helluva lot more fun."

Working on paltry budgets (especially when

compared with the increasingly huge amounts of cash the major studios lavished on their own productions), and yet competing for the same customer's hard-earned buck, the sleaze merchants had to be shrewd showmen first and foremost. To win theater space away from the major studios and draw an audience successfully, they had to be able to smell a trend before its aroma reached the rarefied air of Hollywood, or seize on a subject heretofore untouched by Hollywood due to the self-imposed restrictions of the Motion Picture Production Code by which the major studios continued to live. Then they had to be fast on their feet in exploiting that trend, or tackling that subject matter, by shooting their films and rushing them into distribution with almost lightning speed.

To date, no one has done this better, or with more acumen, than the fifteen sleaze merchants profiled in this book.

The tradition of exploitation filmmaking extends all the way back to the silent era when independent producers ground out pictures dealing with sensational subjects—poverty, race, drugs, prostitution, and so on—their Hollywood counterparts either considered beneath them or just too hot to handle. And somewhat later, men like Kroger Babb, the road-show genius behind the legendary birth-of-a-baby/sex hygiene opus, *Mom and Dad,* and Dwain Esper, the doyen of the drug drama (*Narcotic, Marijuana, Reefer Madness,* et al.), made their marks as well. But the *influence* of the sleaze merchants on the movie business itself is a relatively modern story, which is why this book focuses primarily on the activities of those grand masters, honorable practitioners, and young turks who made their appearance on the exploitation film scene in the 1940s and beyond.

The industry at large has learned much from them. As the walls of screen censorship began to crumble in the late 1960s, the major studios—now able to tackle taboo themes heretofore prohibited to them—did just that and began making big-budget exploitation films of their own geared toward a mainstream audience, a tactic that virtually dominates the movie industry today. The country's scores of independent exhibitors were replaced by a small number of conglomerate-owned theater chains that transformed the nation's movie palaces into multiscreen multiplexes installed in shopping malls that soon deposed the drive-in as the mecca for America's moviegoing youth and curiosity-seekers. These chains continued to prefer Hollywood product over the low-rent work of the sleaze merchants, but they could now have it both ways by offering the public films of the same sensational nature but with big-name stars. However, the advent of home video, which also contributed to the death of the drive-in and the independent "adults only" or "art house" theater, rescued the low-budget exploitation film from oblivion, and today home video remains the primary outlet for such films, both the "classics" and the new.

For all the fun they've had, it's clear that the fifteen sleaze merchants profiled herein have never had an easy time of it. But to paraphrase Bill Holden in *The Wild Bunch* (1969): They probably wouldn't have had it any other way. And that's part of this story, too.

They include:

Edward D. Wood, Jr., the subject of a recent multimillion dollar biopic directed by Tim Burton for Disney, whose penchant for angora sweaters and devotion to Bela Lugosi resulted in two of the most enduring trash-pics of all time, *Glen or Glenda* and *Plan 9 from Outer Space.*

Sam Katzman, the titan of tabloid who could rush a film into production inspired by the day's latest craze or most sensational headlines before the newsprint was even dry.

Herschell Gordon Lewis, the "Godfather of Gore," whose groundbreaking terror trilogy, *Blood Feast, 2000 Maniacs,* and *Color Me Blood Red,* altered the face of screen horror forever.

David F. Friedman, the carny king of soft-core and master of the alliterative ad line, who got 'em inside the theater to see the show by giving 'em most of the show outside.

John Waters, who went from shooting films on a shoestring in which characters eat pooch poop to working for Disney (in whose animal farm pooches *never* poop) without ever losing sight of his artistic ambition of giving bad taste a good name.

Jess Franco, the most prolific sleaze merchant in history, whose films, some say, belong in the garbage, but whose name, all say, belongs in *The Guinness Book of World Records.*

Fred Olen Ray—the heir apparent to AIP, Roger Corman, and just about everyone else who preceded him.

Jim Wynorski, whose trademark mixture of babes, boobs, and belly laughs—even in films where they don't belong—mark him as a long-distance runner in the game.

And many more.

Their profiles, presented in both essay or interview form, are arranged chronologically rather than alphabetically in order to give the reader a sense of how the arena of exploitation film has changed and developed in modern times. Selected filmographies are provided at the end of each profile so that fans and would-be sleaze merchants everywhere can search out most of the films with which each filmmaker has been involved in one capacity or another, either under his own name, or using a pseudonym.

Alternate titles of their work have also been provided as so many of these films have undergone *numerous* title changes over the years in an effort to attract new audiences. That's just *one* of the sleaze merchant's bag of carny tricks you will learn about: the old shell game.

But there are a lot more.

THE
Grand Masters

THE **MONSTER** and THE **GHOUL!**

One deals in wholesale murder . . . the other serves as a torture-master for the living dead! *See it and shudder!*

MONOGRAM PICTURES presents

Bela **LUGOSI** in

"BOWERY AT MIDNIGHT"

with *John* **ARCHER** *Wanda* **McKAY**

Bela Lugosi had one of the meatiest roles of his foundering career in Katzman's *Bowery at Midnight* (1942), a combination gangster and horror film. *(Courtesy Eric Caidin)*

Sam Katzman

BY KEN HANKE

Arguably no producer, or director, in the history of the movies so gloriously exemplifies the joys of exploitation cinema as the legendary Sam Katzman. From Bela Lugosi, the East Side Kids and Jungle Jim to Bill Haley and the Comets, country music superstar Hank Williams to the King of Rock 'n' Roll himself, Elvis Presley, Katzman made movies with or about 'em all in his remarkable four-decade career—a career highlighted by occasional bursts of astonishing creativity given his pitifully low budgets. Katzman made his movies with speed, economy, and a singular lack of concern for plot, logic, or production values. He also evidenced a sheer delight in the filmmaking process for its own sake, an often undervalued quality. As a result, his list of credits—*The Ape Man* (1943), *Voodoo Man* (1944), *Earth Vs. the Flying Saucers* (1956), *Rock Around the Clock* (1956), *The Giant Claw* (1957), and *The Zombies of Mora-Tau* (1957) among many, many others—reads almost like an index of the best of bad cinema.

Born in New York City in 1901, Katzman started out working as a prop boy at Fox Studios in Fort Lee, New Jersey, at the tender age of thirteen. He moved to California in 1924, where he held down a variety of jobs at several major and minor studios, and ascended to the role of independent producer by the time he was thirty-two. His first major accomplishment in this capacity was the serial *Shadow of Chinatown*, made for the low-rent production company Victory Pictures in 1936. The serial marked Katzman's first outing (of ten) with hard-up horror icon Bela Lugosi and boasted a vintage display of wild, woolly, dramatically dubious, and highly entertaining Katzmania. Lugosi plays the mad genius Victor Poten, a Eurasian inventor and crime czar who, according to the dialogue, "hates both the white and Oriental races," each of which he plans to wipe out and replace with a new race of his own creation. Just how he plans to do this is one of the many plot points the script conveniently ignores. But regardless of its narrative shortcomings, the film serves as an excellent introduction to the cinematic world of Sam Katzman with its impressive array of mad-scientist exotica: hypnotic powers, poison gases, a huge mechanical idol that Lugosi uses to crush his victims, and a remarkable device called a "tele-audient machine" that not only bugs whatever room it's placed in, but affords the eavesdropper an unrestricted and slickly edited, shot-by-shot view of the action being "tele-audienced."

Blake of Scotland Yard (1937) and several more serials followed, but it was in 1940 with Katzman's formation of Banner Productions (a subsidiary of Monogram Pictures) that he came into his own by tapping the Dead End Kids (whom he rechristened the East Side Kids) for a series of juvenile delinquency pictures, and acquiring the services of Lugosi for a series of lovably cheesy B horror flicks.

As dubious an acquisition as the East Side Kids may have been, Katzman boasts the distinction of having produced a run of films for them that were comic—at least initially—without being as utterly unrealistic as their later films as the Bowery Boys under producer Jan Grippo. The first, *East Side Kids* (1940), directed by *Shadow of Chinatown*'s Robert F. Hill, marked the start of the series, although the official launch began with the follow-up, *Boys of the City* (a.k.a. *The Ghost Creeps*, 1940), which reintroduced the characters played by Leo Gorcey and Huntz Hall, neither of whom had appeared in the first film. Katzman ground out two to four East Side Kids pictures a year until 1946 when the Kids underwent the transition to the Bowery Boys, then Katzman attempted to launch another youth-oriented series called "Teen Agers," but it proved short-lived.

At their best, the East Side Kids pictures are mindless fun, blessed with occasional outbursts of inspired lunacy, and a genuinely grubby feel of the slums that the later, more sanitized Bowery Boys films tended to downplay. But they pale against the still much-beloved Lugosi pictures Katzman was making at the same time.

By 1941, Lugosi's cinematic fortunes were at low ebb (they had been lower and would be lower still). The horror renaissance begun with *Son of Frankenstein* (1939) had quickly passed the once great star by. Universal Pictures still had him under "special contract," which, roughly translated, meant the studio was free to cast him in slightly inflated supporting parts for very little money and then promote the results as Bela Lugosi films! Enter the great Katzman with an alluring nine-picture contract that would allow Lugosi full-blown *acting* jobs. Never mind that the scripts often made little or no sense, had almost nonexistent budgets, and were slapped together in record time. They gave the thespian artist Lugosi a sense of purpose and accomplishment, for while he was seen by Universal as a character actor suitable only for thankless supporting roles, he was still a name star where Sam Katzman was concerned.

The first of the nine was *The Invisible Ghost* (1941), directed by Joseph H. Lewis, who had made several of the East Side Kids pictures and probably saw the Lugosi film as a somewhat meatier melodrama that offered him a chance to make his mark. In many respects, he did. For a B picture, *Invisible Ghost* is surprisingly elaborate and creative in its direction, which never fails to call attention to itself effectively, and is relatively free of technical and other gaffes.

This entry, however, was but a flash of lucidity in a tidal wave of nonsense to come. For true-blue Katzmania, we must turn to the second film in the Lugosi series, *Spooks Run Wild* (1941), a comic horror picture that pitted Lugosi against the East Side Kids.

This is a Sam Katzman production straight up. What plot there is—the East Side Kids go to summer camp where they get mixed up with magician Lugosi, whom they mistake for the "Monster Killer" terrorizing the countryside—makes very little sense, and the dialogue is wonderfully inane. For example, when one of the kids is shot at by an overzealous cemetery keeper, the sheriff offers the ludicrous assessment "He just used buckshot—he couldn't have hurt anyone bad!" There is also a high quotient of blown lines neither Katzman, nor director Phil Rosen saw fit to retake. The result is an unintentional laugh-a-thon like few others. And yet there is an undeniable atmosphere to some of the film's more unconnected moments as when Lugosi and similarly dressed, albeit dwarfish, sidekick Angelo Rossitto wander the corridors of the film's budget-conscious old dark house for no apparent reason, and a scene involving a wholly arbitrary visit to a cemetery. These scenes have a resonance the bulk of the film lacks; it's almost as if they were lifted from another project entirely, a project that may have been started then cancelled abruptly in mid-production, which is by no means an untenable theory given the frugal, never-let-any-footage-go-to-waste (even if it doesn't fit) style of producing Sam Katzman embodied.

Spooks Run Wild, however, is a model of intelligent filmmaking compared with its follow-up, *Black Dragons* (1942), which Lugosi described in a publicity item of the time as "the most frightening film" he'd ever made. Perhaps he was referring to the actual production of the film, since he surely could not have meant the nonstop smorgasbord of inanity that is the film itself.

Shot cheaply and in apparently more haste than the usual Katzman production, the film offers Lugosi as the mysterious Monsieur (with *that* accent?) Colomb, who is blissfully running around Washington, D.C., knocking off a group of Japanese saboteurs masquerading as American industrialists. We know from the onset that these boys are Axis spies, since they say things like, "I wish we could blow up more ammunition dumps before we have to leave." Remarkably slipshod and chock-full of overzealous canned music, *Black Dragons* also falls back on the use of stock footage, including some newsreel shots of the riots at Rudolph Valentino's funeral (which, presumably, was also the work of Japanese saboteurs). These flaws, of course, are the very reason why the film has achieved its magnificently well-earned reputation as a bona fide classic of *le bad cinema*. Perhaps Lugosi was right after all in "defying" the viewer to see this film.

The Corpse Vanishes and *Bowery at Midnight* (both 1942) were definite steps up (how could they not have been?). Helmed for Katzman with a remarkably cold-blooded attitude toward violence by Wallace Fox, although lacking the stylishness of *Invisible Ghost*, they are not inconsiderable little achievements which somehow work as horror thrillers, while not being especially more coherent or logical than any of the other films in the Katzman-Lugosi series.

Without question, *The Corpse Vanishes* is the lesser of the two vehicles, if only because it sticks most closely to the established horror film formula. (In fact, the scriptwriters toss in every cliché and plot convention of the genre imaginable, without even passing regard for suitability, or even believability.) Lugosi is Dr. Lorenz, a brilliant doctor who induces catatonia in young brides at the altar by presenting them with orchids that he has specially grown for just this nefarious purpose. He then steals their "corpses," spirits them to his subterranean laboratory, and extracts vital glandular fluids from them in order to keep his incredibly bitchy and foul-tempered wife perpetually young (well, moderately young anyway). It's a cushy little setup until plucky girl reporter Luana Walters gets wise to it and helps engineer his downfall. Until that happens, we are treated to an amazing array of singularly bizarre notions (to anyone but Ed Wood's pal Criswell, that is), such as Mr. and Mrs. Lugosi sharing twin coffins in their bedroom ("I find a coffin much more comfortable than a bed! Many people do so," he explains without volunteering who these "many people" might be!), and a climax with enough stabbings and stranglings to warm the heart of the most flamboyantly morbid composer of Italian opera. *The Corpse Vanishes* is undeniably one of the most outlandish of Katzman's pictures.

But *Bowery at Midnight* is even better—if only because it afforded Lugosi one of the meatiest roles of his career. He plays Dr. Brenner (alias Karl Wagner), a college sociology professor moonlighting as the kindly owner of a Bowery mission (in reality a front for his criminal activities). Realizing somewhat late that the film was supposed to be a horror picture not a gangster flick, the scriptwriters quickly inserted a drug-addicted mad doctor (Lew Kelly) and a basement cemetery (in reality the entrance to a subbasement full of Lugosi's victims, skillfully revived by the junkie medico!) into the proceedings. A wholly ludicrous idea? Of course, but it affords Lugosi the classically tasteless line, "Doc, how many times have I told you to keep that cat from desecrating my graves?"

Katzman's next outing, *The Ape Man* (1943), is probably the most famous and best loved of his Lugosi series, and quite possibly the most concentrated sixty-four minutes of sheer insanity ever committed to film by otherwise apparently rational human beings. There is, admittedly, a

Sheer insanity on celluloid, *The Ape Man* (1943) remains the most famous and best-loved film in Katzman's Lugosi series. *(Courtesy Eric Caidin)*

The Voodoo Man (1944), featuring George Zucco and Bela Lugosi, involves a screen-writer working for a producer referred to as "S.K.," who gets mixed up in a kidnapping and voodoo plot. *(Courtesy Eric Caidin)*

slight possibility that the whole affair was deliberately made tongue-in-cheek, but one tends to doubt it. This round, Lugosi is Dr. James Brewster, a noted scientist who has supposedly disappeared, but who, in reality, is squirreled away in the family mansion, owing to the fact that his experiments with "ape fluid injections" (whatever for is not explained) have turned him into the title character. A Katzman budget being a Katzman budget, Lugosi's makeup consists of an abundance of crepe hair stuck on him. He walks in a constantly stooped position, while his new-found simian tendencies are expressed (with typical Katzman logic) by having him cozy up in a cage with a bona fide gorilla (Emil Van Horn). Mayhem ensues when Lugosi hits upon the bright notion that injections of human spinal fluid might cure him—or at least improve his posture. So, Lugosi and the gorilla go on a rampage throughout the city, securing the precious fluid by killing people. Eventually, Lugosi's ape arbitrarily turns on him just in time to prevent heroine Louise Currie from feeling the sting of the hypodermic. None of this is made to seem even remotely credible, and in seeming acknowledgment of that fact, the scriptwriters and/or Katzman critique themselves by inserting a

character who is ultimately revealed as the author of the story, which he terms a "Screwy idea, wasn't it?" The effect is almost surreal.

It is best to pass over the tedious Lugosi–East Side Kids follow-up, *Ghosts on the Loose* (1943), in relative silence, except to note that it is the first film where Katzman actually worked his name into the dialogue. In a sequence where the boys try to get a police escort for the wedding of Huntz Hall's sister (played by a young Ava Gardner), they cook up a story about how "the Katzman mob" have threatened to sabotage the affair. In his next Lugosi romp, *The Voodoo Man* (1944), Katzman went himself one better by concocting a story revolving around a screenwriter for Banner Pictures (the name of Katzman's own production company) who becomes unwittingly involved in the kidnapping and voodoo ceremony antics of Messrs. Lugosi and Zucco. Moreover, the film manages to include two scenes actually set at Katzman's Banner Pictures studio where the writer encounters his boss, referred to as "S. K.," although the character is not played by the Great Man himself.

The on-screen Katzman and the possibility that *The Voodoo Man* is a true story aside, the film itself is, if anything, loopier than *The Ape Man* and

frozen (in cellophane by the looks of it) prehistoric man and the expected mayhem that ensues from this. The title isn't the only cheat, since the credits (which were apparently shot before the film itself) claim that both Frank Moran and George Zucco play the caveman. Zucco—perhaps having read the script—became ill and bowed out; only Moran appears in the film.

Despite strong support from John Carradine, the film is rather indifferently made. It moves fast enough and has its share of Katzmaniacal gaffes (the cellophane ice, some lovably shaky rear-screen work of the Frozen North, the often visible long underwear on the prehistoric gent, et cetera), but it isn't quite as much fun as most of its predecessors. Perhaps Katzman had grown tired of the series, of making films at low-rent Monogram, or both. In any case, by 1948, he was back in his element with the Jungle Jim series, which he filmed at the classier new home of Columbia Pictures. Not surprisingly, Katzman didn't rise to the level of his new studio, but perversely brought the studio down to his own level. Not since the early '30s (serials exempted) had Columbia leant its name to anything as conspicuously bargain

quite as much fun, though it has never attained that film's legendary status (probably owing to the curious fact that it's not generally available). The story line, largely recycled from *The Corpse Vanishes*, offers us Lugosi as Dr. Richard Marlowe, a vaguely mad scientist with a zombie wife, who has turned to the assistance of gas station owner and part-time witch doctor George Zucco to revive the lady. Since Mrs. Marlowe has been in this state for twenty-two years according to the script, one really must admire his tenacity, while simultaneously questioning the credulity of a man who can spend twenty-two years listening to Zucco's lame excuses as to just exactly *why* the idiotic voodoo ceremonies have never produced any results.

Katzman and Lugosi had one more tandem project up their sleeves, *Return of the Ape Man* (1944), which, despite its title, had nothing to do with *The Ape Man*. Rather, it involves the experiments of Lugosi's Professor Dexter to revive a

Laurie Carroll is menaced by waterfront thugs in Katzman's straight-from-the-headlines saga of juvenile delinquency and gangland corruption, *Rumble on the Docks* (1956). *(Copyright © 1956 Columbia Pictures)*

Scientific experiments turn luckless drifter Steven Ritch into *The Werewolf* (1956), directed by the prolific Fred F. Sears. *(Copyright © 1956 Clover Productions)*

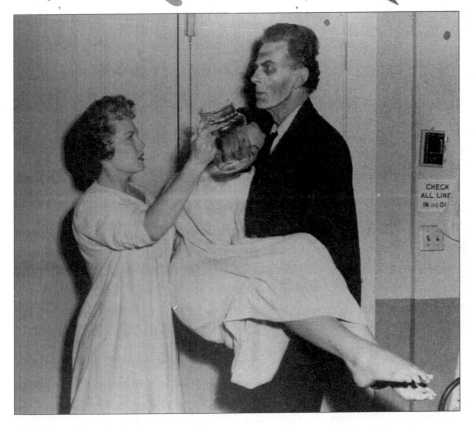

novelty of the casting, however, it was not one of the better entries. Altogether more in the Katzman vein was 1950's *Mark of the Gorilla*, which was bizarre enough to resemble one of Katzman's more offbeat Monogrammers. It tells the story of a bunch of murderous Nazis who commit their nefarious deeds dressed up in gorilla suits! This was exactly the sort of Katzman-styled nonsense required to propel the series through another dozen movies, including such classics as 1950's *Pygmy Island* (featuring Billy Barty as the leader of a tribe of pygmies); 1952's *Jungle Jim in the Forbidden Land* (giants this time, along with lots of stock footage); 1953's *The Killer Ape* (evil scientists and germ warfare); 1954's *Cannibal Attack* (vaguely East European secret agents disguised as crocodiles); and 1955's *Jungle Moon Men* (an H. Rider Haggard–like immortal princess). The series was popular enough and Weissmuller appears to have been reasonably pleased with it, since he ultimately dropped the Jungle Jim moniker and played the last few entries under his own name, which can be viewed now, perhaps, as a perverse kind of immortality.

By 1955, the jungle picture must have been wearing out for Katzman, and he turned to two

basement as Katzman's Jungle Jim films. The only thing the series actually had going for it was the appearance in the title role of former screen Tarzan Johnny Weissmuller, who had gotten frankly too old and too fat for the role of the movies' most famous "apeman." So, the ever-resourceful Katzman tapped him to star in this khaki-and-pith-helmet variation inspired by a comic strip instead, not mindful of the fact that Weissmuller's acting ability had never gone much beyond the "Me Tarzan—You Jane" level under the best of circumstances. The part of Jungle Jim required Weissmuller to speak more dialogue than usual, and his inability to do so made his character come across as slightly moronic.

As was often the case with Katzman's series films, the first entry, *Jungle Jim* (1948), was relatively sober and restrained. The second installment, *The Lost Tribe* (1949) was a bit wilder and worked around its stars' acting ability (or lack thereof) by concentrating on action scenes, while the third entry, *Captive Girl* (1950), tried to score *its* points with the casting of another former screen Tarzan, Buster Crabbe, as Jim's nemesis. Apart from the

Katzman returned to the rock musical genre he had created in *Don't Knock the Rock* (1957), featuring Alan Freed and a bevy of '50s rock superstars. *(Copyright © 1957 Columbia Pictures)*

other genres he considered ripe for exploitation: rock and roll and science fiction. To the great S. K. goes the credit for what might be called the first rock movie musical, *Rock Around the Clock* (1956). It wasn't much of a film then and it certainly hasn't improved with age, but it did showcase Bill Haley and the Comets and, to a lesser degree, the Platters, with such early rock standards as "See You Later, Alligator," "The Great Pretender," "Only You," and, of course, "Rock Around the Clock." As was typical of nearly all American rock films of the period, it was a fairly shoddy affair made by men who didn't really understand the music or its fans. Katzman—never one to waste *anything*—liked the paper-thin plot well enough, however, to recycle it a few years later in an effort to cash in on a new phenomenon with *Twist Around the Clock* (1961), featuring Chubby Checker, the Marcels, and Dion in place of the earlier rockers. Prior to this retread, he had also tried his hand at promoting calypso music in much the same manner with *Calypso Heat Wave* (1957). Whatever may be said of these films, the man's ingenuity for anticipating and/or quickly cashing in on the craze of the moment was downright astonishing!

Perhaps more enduring are Katzman's string of 1950s horror/science-fiction films, two of which—*Earth Vs. the Flying Saucers* (1956) and *The Giant Claw* (1957)—are considered "classics" of their type, albeit for different reasons. Special effects aficionados single out *Earth Vs. the Flying Saucers* as the better of the duo because of its Ray Harryhausen–produced effects and occasionally above-average script and acting. Perhaps. But plaudits for the script have been exaggerated and the effects, while ingenious, are only intermittently convincing due to the project's budgetary restrictions. It's also too sober and restrained to be considered a prime example of the Katzman oeuvre.

The Giant Claw remains more memorable, and more typically Katzman, because it's a whole lot goofier. In fact, it is quite possibly the most delirious of the giant atomic mutation pictures to come out of the 1950s. Plot-wise, the film is almost identical to *Earth Vs. the Flying Saucers*. Once again, Katzman's house director, the prodigious Fred F. Sears (who died of a heart attack the same year at the young age of forty-four) was in control of the proceedings, leading an impeccable 1950s sci-fi cast (Jeff Morrow, Mara Corday, Morris

THE SLEAZE MERCHANTS

22

A throwback to his Monogram days, albeit with marginally better effects and production values: *Zombies of Mora-Tau* (1957). (Copyright © 1957 Columbia Pictures)

After rocking America's youngsters around the clock, Katzman quickly counseled them *Don't Knock the Twist* (1962). *(Copyright © 1962 Columbia Pictures)*

its own quirky way, *The Giant Claw* is perhaps the ultimate justification of the Katzman approach: Take a well-worn plot, tweak it to make it absurd, spend as little as possible bringing it to the screen in order to ensure a fast profit, *et voilà*, instant cult classic! Partisans may argue that *Earth Vs. the Flying Saucers* is the better of the two films, but there's no denying that *The Giant Claw* has found a more permanent position in the pantheon of truly lovable bad monster movies.

Katzman managed to sandwich a number of exploitative horror/sci-fi gems in between these two "classics," the most notable being: *The Werewolf* (1956), *The Man Who Turned to Stone* and *Zombies of Mora-Tau* (both 1957). Despite a simple-minded plot involving shipwrecked zombies who can only be appeased by the return of some pilfered diamonds they've been guarding, *Mora-Tau* actually generates a modicum of atmosphere. However, the truly odd thing about this film (and to a lesser degree the other two as well) is that it seems like a throwback to Katzman's Monogram days—albeit with marginally better effects and production values. It seems like a picture very much out of its time.

Ankrum) in a story that defies logic and is burdened with possibly the worst special effects ever seen. According to legend, the actors walked out of the screening room in consternation when they saw the mutated "Giant Claw" of the title, an hysterically unrealistic bird puppet, which, in common with the extraterrestrials of *Earth Vs. the Flying Saucers*, seems to prefer attacking national landmarks. The Washington Monument and the Capitol Dome took it on the chin in the earlier film, but befitting its size Katzman's big bird takes on the whole world this time around by pecking a gaping hole in the UN Building! The truth be told, however, *The Giant Claw* is a great deal of fast-moving fun and its abominable effects are so sufficiently ridiculous as to be charming, as is the script's kindergarten-level view of science with its fantasticated "atomic cannon" that ultimately blasts the beaky one out of the sky with an atom bomb fired at close range (with no harm to the beast's nearby assailants, it should be added). In

One almost wishes that Katzman's producing career had ended at this point (on a high note, as it were), since nothing in his subsequent filmography quite came up to the standards of truly tacky wondrousness that had marked his work up through *The Giant Claw*. The tackiness was certainly present in his later films, but the fun was missing. His Elvis movies in the '60s were quite possibly the worst the singer ever made, though the first of them, 1964's *Kissin' Cousins* (an unabashed rip-off of Al Capp's Lil' Abner comic strip), did offer the horrifying spectacle of two Elvises for the price of one (even if one of them boasts the most ghastly blond dye job of all time),

as well as the usual quota of forgettable songs. The fascination it and its follow-up, the even more lame *Harum Scarum* (1965), continue to engender is roughly akin to gawking at the pickled cranium of a two-headed cow in a sideshow.

Trouper that he was, Katzman kept his hand in making films for Columbia, for American-International Pictures, and for any other studio that would have him until his death in 1973. But his last efforts (a number of them produced by his son, Jerry) have almost none of the oddball charm we associate with his earlier works. In fact, they are all too typical signposts that Katzman's time had come and gone, that he had outlived his era.

Katzman exploited a different type of music and music superstar in *Your Cheatin' Heart* (1964), a biography of country-and-western legend Hank Williams (George Hamilton). *(Copyright © 1964 MGM)*

S A M   K A T Z M A N

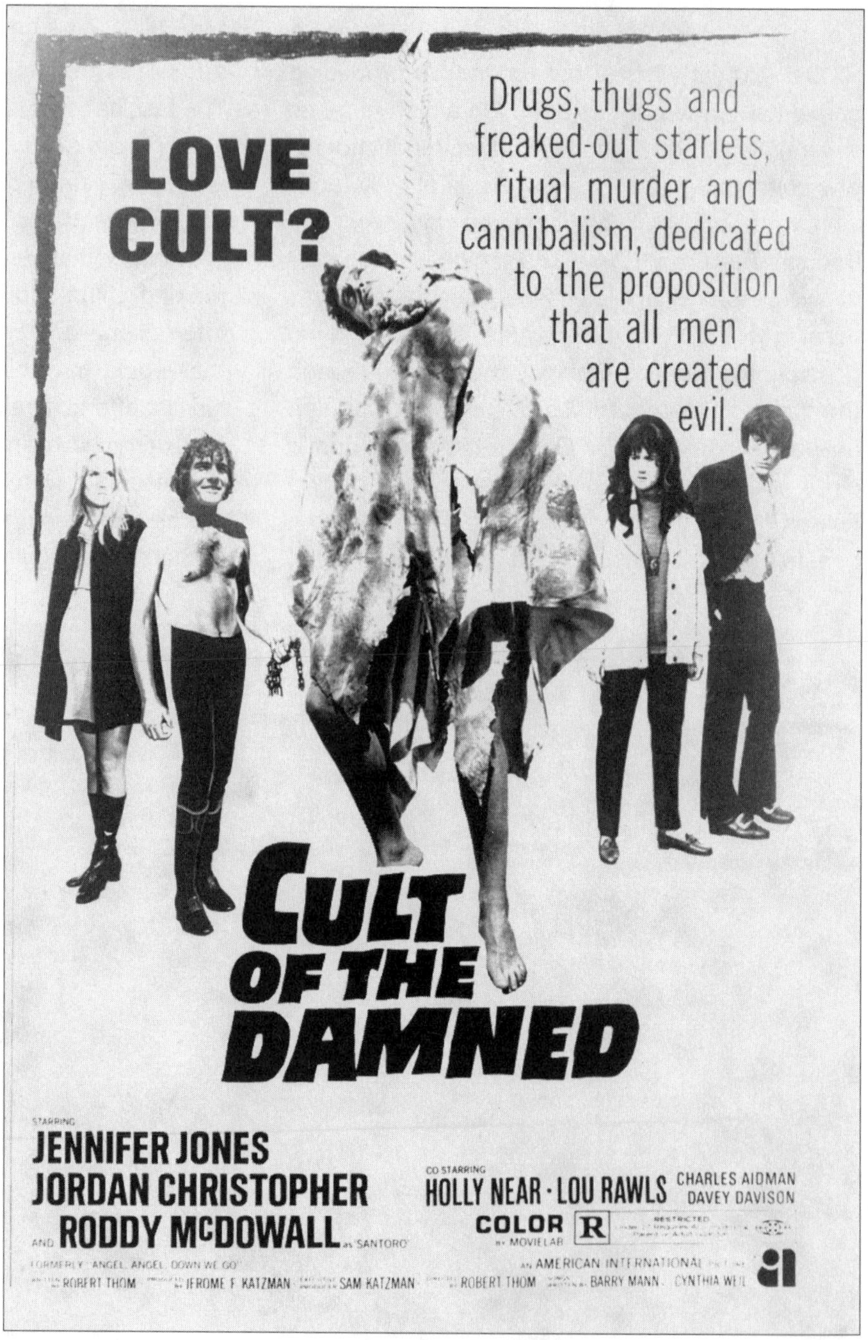

Katzman's son, Jerry, carried on the family tradition by rushing *Cult of the Damned* (1969, a.k.a. *Angel, Angel, Down We Go*), a thinly veiled look at the Manson family murders, into theaters before the headlines were even dry. *(Copyright © 1969 American-International Pictures)*

LOVE CULT?

Drugs, thugs and freaked-out starlets, ritual murder and cannibalism, dedicated to the proposition that all men are created evil.

CULT OF THE DAMNED

STARRING
**JENNIFER JONES
JORDAN CHRISTOPHER**
AND **RODDY McDOWALL** as SANTORO

CO STARRING
HOLLY NEAR · LOU RAWLS CHARLES AIDMAN
DAVEY DAVISON
COLOR BY MOVIELAB **R** RESTRICTED

FORMERLY "ANGEL, ANGEL DOWN WE GO"
WRITTEN BY ROBERT THOM · PRODUCED BY JEROME F. KATZMAN · EXECUTIVE PRODUCER SAM KATZMAN · DIRECTED BY ROBERT THOM · MUSIC BY BARRY MANN · CYNTHIA WEIL
an AMERICAN INTERNATIONAL Picture

Katzman may have worked for the smaller studios—or at the bottom end of the scale at larger ones—but he, like many of his generation of producers, exploitation or otherwise, was ultimately dependent on some kind of studio support for facilities, financing, and/or distribution. The growing move in the '60s and '70s away from the studio system into one-shot independent filmmaking deals did not work for him, nor for that matter did his style of quirky, but basically traditional, film with its relatively innocent worldview adapt to the increasingly worldly content of the exploitation film as the decades progressed. Katzman may have dealt in sleaze, but it was the sleaze of an altogether different era, an era now gone.

One can only wonder if the work of today's more overt sleaze merchants will eventually take on the same nostalgic hue time has so generously awarded the best of the worst and the worst of the best work of the immortal S. K. It seems unlikely, but it would have probably seemed the height of absurdity to Katzman himself that his old movies would even be watched fifty years down the road, much less enjoyed and discussed in books like this one.

SELECTED FILMOGRAPHY

1933: Ship of Wanted Men; **1934:** A Demon for Trouble, Brand of Hate, Hot Off the Presses, Danger Ahead; **1936:** Put on the Spot, Rio Grande Romance, Kelly of the Secret Service, A Face in the Fog, Shadow of Chinatown; **1937:** Blake of Scotland Yard, Two Minutes to Play, Million Dollar Racket, Tombstone Terror, Western Justice, Big Calibre; **1938:** Flying Fists, Silks and Saddles, Lightning Carson Rides Again; **1940:** East Side Kids, Straight Shooter, Boys of the City, That Gang of Mine; **1941:** Spooks Run Wild, Pride of the Bowery, Flying Wild, The Invisible Ghost, Bowery Blitzkrieg, Zis Boom Bah; **1942:** The Corpse Vanishes, Mr. Wise Guy, Black Dragons, Let's Get Tough!, Smart Alecks, Bowery at Midnight, 'Neath Brooklyn Bridge; **1943:** Spotlight Scandals, Kid Dynamite, The Ape Man, Clancy Street Boys, Ghosts on the Loose, Mr. Muggs Steps Out; **1944:** The Voodoo Man, Million Dollar Kid, Follow the Leader, Return of the Ape Man, Three of a Kind, Block Busters, Bowery Champs, Crazy Knights; **1945:** Docks of New York, Come Out Fighting, Mr. Muggs Rides Again; **1946:** Betty Co-Ed, High School Hero, Freddie Steps Out; **1947:** Last of the Redmen, Son of Zorro, Jack Armstrong, Little Miss Broadway, Vacation Days, Sweet Genevieve, Two Blondes and a Redhead; **1948:** Superman, Glamour Girl, Racing Luck, Triple Threat, I Surrender Dear, Jungle Jim, Congo Bill; **1949:** Manhattan Angel, The Mutineers, Bruce Gentry, Barbary Pirate, Chinatown at Midnight, Batman and Robin, The Lost Tribe; **1950:** Last of the Buccaneers, Captive Girl, Atom Man Vs. Superman, Mark of the Gorilla, Cody of the Pony Express, Pirates of the High Seas, Adventures of Sir Galahad, Tyrant of the Sea, State Penitentiary, Chain Gang, Pygmy Island, Revenue Agent; **1951:** A Yank in Korea, Purple Heart, Roar of the Iron Horse, Fury of the Congo, Jungle Manhunt, Captain Video, Hurricane Island, The Magic Carpet, When the Redskins Rode; **1952:** The Golden Hawk, California Conquest, Jungle Jim in the Forbidden Land, Voodoo Tiger, Thief of Damascus, Brave Warrior, King of the Congo, Yank in Indo-China, The Pathfinder, Last Train from Bombay, Mysterious Island; **1953:** Savage Mutiny, The Killer Ape, Valley of the Head Hunters, Fort Ti, The Lost Planet, Siren of Bagdad, Jack McCall, Prince of Pirates, Serpent of the Nile, Sky Commando, Slaves of Babylon, The 49th Man, Flame of Calcutta, Conquest of Cochise, Prisoners of the Casbah; **1954:** The Miami Story, Drums of Tahiti, Adventures of Captain Africa, Jungle Maneaters, Cannibal Attack, The Saracen Blade, Jesse James Vs. The Daltons, Battle of Rogue River, Charge of the Lancers, The Law Vs. Billy the Kid, Masterson of Kansas, The Iron Glove; **1955:** Jungle Moon Men, Devil Goddess, Pirates of Tripoli, New Orleans Uncensored, Seminole Uprising, The Gun That Won the West; **1956:** Rock Around the Clock, Rumble on the Docks, Earth Vs. the Flying Saucers, The Werewolf, Utah Blaine, Blackjack Ketchum, Uranium Boom, The Houston Story, Miami Expose, Cha-Cha-Cha-Boom!; **1957:** Calypso Heat Wave, Escape from San Quentin, The Man Who Turned to Stone, The Giant Claw, Don't Knock the Rock, The Tijuana Story, The Zombies of Mora-Tau, The Night the World Exploded, The World Was His Jury; **1958:** Crash Landing, Going Steady, Juke Box Rhythm, Life Begins at 17; **1959:** The Last Blitzkrieg, The Flying Fontaines; **1960:** The Enemy General, The Wizard of Bagdad; **1961:** Twist Around the Clock, Pirates of Tortuga; **1962:** The Wild Westerners, Don't Knock the Twist; **1963:** Hootenanny Hoot; **1964:** Kissin' Cousins, Your Cheatin' Heart, Get Yourself a College Girl; **1965:** Harum Scarum, When the Boys Meet the Girls; **1966:** Hold On!; **1967:** Riot on Sunset Strip, The Fastest Guitar Alive, Hot Rods to Hell, The Love-Ins; **1968:** The Young Runaways, For Singles Only, A Time to Sing; **1969:** Angel, Angel, Down We Go (a.k.a. Cult of the Damned); **1972:** How to Succeed with Sex, The Loners.

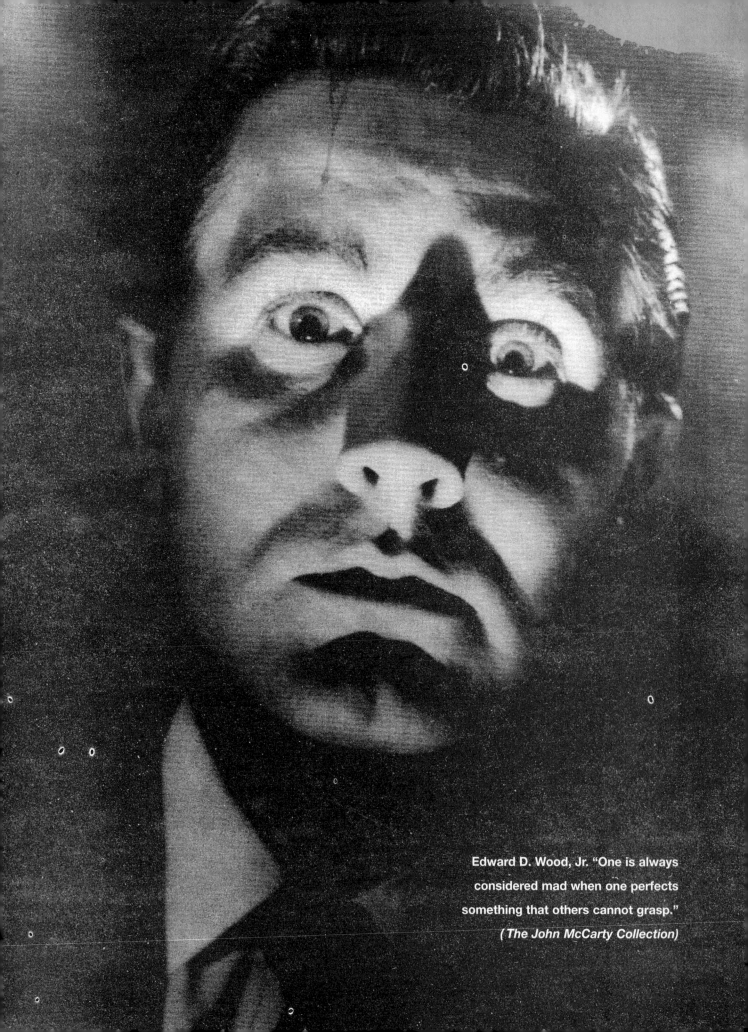

Edward D. Wood, Jr. "One is always considered mad when one perfects something that others cannot grasp." *(The John McCarty Collection)*

Edward D. Wood, Jr.

BY KEN HANKE

The movies' only outspoken champion of trans-vestism, Ed Wood (himself a cross-dresser, known for occasionally helming a picture in full drag battle regalia) was quite possibly the most blindly optimistic filmmaker who ever lived. According to everyone who ever knew him, Wood never wanted to be anything but a filmmaker, and nothing in his wildly disorganized and frequently depressing life swayed him from his ambition—an ambition that resulted in (at least) three of the most enthusiastically awful, best-loved bad movies of all time—*Glen or Glenda* (a.k.a. *I Changed My Sex,* 1953), *Bride of the Monster* (1955), and *Plan 9 from Outer Space* (1956).

Ed Wood typifies the ultimate in filmmaking independence. Literally, he did it *all* on his own, though not necessarily by choice or design. He never threw away a solid career working for the studios to assert his independence. Rather, inde-pendence was foisted upon him by circum-stances. His approach to filmmaking was simple: If no studio would hire him or finance his projects (which they wouldn't and didn't), he'd make them himself, obtaining money from any possible source. The remarkable thing is that he did. Say what one will about the threadbare, illogical plots of his films, their abysmal acting, ludicrous paint-ed flats, mismatched shots, wholesale use of stock footage, complete lack of technique, and hysterically inept special effects, Wood *made movies*—in spite of all obstacles—by optimistically

barging in where more timid, yet more talented, would-be filmmakers feared to tread.

Born in Poughkeepsie, New York, in 1924, Wood fell in love with the movies at a very young age, and began making his first films in 8 mm even before he'd reached his teens. Following a stint in the Marine Corps during World War II, where, according to legend, he stormed the beaches at Tarawa wearing ladies' underwear beneath his battle dress, he journeyed to Hollywood to realize his boyhood dream of making it big in the movie business.

He wrote and directed his first film, a Western short called *The Streets of Laredo*, in 1948. Though the film was never completed and lacked a soundtrack, it's abundantly obvious that Wood emerged in full flower with this project. It had no budget and the money for it was constantly being wrangled at the last minute when existing funds ran out. Wood, it seems, could not ride a horse at all, but this did not keep him from casting himself as the villain in the piece. When the script called for a coffin, Wood simply knocked one together out of cardboard—although it proved to be a foot too short! For a filmmaker whose most identifying signature was a very personal brand of ineptitude on an almost cosmic scale, this was truly an aus-picious beginning.

A more properly completed (at least it had a soundtrack) short called *The Sun Was Setting* arrived in 1951, followed by Wood's pseudony-

mous script for *The Lawless Rider* in 1952, but it was with the George Weiss–produced exploitation feature on sex-change operations, first known as *Behind Locked Doors*, then as *Transvestite*, and then as *Glen or Glenda* (not to mention a myriad of alternate titles affixed to it by states' rights distributors over the years), that Wood came into his own. What Weiss originally intended as a sensationalistic "documentary" on the life of transsexual Christine Jorgensen ultimately became a kind of self-portrait of Ed Wood himself, a classic apology for cross-dressing, and a fetishistic paean to the delights of wearing angora sweaters.

Any movie that casts Bela Lugosi in the role of God must, however, have something going for it, and *Glen or Glenda* most assuredly does, since this singular notion is in fact one of the more rational ones in the film. Lugosi was not exactly an enthused participant, feeling that the exploitative tone of the film was demeaning, which may seem a bit odd coming from the man who had just allowed himself to be exploited in *Bela Lugosi Meets a Brooklyn Gorilla* (1952). But at this point in Lugosi's sagging career, a fast thousand dollars (some sources say five hundred dollars) was not to be shrugged off.

On the one hand, Wood's rationale for casting Lugosi was clearly a mixture of commerce and the outgrowth of his own adolescent attachment to the once-great horror film star. But on a thematic level (and whatever his shortcomings as a filmmaker, Wood was an obsessive, whose work *does* have a certain thematic consistency) there is something much deeper at work here. The idea of having the controlling spirit/God/mad scientist that Lugosi plays at the center of things takes the burden of transvestism off the shoulders of Wood's Glen character, making it abundantly clear that he is himself in no way responsible for his addiction to angora pullovers and open-toed pumps. Rather, according to the film, the transvestite is *born* with these peculiarities. As absurdly as it may be presented in the film, this message was a very forward piece of thinking for 1953.

However, what is most striking about *Glen or Glenda*, and what keeps the film in our collective consciousness, is its uniquely Woodian blend of obsession and ineptitude. Wood veteran Gregory Walcott (*Plan 9 from Outer Space*) has remarked that "Ed had poor taste and was undisciplined. He had no taste. If he had ten million dollars it [*Plan 9*] would have been a piece of

"And what are little boys made of? Is it snakes and snails and puppy dogs' tails? Or is it brassieres! And corsets!" The cross-dressing maestro himself as the star of *Glen or Glenda* (1953). *(The John McCarty Collection)*

EDWARD D. WOOD, JR

tasteless shit." This is certainly true of Wood's own dress sense, as well as the styles of dress in which he attired his films' actresses and assorted transvestites. In fact, it is often hard to tell which is which, since all are dressed in cheap and obvious outfits, resulting in a kind of grotesque parody of womanhood, regardless of the actual gender.

As if this weren't enough to sink *Glen or Glenda* on an artistic basis, there is also what might be termed Wood's "gift" for dialogue. Here we have a man ostensibly trying to craft a serious statement on transvestism who includes such lines as "And what are little boys made of? Is it snakes and snails and puppy dogs' tails? Or is it brassieres! And corsets!" Not to mention Lugosi's classic warning of, "Bevare! Bevare of the big green dragon that sits on your doorstep! He eats little boys!" There's no doubt that this kind of insanity is endearing, but it goes a long way toward illustrating how easily Wood could (and would) scuttle his work's intentions through his utter lack of taste and logic.

Except for Lugosi, the general level of the acting in *Glen or Glenda* (indeed, in *all* of Wood's pictures) is somewhere between bad and awful. Wood himself stars as Glen under the pseudonym of Daniel Davis and his performance is more wooden than any ever given by Nelson Eddy at his cigar-store Indian worst. He comes alive on-screen only when he comes in contact with a nice, fuzzy sweater. A wooden Wood, though, is preferable to the animated histrionics of his co-star, Dolores Fuller, whose nasal delivery of all her dialogue is grotesquely annoying. The film's high point in stupefying dramaturgy, however, is surely the big set-piece nightmare sequence wherein Wood is accosted by all manner of persons (led by a picture-book devil) pointing an accusatory finger at him and his little weakness. No one involved on-screen seems to have a clue to what the scene is all about or what point it is trying to make, but they carry on gamely like indulgent relations in a quirky home movie that got out of hand. That the devil is played by the same man (the improbably

named Captain De Zita) who plays Glen's father was no doubt a matter of simple economics, but it certainly suggests a pent-up paternal hostility on Wood's part, which is very much in keeping with a man who so obviously considered himself a martyr to end all martyrs. (Wood even went so far in this area as to make himself up and pose as Christ—in 3-D no less—for a personalized Christmas card.)

The most astounding aspect of *Glen or Glenda*, though, is how very little film was actually shot to make it. Wood had perhaps enough actual filmable material in his screenplay for roughly fifty minutes of movie, but fifty minutes was not enough for a feature. Enter one of Wood's more curious stylistic trademarks—the use of stock footage. Intimates of Wood have indicated that the director would screen whole libraries of stock footage, making notes on how to build a comprehensible (in the Ed Wood sense) story line inexpensively out of what he unearthed. The approach was certainly not new, as every fan of the B picture knows, but Wood made it into a kind of art form. In *Glen or Glenda*, for example, Wood took a lengthy sequence lifted from a documentary on a steel mill, overdubbed it with a conversation in which two steelworkers discuss wearing women's underclothes, and inserted it to pad out his film's running time. A series of scenes in *Glen or Glenda* depicting the trials and tribulations of the transvestite was similarly accomplished with other stock shots and the overdubbed voice of a woman requesting a divorce because her husband has stretched all of her clothes out of shape. There is even a priceless moment where—for no apparent reason—Wood inserts a shot of a buffalo stampede with Lugosi's off-screen voice shouting, "Pull the strings! Dance to that for which you were made!" The effect of these and other sequences is certainly slipshod and cheap, but also mesmerizing in a way that many "normal" films are not.

Wood always tended to think of *Glen or Glenda* as a documentary, which may have been his original intention (as it was producer Weiss's). But the end result was something else entirely. A

Left to right: Herbert Rawlinson, Steve Reeves (later of *Hercules* fame) and Lyle Talbot in *Jail Bait* (1954), Wood's tale not of a teenage sexpot but of a gangster who undergoes plastic surgery to escape the police. *(The John McCarty Collection)*

sequence involving a sex-change operation aside, about as clinical as *Glen or Glenda* gets is its dubious explanation about the joy and comfort of wearing women's clothing, or the frequently deleted segment wherein one learns that it is possible to tell the mere transvestite from the outright homosexual by how long the person holds your hand when getting a light for a cigarette. In this respect, it is possible to take the film as somewhat educational, but in nearly every other respect *Glen or Glenda* is a phantasmagorical nightmare that has nothing to do with science or education. It's more like the ultimate bad trip.

When television arrived on the scene, Wood tried (unsuccessfully) to sell a pilot for a series called "Crossroad Avenger" (1953), starring former cowboy actor Tom Keene as a character called the Tucson Kid and another former star of B Westerns, Tom Tyler, as his sidekick *(Glen or Glenda* veteran Lyle Talbot was in the cast as well). Considering the often amateurish calibre of

a great deal of early '50s television, it's almost a surprise that this did not sell. But Wood—a diehard fan of the B and C Western—had sufficient faith in it that he actually shot a sequel called *Boots* (1953), which also failed to sell. In the wake of these two failures to go mainstream, Wood returned to exploitation with a little opus called *Jail Bait* (1954), the concept of which may have been borrowed from a 1935 gangster picture called *Let 'Em Have It*, the '47 Bogart-Bacall film *Dark Passage*, or both. The plot, which recounts the adventures of a gangster (Timothy Farrell) who undergoes plastic surgery

EDWARD D. WOOD, JR

23

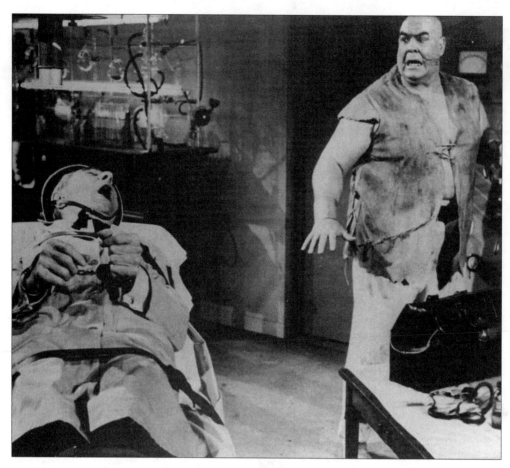

Bela Lugosi and Tor Johnson in *Bride of the Monster* (1955), the closest Wood ever came to making a coherent feature film. *(The John McCarty Collection)*

to escape his just deserts, wasn't the only thing Wood borrowed. He cribbed the music score from a 1952 sci-fi/girlie picture called *Mesa of Lost Women* and pilfered a vaudeville routine from an early "blaxploitation" movie called *Yes, Sir, Mr. Bones!* The results lacked the almost hypnotic conviction of *Glen or Glenda*, however, since the project was obviously much less personal to the director.

Armed with a broken-down rubber octopus previously seen in a Republic Pictures John Wayne movie called *Wake of the Red Witch* (1948), a narcissistic leading man (Tony McCoy) who couldn't act (but whose father provided some of the financing), Bela Lugosi, Tor Johnson, and a somewhat better than usual script, Wood next created *Bride of the Monster*, an attempt at a horror picture in the style of the classic Universal films Wood had grown up on. What he achieved, however, was closer in spirit to the low-rent series of Lugosi horror flicks turned out by Sam Katzman

and Monogram Pictures in the 1940s: an exercise in lunacy chock-full of (mostly unintentional) laughs and chills. Still it's the nearest Wood ever came to making a cohesive—and coherent—feature film. This is not to say that the finished product is without an abundance of Woodisms. There are many, including a mad scientist lab with painted flats palmed off as stone walls, a full kitchen setup created only to fill up empty space, and a photographic enlarger as the lab's principal piece of equipment!

Still, *Bride of the Monster* is noteworthy for giving the fragile, aged Lugosi the meatiest role of his saddening 1950s career. Cast as Dr. Eric Vornoff, a vaguely Russian scientist who dreams of perfecting a race of "atomic supermen" with which he plans to "conquer the world," Lugosi is in good form, and for the record, does *not* claim that Tor Johnson is "as gentle as a 'kitchen.'" Despite popular legend, he clearly says "kitten." No doubt Wood was thinking of his martyred view of himself when he penned such lines for Lugosi as "Home—I have no home. Hunted . . . despised . . . living like an animal! The jungle is my home." But the words could apply to Lugosi as well, who had gone from being the reigning king of the horror film to an almost unemployable alcoholic and drug addict. Perhaps the most telling and resonant moment in the film, however, is Lugosi's big speech, where he says "Here in this forsaken jungle hell I have proven that I am *all* right," which, in fact, his performance demonstrated was true. On the other hand, Wood himself seems best summed up by Lugosi's pronouncement that "One is always considered mad when one perfects something others cannot grasp."

Wood seems not to have cared much for the resulting film, always citing *Plan 9 from Outer Space* as his masterpiece. The reason for this may have been that he lost control over many aspects of the production of *Bride of the Monster* to lead-

ing man Tony McCoy's father, who held the purse strings. According to Wood, the younger McCoy was the worst actor he ever directed (a tall claim indeed) and some scenes were compromised by this fact. Without a doubt, the younger McCoy must have been responsible for such idiocies as the wholly arbitrary scene where his fight with Tor Johnson results in his shirt (but not his suspenders) being ripped away to allow for a gratuitous bit of beefcake. The elder McCoy, however, seems to have been responsible for the ludicrous inclusion of stock footage of an atomic bomb going off when Lugosi is struck by lightning at the film's climax. Regardless, there is certainly a *lot* of Ed Wood in the film, too—ranging from such felicitous moments as Lugosi examining a potential "atomic superman," discovering a bruise, and slapping Tor Johnson while exclaiming, "Lobo! You're too rough with my patients!" to the hero's being menaced by stock shots of alligators. The

Wood's chiropractor Tom Mason doubles for the late Bela Lugosi in the director's self-proclaimed masterpiece *Plan 9 from Outer Space* (1956). *(The John McCarty Collection)*

Resurrected corpse Tor Johnson goes on the rampage in *Plan 9 from Outer Space* (1956), often hailed by Ed Wood detractors as the worst film ever made. *(The John McCarty Collection)*

film's ultimate absurdity, though, is definitely the "atomic octopus" scene wherein several actors have to struggle gamely just to suggest they are being attacked by this obviously immobile prop—the unrealistic hokeyness of which Wood typically calls attention to by lingering his camera on it for much too long.

At this late date, it is impossible to sort out the truth from the fiction concerning who owned *Bride of the Monster*, who got what out of it, and who screwed whom over its production and distribution. Conflicting stories suggest that American-International Pictures producer Samuel Z. Arkoff "stole" the film from Wood (along with the idea for a subsequent AIP film, *How to Make a Monster* [1958]) and used the profits to found his picture-making empire; that Wood sold far more than 100 percent of the picture to get it financed and was therefore at the mercy of McCoy the Elder and a lot of other investors; and so on. Only one thing *is* clear: Ed Wood never saw a nickel out of it. His

entire financial gain from the film was his original director's fee—$350.

Shortly after *Bride of the Monster*, Lugosi checked himself into a drug rehabilitation clinic to kick his morphine habit, living mostly on the hope of making a comeback in forthcoming projects from Ed Wood. Their relationship was indeed a strange one—the once-great star and the no-budget director; as a result, there has been a tendency in recent years to romanticize Wood as somewhat of a savior where Lugosi was concerned. But the relationship was, at best, a symbiotic one. Wood *did* offer the actor the chance to work when no one else would. But he benefited too because Lugosi's name still had some marquee value.

For many filmgoers *Plan 9 from Outer Space* is the film most closely associated with Ed Wood, although not for the reasons Wood may have wished. The film has earned the reputation over the years as the worst ever made, which isn't true, but neither is the claim very far afield, for *Plan 9*'s

Wood bounced back from the failure of *Plan 9 from Outer Space* with the screenplay for *The Bride and the Beast* (1958), the wild and Woody story of a young woman (Charlotte Austin) who is attracted to her husband's (Lance Fuller) pet gorilla. Adrian Weiss produced and directed. *(Courtesy Eric Caidin)*

shortcomings are legion. Wood's primary reservation about the film stemmed from the necessary shortening of Lugosi's role when the actor died during shooting. And the scenes in which Lugosi does appear look suspiciously like a combination of home movie and test footage. (Lugosi comes out of a house, walks down a sidewalk, and exits the frame. The narrator comments, "The old man left home," which is followed by the noise of squealing tires on the soundtrack and the further narration, "Never to return!")

The story line of *Plan 9 from Outer Space* (or, as Wood wanted to call it, *Grave Robbers from Outer Space*) is actually no better or worse than any number of 1950s science-fiction films. The title refers to a plot to resurrect the dead, explains ultra-campy John "Bunny" Breckinridge as "The Ruler" of a race of aliens bent on conquering the world. There are certainly worse premises to base a film on, but it took someone of Wood's peculiar vision to come up with *Plan 9*. His aliens arrive in flying saucers made from plastic toy UFO model kits obviously suspended on wires. His singularly unprepossessing "army of the undead" consists of Lugosi, Tor Johnson, Vampira, and a chiropodist turned "actor" named Tom Mason who doubled for Lugosi after the star's demise (Wood "disguises" the fact that Mason looks *nothing* like Lugosi by having him hold his cape over his face). Moreover, as if hell-bent on proving Gregory Walcott's statement that he had absolutely no taste, Wood explains that they are the "resurrected dead" by having another member of the cast comment on their "awful smell." On top of this, Wood's spaceship interior is clearly a lamely disguised soundstage decked out with a shower curtain and some other "futuristic" touches, while his "big" speech for the oddly named head alien, Eros (Dudley Manlove), is merely line upon line of nonsense that goes on forever. (Wood thought it was brilliant writing, of course.) These shortcomings, however, are precisely the reason why *Plan 9* has outlasted many better-made films of the era in the public's mind.

One of Wood's more unique ideas was to add newscaster-turned-"psychic" Criswell to the cast as narrator for the purpose of lending authenticity to what is presented as a true story "based on the secret testimony of the miserable souls who survived this terrifying ordeal." A flamboyant and brazenly phony psychic, who according to his friends, liked to sleep in a coffin, Criswell was mostly a professional hanger-on, who specialized in predicting intentionally ridiculous events such as the city of Denver's eventual turning into Jell-O (it hasn't as of this writing). He never for a moment took himself or his prophetic abilities seriously and seems to have been quite astonished that anyone else did. Criswell was, however, a genial ham and his pseudo-authoritative presence lends just the right touch of insanity to *Plan 9*. "Can you prove it didn't happen?" he asks at the end—and can we?

The making of *Plan 9* was even weirder than the film itself. Wood had previously dealt with exploitation specialists like George Weiss and the "moneyed" fathers of wanna-be movie stars to bankroll his films. To finance *Plan 9*, however, he turned to a Baptist minister named J. Edward Reynolds, who saw the film as an opportunity to get into the movie business, and use the profits from the film to finance a series of "edifying" religious films. Anyone looking at Wood's track record might have had some serious reservations about this scheme, but Wood was apparently a very persuasive salesman. In return, Wood agreed to have the cast and crew baptized into the "proper" faith by Reynolds prior to production. Soon he found his personal life and dress sense under fire from Reynolds, who also insisted that the film's original title be changed. Ultimately, according to Wood's widow, Kathy, Reynolds honed in on Wood's alcoholic tendencies and constant penury, and used them as a wedge to buy full control of the finished film for one dollar, after which the film sat on a shelf for three years, unable to find a distributor.

Ripped off on his best film (*Bride of the Monster*), his most impressive star now dead, and

A COMPULSIVE KILLER STRIKES TERROR...

...in every woman's heart

SINISTER URGE OF A COMPULSIVE KILLER

"LET'S SEE THOSE LEGS...FROM THE TOES RIGHT UP TO YOUR HAT"

A GIRL IN A PHOTOGRAPH A PSYCHO MADMAN A SLASH OF A KNIFE

PORNOGRAPHY... CREATOR OF CRIME AND SEX HEADLINES

POSTMARKED FOR DEATH.. BY A 'SMUT' PICTURE THRU THE MAIL

THE SINISTER URGE

A HEADLINER PRODUCTION

with
KENNE DUNCAN   JEAN FONTAINE
JAMES MOORE   CARL ANTHONY
DINO FANTINI

A PSYCHO
WITH THE
URGE
TO KILL

A Beautiful Girl
A Photograph
A Compulsive Urge
A Slash of a Knife

MISTRESS TO HIS
COMPULSIVE MADNESS
....HIS TOUCH MEANT DEATH

FRANK...DARING...TERRIFYING REALISM

ring Duke Moore that Wood turned into an unsold pilot for a proposed TV series to have been called "Portraits in Evil," and *The Night the Banshee Cried* (1957). He also penned the screenplay for *The Bride and the Beast* (1958), a wild and Woody extravaganza that he originally wanted to call *Queen of the Gorillas*. Produced and directed by Adrian Weiss, the film centers on the attraction of a young wife (Charlotte Austin) to her husband's (Lance Fuller) pet gorilla, which is named Spanky (the part was played by former serial and B cowboy movie star Ray "Crash" Corrigan).

The next feature Wood directed himself was *Night of the Ghouls* (1958), starring former cowboy movie heavy Keene Duncan and Tor Johnson. As with *Plan 9* Criswell opened the film with a warning speech about what was to come, a story "so astounding some of you may faint!" Once again, Wood thought he was in Universal's classic monster territory, and once again he fell more than a little shy of his intended mark.

This round, Wood secured financial support by getting drunk with a Fuller Brush salesman who subsequently convinced a friend to pass up a potentially lucrative real-estate investment to put money instead in Wood's latest cinematic delirium. Of course, the money wasn't really enough to cover the making of the film, and the production was constantly on the verge of collapsing. Tor Johnson apparently got so fed up that he insisted on being paid *before* each day's work. Forced to shoot in a severely cramped studio, Wood hastened to complete the film before the electric bill (which he couldn't pay) came due. Amazingly, something resembling a film came out of this. Not so amazingly, Wood thereafter lost control of the final product. In Rudolph Grey's biography of Wood, *Nightmare of Ecstasy* (Feral House, 1992), the film's leading lady, Valda Hansen, recalled the image of the heartbroken director standing in the rain, crying,

having lost ownership of his as-yet-unreleased "masterpiece," Wood might have been inclined to throw in the towel, but such a consideration was not apparently in the indomitable man's makeup. Instead, he cooked up a pair of short films: *Final Curtain* (1957), a former Lugosi project now star-

and telling her that "they" were going to "do me a *Plan 9* all over again," a tragic moment of self-perception in Wood's usually blindly optimistic existence.

From *Night of the Ghouls* Wood plunged into *The Sinister Urge* (1960). Billed as a "smut picture" and "portrait of a psycho killer," this is probably his most accomplished non-horror film. The film is intended as a cautionary tract on the dangers of pornographic films, which, Wood's script suggests in all seriousness, have the power to turn normal young men into hot-blooded sex maniacs and killers. But the most noteworthy thing about it was the relative ease with which it was made. With exploitation producer Roy Reid at the helm, the money did not run out and Wood brought the film in as planned. For his director's chores, he picked up a whopping one thousand dollars. The film saw release as the top half of a double bill with a reissue of *The Violent Years* (1956), a film Wood had written. Despite the obvious toll that alcohol was taking on him (it is hard

Guns blazing and hormones raging, a gang of teenage girls runs amok in the Wood-scripted *The Violent Years* (1956), directed by William M. Morgan. (Courtesy Eric Caidin)

UNTAMED GIRLS OF THE PACK GANG!

TEENAGE KILLERS TAKING THEIR THRILLS UNASHAMED!

THE VIOLENT YEARS

THRILL GIRLS OF THE HIGHWAY!

EDWARD D. WOOD, JR

Jack Searl and Jenny Maxwell in the Ed Wood–scripted white trash opus *Shotgun Wedding* (1963). *(The John McCarty Collection)*

to believe that the slightly bloated and rapidly aging Wood seen in production stills from the late '50s is the same handsome Ed Wood who starred in *Glen or Glenda*), he had at last proved himself capable of turning out a releasable property.

Unfortunately, success did not follow in its wake, and Wood found himself turning out instructional films for the government. He also wrote the script for a sleazy "white trash" exploitation opus called *Shotgun Wedding* (1963). By 1965 he had bottomed out and was entering the final phase of his career: pornographer. Beginning in 1963 with an opus titled *Black Lace Drag,* he had helped support himself by churning out so-called adult novels. This peculiar form of generic writing (still in existence today) was an area of literary endeavor that had about as much relation to professional writing as Wood's movies had to traditional filmmaking. Wood simply supplied "x" number of words on a flat-rate basis to the publisher, and surrendered all rights to the material. In

1965 he also penned the script for a combination horror-porno flick *Orgy of the Dead*, which he later novelized.

It wasn't until 1970 that he directed his own "nudie" feature, *Take It Out in Trade*, in which Wood himself once again donned the old angora sweater and appeared in the role of "Alecia." From descriptions of the film, it would seem that Wood had lost none of his particular vision in the ten years that separated this picture from *The Sinister Urge*. Indeed, if anything, it seems that Wood's approach to the soft-core sex film was possibly more inventive than his more "mainstream" earlier work—albeit no more coherent. His signature lack of coherence may well be why the film was never picked up for distribution. Nevertheless, he quickly followed it up with the harder-core *Necromania* (1971), from which it was only a small step to the world of 12-minute porno "loops" and more of the same up to his untimely death in dire poverty in 1978 at the age of fifty-four.

The saga of Ed Wood can be viewed as a depressing tale of a strange man who simply never accepted the fact that what he wanted most to do in life, he really lacked the talent for doing. And yet Wood and his delirious movies continue to exert an almost inexplicable fascination on us. In some perverse and not unsatisfying manner, this is Wood's justification and claim to cinematic immortality—an immortality now assured by director Tim Burton's multimillion-dollar biopic of the auteur of sleaze merchants, *Ed Wood* (1994), starring Johnny Depp in the title role.

It comes as little or no surprise that Wood's life story would appeal to the individualistic talent behind the gentle fable *Edward Scissorhands* (1990) and the dark fables *Batman* (1989) and *Batman Returns* (1992), for in many ways Wood's story is a combination of the two. It's the saga of a bizarre person obsessed with something no one cares about even slightly—yet who ultimately forces us to recognize him and his obsessions because of his indomitable—and wholly un-shared—belief in himself. In this respect, Ed Wood may be the ultimate Tim Burton hero—and a hero-ic figure for all of us, despite the cautionary nature of that heroism.

No filmmaker—indeed, no artist of any kind—can ever quite escape a "there-but-for-fortune-go-I" feeling of discomfort at the very thought of Ed Wood. Burton's film may help to put this feel-ing into some kind of perspective, although there is a large degree of irony in the fact that five min-utes of *Ed Wood* probably cost more to make than the entire Wood oeuvre.

SELECTED FILMOGRAPHY

1948: The Streets of Laredo* (a.k.a. Crossroad of Laredo); **1951:** The Sun Was Setting* (a.k.a. The Sun Also Sets); **1952:** The Lawless Rider; **1953:** Glen or Glenda (a.k.a. I Changed My Sex), Crossroad Avenger: The Adventures of the Tucson Kid, Boots; **1954:** Jail Bait (a.k.a. The Hidden Face); **1955:** Bride of the Monster (a.k.a. Bride of the Atom); **1956:** The Violent Years, Plan 9 from Outer Space; **1957:** Final Curtain*, The Night the Banshee Cried*; **1958:** The Bride and the Beast, Night of the Ghouls (a.k.a. Revenge of the Dead); **1960:** The Sinister Urge; **1963:** Shotgun Wedding; **1965:** Orgy of the Dead; **1969:** For Love Or Money, One Million AC/DC, Operation Redlight, Gunrunners, The Photographer; **1970:** Take It Out in Trade; **1971:** Necromania, The Only House; **1972:** Class Reunion, The Cocktail Hostesses, Dropout Wife; **1974:** Fugitive Girls (a.k.a. 5 Loose Women); **1975:** The Beach Bunnies.

*Short film

Herschell Gordon Lewis (Courtesy Daniel Krogh)

Herschell Gordon Lewis

BY JOHN McCARTY

In his roughly decade-long career (1960–1972) as an exploitation filmmaker, Herschell Gordon Lewis turned out thirty-seven feature films whose enduring popularity—and influence on exploitation filmmakers who followed—place him at the top of the heap as one of exploitation cinema's reigning grand masters.

Lewis had an almost uncanny ability to spot a trend and exploit it before anyone else did. While Hollywood and even many of his own compatriots in the exploitation film arena continued to grind out one monster movie after another to capitalize on the American teenager's apparently insatiable appetite for such fare, Lewis envisioned the death of that genre as well as its next evolutionary step. And so, he and his then-partner Dave Friedman began making *gore* films. This was in 1963, almost twenty years before the major Hollywood studios would take the same route with *Friday the 13th* (1980) and its like. Similarly, Lewis made his first nudie in 35 mm before Russ Meyer did and even turned out a series of Southern-fried, "good ole boy" action melodramas in the Burt Reynolds mold well before the name Burt Reynolds lit up its first marquee.

Rivaling the energies of some of filmdom's better-known auteurs, Lewis not only wrote, produced, and directed many of his films, but photographed and scored them as well, often under several pseudonyms, including: Lewis H. Gordon, Sheldon Seymour, Georges Parades, Armand

Parys, and R. L. Smith. Then he went on to devise their advertising campaigns and sell his films—none of which failed to return a profit—on a state-by-state basis from his home base of Chicago, where, in his spare time, he also ran an advertising agency that was billing a million dollars a year.

As a result of his efforts, Herschell Gordon Lewis became the first significant—and influential—filmmaking force the Windy City had seen since the silent film era, and a pioneer in the concept of regional filmmaking.

Today, Lewis has achieved folk-hero status. Exploitation and gore film fans continue to seek out his films as objects of American folk art. And aspiring filmmakers in exploitation look upon him with reverence as not only a major influence upon them but as a man who could teach them a trick or two about how to get their own films off the ground.

Long retired from the exploitation film business, Herschell Gordon Lewis today enjoys a comfortable semiretirement in Florida, where he operates a highly successful advertising agency specializing in direct mail—a subject he has written several acclaimed how-to books about.

Q: You started out as a college professor. How did you make the leap from that to the exploitation film business?

HGL: When I got out of school, I was convinced that the only civilized job was teaching. It's quite a good life with very little pressure and a certain amount of prestige. The academic life has a certain cachet in social circles. But one thing one does not do in academic circles is make a lot of money. I was teaching journalism, English, and the humanities at the University of Mississippi—which was not then one of our major centers of culture—when a friend of my then-father-in-law approached me with the idea of producing advertising materials on an ongoing basis for his chain of thirty-two retail stores. I liked the idea, and in order to pursue it I didn't renew my contract with the school. But by the time I was available to make the move, he was out of business, so I was left in the lurch. I began answering ads in *Advertising Age*, *Broadcasting*, and everywhere else and got two semiconcrete offers, one from the Cotton Council of Memphis, which was looking for a public relations director, and the other from a radio station in Pennsylvania, which was looking for a person to be on the air from six to nine in the morning and sell time the rest of the day. The Cotton Council hemmed and hawed and the radio station made me a firm offer. So, in the interest of keeping food on the table, I went to Pennsylvania. The first month I made sixty-eight dollars and immediately began looking for another job, which I landed, shortly thereafter, at a radio station in Racine, Wisconsin. I moved there with gusto and a couple of weeks later, they made me manager of the station, which meant I was suddenly a person of position again with decision-making capabilities and so on. People then started asking me why I was in radio and not the growing medium of television, so I got interested in TV and joined a TV station, WKY, in Oklahoma City as TV producer. Later, a fellow I'd gone to school with at Northwestern invited me back to Chicago to become the TV director of his advertising agency, and while I was there, Martin Schmidhofer, the fellow who owned the studio where we shot most of our TV commercials and industrial films, told me he was looking for a partner. Since the agency was

beginning to look a little rocky at the time, I bought a half-interest in the studio. We changed the name of the studio to Lewis and Martin Films, and soon after moved to a bigger building at 1431 North Wells Street. Originally, we had nothing but 16-mm film equipment. But for some of the projects we had to shoot for the government and the larger advertising agencies, we eventually bought 35-mm equipment, which is what prompted us to start thinking about the idea of branching out into features. Back then, it would have been impossible to shoot features without 35-mm because if you didn't get your film booked into a theater, there was no way to make your money back, so one thing simply led to another.

Q: Yes, this was before the age of video and all the other outlets filmmakers now have for distribution. Forgetting the equipment factor, what made you think you could actually pull it off and get your film released?

HGL: I met a Chicago distributor named Erwin Joseph who owned a company called Modern Film Distributors. (Dave Friedman worked for Joseph, and that's where I met him, too.) Joseph told me that if I could put together a film that would run through a projector and had a quantity of dialogue and action in it, he would have no problem distributing it on what was then called a states' rights basis. Here's how that worked. Thirty-two exchange areas existed across the country. Within each exchange area, the major companies such as MGM, Warner Brothers, Twentieth Century–Fox, and so on had their own offices, and a number of smaller, independent distributors coexisted with them. Erwin Joseph was well known among the independents and was eager to have a situation in which he could be not a subdistributor but a master distributor, but he'd never had the opportunity to be the master distributor of a movie of any consequence—not that mine were of any consequence. So I formed a company, Mid-Continent Films, to make a picture for which Joseph would act as master distributor. It was called *The Prime*

"They wanted a teenage picture with lots of action and sex." From H. G. L.'s debut feature as a producer, *The Prime Time* (1960), starring Jo Ann LeCompte and James Brooks. *(Courtesy Daniel Krogh)*

Time [1960]; Karen Black made her screen debut in that picture in a bit part by the way. When it was finished, Erwin Joseph and Dave Friedman immediately began to exploit the thing to sub-distributors exchange area by exchange area, state by state. Armed with what appeared to be the early results, Mid-Continent made a second film for Joseph to distribute called *Living Venus* [1960], which I directed. I hadn't directed *The Prime Time*. A man named Gordon Weisenborn directed that one. I was the producer, which goes to show you how much I knew in those days. *Living Venus* turned out to be five times

the movie for about half the cost. But as it was going into distribution, Modern Film Distributors went bust. And when it went bust, Mid-Continent Films immediately went out of business, too, because the only assets the company had were those two movies, and, in fact, we were depending on income from Modern Film Distributors to pay off some lab bills on *Living Venus*. So that's how I got into the film business. As Shakespeare said: "Sweet are the uses of adversity."

Q: How was it determined what kind of film to make the first time out?

HERSCHELL GORDON LEWIS

37

HGL: That decision was made quite cold-bloodedly by Erwin Joseph and Dave Friedman. They outlined exactly what they wanted. For *The Prime Time*, they wanted a teenage picture with lots of action and sex. A guy named Robert Abel wrote the script to their specs. I was the producer —which essentially meant the check writer. *Living Venus* on the other hand was entirely my idea. It was the story of the rise and fall of a fellow roughly patterned after Hugh Hefner. We didn't shoot in a studio, but on locations all over Chicago. Harvey Korman was in the cast. A man named Jim McGinn and I wrote the script, which I felt had more bite to it than *The Prime Time*.

Q: What do you mean by *more bite*?

HGL: It was a more playable picture. The dialogue was more like dialogue. The action was more like action. There was a certain amount of real sexiness to it, although today it would be no worse than a PG-or maybe even a G-rated picture.

Q: Did you regard these pictures as exploitation films, and actually use that word to describe them?

HGL: Oh, yes. They were absolutely regarded as exploitation pictures. As you pointed out, we had no video or cable back then, so you either

made it in the theaters or you didn't make it at all. Now let's say you're a theater owner. In comes MGM with *Ben-Hur* [1959] and in comes Mid-Continent Films with *Living Venus* with a lot of exploitable elements. They both say play my picture. What decision are you going to make? Well, if MGM wants seventy percent of the box office on their picture, and Mid-Continent only wants thirty-five percent and hands you a complete marketing campaign, maybe you'll give Mid-Continent a shot.

Q: What's your definition of an exploitation film?

HGL: An exploitation film is a motion picture in which the elements of plot and acting become subordinate to elements that can be *promoted*. In that respect, I would regard *Jurassic Park* [1993] as the ultimate exploitation film. If you look at *Jurassic Park* with a cold-blooded eye, the acting level is junior high school. People read their lines as though they're seeing them on a TelePrompTer for the first time. But that's not what it's all about. A film like *Cyrano de Bergerac* [1950] with José Ferrer—now, *that's* a motion

"The story of the rise and fall of a fellow roughly patterned after Hugh Hefner." From *Living Venus* **(1960), produced and directed by Herschell Gordon Lewis.** *(Courtesy Daniel Krogh)*

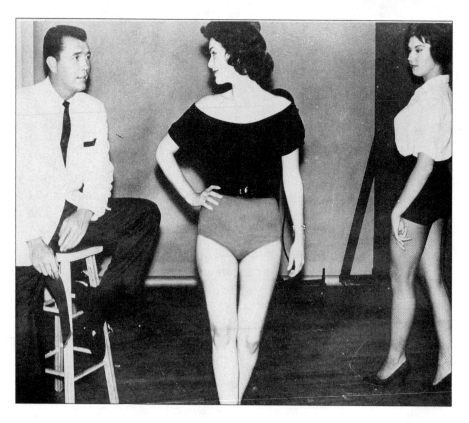

picture. There are no exploitation values at all. It's not an exploitation picture. There are no dinosaurs eating people or chomping off arms. *That's* exploitation—elements the promoter can grab on to and shake in the face of theater owners to get them to play the picture and in the face of the public to get them to see it.

Q: Who was the audience for your films? Paint me a word portrait if you can.

HGL: A typical audience member would live south of the Mason-Dixon line, would be between twenty-five and forty-five, would live in rural rather than urban circumstances, would probably be male, would not be highly educated, and would have a terrific number of prejudices. Oddly enough, the fans I run into now in my posthumous appearances as an historical figure—a cult figure like the late James Dean—are exactly the opposite. They're under forty-five. They're highly educated. And they're totally *without* prejudice. Strange, isn't it?

Q: Yes, it is strange. Perhaps exploitation films have some socially

redeeming value, after all. Tell me how you got into the gore business.

HGL: After *The Prime Time* and *Living Venus*, Dave Friedman and I moved into the area of nudies with such films as *The Adventures of Lucky Pierre* [1961] and *Daughter of the Sun* [1962], and we were quite successful, but after a time I became increasingly disenchanted with them. After all, there were only so many ways to show girls in a nature camp playing volleyball. I told Dave I didn't want to make any more nudies. I felt that our picture *BOIN-N-G!* [1963] was the best one yet made and that we weren't going to beat it. I also told him I could see the grosses dropping. We sat down to figure out what else might suit us, and we put down, tentatively, the stark single word *gore*. If you visualize the film industry of 1963, it wasn't then as it is now. The independent low-budget production could get playing time only if it were one the major companies couldn't or wouldn't touch. Gore fit that narrow strait, so we settled on gore. I wrote a script that was little more than a fourteen-page outline, although as we sometimes did, we credited one of the crew with the script, which was about an insane Egyptian caterer named Fuad Ramses who murders and dismembers several

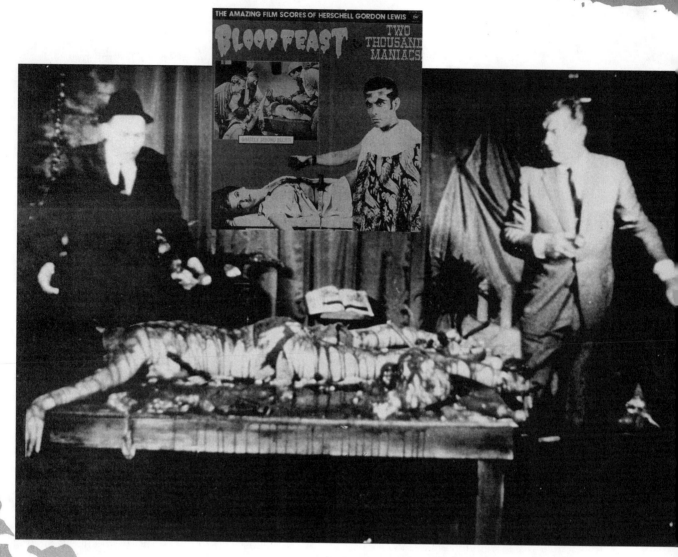

A police captain (Scott H. Hall, left) and hero Bill Kerwin (using the pseudonym Thomas Wood) find a woman's mutilated body in H. G. L.'s splatter groundbreaker, *Blood Feast* (1963). *(Courtesy Daniel Krogh)*

hapless young women for the titular repast. With our usual contempt for the finer points of production, we used as our cast the same people we had used in *Bell, Bare and Beautiful* [1963], a nudie we'd just made. Our principal concern wasn't acting talent but effects. I gave the film the title *Blood Feast* [1963] and knew some newspapers would reject that title, since the word *blood* was controversial in those antediluvian times, but that for theaters it would be a whole new world. More important than plot or cast was blood. The traditional kind of stage blood we'd used in some of our earlier films looked purple, which didn't matter in a black-and-white film but we intended to make *Blood Feast* in color. So,

we went to a cosmetics laboratory in Coral Gables (we were shooting in Florida), and together with the massed brainpower at Barfred Laboratories we came up with stage blood that as far as I know the laboratory is still selling, regrettably and perhaps unfairly with no royalties to us. The base of our stage blood was Kaopectate, but we never told the actors that. We simply told them it was edible.

Q: Did you have any idea you were making a classic?

HGL: Not a classic, no, but I knew as we were cutting *Blood Feast* that we had an extraordinary exploitation film on our hands. We'd ask people to look at a rough cut on the Moviola. Here was a beat-up print, covered with grease pencil marks and patched with tape, together with a half-finished soundtrack. Even though we were laughing and joking as we ran the footage, people would turn green, avert their heads, say "Yucch!" or actually scream. We opened the film at a drive-in in Peoria, feeling that if we dropped dead in Peoria no one would know. The film opened on a Friday. Saturday we couldn't stand it any longer, and we drove down to Peoria. Even though there was a major fair in town, theater traffic was backed up so far the state police were directing it. We were still about a quarter-mile from the theater when I turned to Dave, held out my hand, and said, "I guess we've started something."

Q: What other tidbits do you remember from the production of *Blood Feast*?

HGL: If you remember *Blood Feast*, you'll recall the leads go to a lecture on ancient Egyptian religious cults at one point. The guy we cast as the lecturer was an old carny friend of Dave Friedman's named Al Golden. He kept

saying "indentify" instead of "identify." After thirty-five takes, I was ready to give up, but he got it on the next take. We also burned a hole in a street in Miami. For one scene, we needed an arm that was to be found baked in a pizza oven. To get it to look baked, we took it out into the street and doused it with gasoline. The gasoline can caught fire, and we couldn't put it out. By the time we did get it put out, it had burned a nice round hole in the asphalt street. We tried to melt some asphalt to run into the hole so no one would break an axle, but were only partially successful.

Q: From that auspicious beginning you moved on to *2000 Maniacs* [1964], which, in many ways, is a gore-filled variation on the plot of the musical *Brigadoon*.

HGL: Yes, the plot's about a small Southern town whose citizens were massacred by Union troops during the Civil War that magically reappears a hundred years later to wreak revenge on six Northern tourists who get detoured off the main road. The funniest thing I can remember about making that film was we stuck this banner across the main street of a town called St.

"A BLOOD-SPLATTERED STUDY IN THE MACABRE [AND] A FILM IN WHICH YOU DARE NOT BECOME TOO INVOLVED!" From *Color Me Blood Red* (1965), the concluding film in Lewis and Friedman's "gore trilogy." *(Courtesy Daniel Krogh)*

"A TOWN OF MADMEN CRAZED WITH BLOOD LUST!" From *2000 Maniacs* (1964), Lewis's gore-filled variation on the plot of the musical *Brigadoon.* (Courtesy Daniel Krogh)

Cloud, Florida. The banner said, "Pleasant Valley Centennial—1865–1965." We shot the picture in 1963. Well, I came out on the porch of the hotel where we were all staying one day, and two guys are looking up at this banner. One guy said, "I wonder why Pleasant Valley is having its centennial here?" And the other guy said, "What I don't get is why they put the banner up so far ahead of time." We had a real good time making that picture. It's one of my favorites. It was an excellently contrived picture, and the best acted picture I did outside of the later *A Taste of Blood* [1967], which is a much more polished production overall.

Q: *Color Me Blood Red* concluded your gore trilogy with Dave Friedman. Since you were such a successful team, why did you and Dave break up?

HGL: Those three movies were produced by a quartet—me, Dave Friedman, Sid Reich, and Stanford Kohlberg, who was a theater owner in Chicago. Kohlberg represented to us that he could get the Exchange National Bank of Chicago to fund a permanent film production company, which was my then-ultimate dream. But to do that, he said, we had to let monies accrue, so we quit taking money out —it was pouring in

from *Blood Feast* and *2000 Maniacs*; we had not yet finished cutting *Color Me Blood Red*. Weeks and weeks went by and I finally called a guy I knew at the Exchange Bank to find out what was going on, and he told me he knew nothing about the production company venture whatsoever. So, the three of us wound up suing Kohlberg. Since our income was cut off, I said to Dave we better make another picture to get some cash flowing in. The picture I intended to make was an exact match for our audience called *Moonshine Mountain* [1964]. As we prepared to make it, I set up a deal with my distributor in Charlotte, North Carolina—a very nice fellow named Harry Kerr— to help us on location in exchange for additional distribution rights in Atlanta and Jacksonville— prime territory for our movies. So, I'm getting ready to shoot, and suddenly Dave Friedman simply disappeared. He vanished. In a couple of weeks I discovered he had privately settled with Kohlberg and moved to California to work with a fellow named Dan Sonney, who was an old-line film distributor. I was furious with Dave that he

Some backwoods mayhem from *Moonshine Mountain* (1964), a film "Directed by Herschell Gordon Lewis, who ought to know better but don't." (Courtesy Daniel Krogh)

HERSCHELL GORDON LEWIS

43

had privately settled with Kohlberg. It destroyed the preplanning on *Moonshine Mountain*, but I was determined to go ahead so I made a deal with Kerr to get advances from some of his sub-distributors—it was almost like Esau selling his birthright for a mess of pottage—and shot *Moonshine* on my own. I was both producer and director on that movie. Before, Dave was the producer and I was the director, although the titles really meant nothing. We also doubled as soundman and cameraman, respectively. I was obviously in a pickle making this movie on my own, but fortunately it turned out to be a real smash. The lawsuit with Kohlberg went on and on, and I was totally out of touch with Dave Friedman. About a year later, Sid Reich died and his son settled immediately with Kohlberg—the family wanted no litigation hanging over their heads, the IRS had stepped in and so on—so here I was the sole dog in the manger, the only plaintiff left. So, I finally settled with Kohlberg too because it was quite obvious to me that the legal fees would amount to more money than I would ever get back. At some meeting years later at the Theatre Owners of America in Los Angeles, I finally ran into Dave and we made up. And we've been good friends ever since. In fact, we're better friends now than we were before. But that's the reason we split up and I went out on my own.

Q: I've always liked the screen credit you gave yourself on *Moonshine Mountain*. If I remember correctly, it reads: "Directed by Herschell Gordon Lewis, who ought to know better, but don't."

HGL: That's right.

Q: It sort of cuts your critics off at the knees. Tell me a little about *A Taste of Blood*.

HGL: That was, as I have said, my best picture. We had cooperation on that picture that no one has had before or since. We had production values on that picture, which is two hours long!

Q: Your *Gone With the Wind* of gore.

HGL: It really is.

Q: Did you have any trouble getting that big ocean ship to unload the vampire's coffin for the film?

HGL: Absolutely none. That was the height of splendid cooperation. We told them exactly what we were doing: making a horror film, a *Dracula*-type picture, and they hoisted that box with the casket in it for us. They even stopped the people from getting off the boat so that we could get

Lewis in full makeup for his cameo in *A Taste of Blood* (1967). *(Courtesy Daniel Krogh)*

HERSCHELL GORDON LEWIS

45

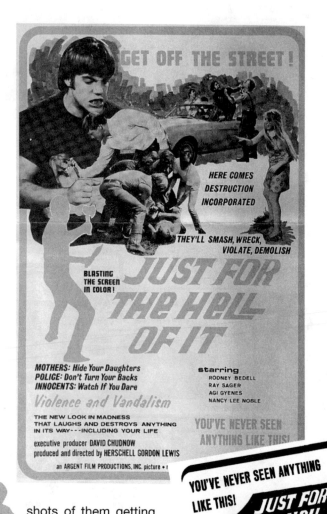

GET OFF THE STREET!

HERE COMES
DESTRUCTION
INCORPORATED

THEY'LL SMASH, WRECK,
VIOLATE, DEMOLISH

BLASTING
THE SCREEN
IN COLOR!

JUST FOR THE HELL OF IT

MOTHERS: Hide Your Daughters
POLICE: Don't Turn Your Backs
INNOCENTS: Watch If You Dare

Violence and Vandalism

THE NEW LOOK IN MADNESS
THAT LAUGHS AND DESTROYS ANYTHING
IN ITS WAY···INCLUDING YOUR LIFE

executive producer DAVID CHUDNOW
produced and directed by HERSCHELL GORDON LEWIS

an ARGENT FILM PRODUCTIONS, INC. picture • 1

starring
RODNEY BEDELL
RAY SAGER
AGI GYENES
NANCY LEE NOBLE

YOU'VE NEVER SEEN
ANYTHING LIKE THIS!

YOU'VE NEVER SEEN ANYTHING LIKE THIS! **JUST FOR THE HELL OF IT**

their Mars lights flashing. We had a lot of explaining to do at that moment, which was about four-thirty in the morning.

Q: After that you made *The Gruesome Twosome* [1967].

HGL: Yes. At the tail of the picture for the scene where the heroine is supposed to poke out the eye of the homicidal son, our prop person, Allison Louise Downe, came up with cow eyeballs which were about thirty-seven times larger than a human eyeball. So, we were scrambling around for something we could use, and all we could find was a fish. We ended up using fish eyeballs, which looked pretty real by the way.

Q: Any memories of your two back-to-back motorcycle gang, juvenile delinquency movies, *She-Devils on Wheels* [1968] and *Just for the Hell of It* [1968]?

HGL: There was this girl, Agi Gynes, that we used in *Just for the Hell of It*. She was supposed to say, "They shouldn't listen to that senile old woman." Instead, she kept saying, "They shouldn't listen to that senile old wo . . . MAN!" We did that scene all afternoon. Later, I said to myself, "You jerk, why didn't you just change the line?" She never did get it. That girl was our jinx on that picture. She was trying to prove she could ride a motorcycle because she wanted to be in *She-Devils*, which we were shooting at the same time. She borrowed a 125-cc bike from another girl, who we called Fang because she only had one tooth, and drove the damn thing right into the swimming pool of the motel where we were staying. "Look at me, Mr. Lewis, I can do wheelies!" And into the pool she went. As I remember, she pulled a dying swan routine, but no one gave a hoot for her. They were all more concerned with the bike and the pool, which I thought was very funny.

shots of them getting off. We did it with the public relations people of, I think it was, Emerald Lines.

Q: You also acted in that picture.

HGL: Right, the actor I hired didn't show up. So, we made a fake mustache for me, and I pulled a cap down over my head and spoke in a thick British accent. I figured nobody would know who it was. I was horrified at the mix to have a guy turn to me and say, "Hey, what are you doing in this thing?" Oh, Jesus, I thought, my cover is blown. Also on *A Taste of Blood*, in the middle of the night we had these prop police firing blanks. I didn't want to stop them because they were doing it well, and they weren't professional actors. But surer than hell, that racket in the middle of the night brought out a whole passel of real on-duty police with their sirens wailing and

Q: *She-Devils on Wheels* was about an all-girl gang of bikers, The Maneaters, and is the more

Lewis's obscure *Blast-Off Girls* (1967), a tale of the '60s rock music scene, remains one of his most polished productions. (Courtesy Daniel Krogh)

famous of the two films. I understand American-International Pictures wanted to pick it up for distribution.

HGL: They did distribute it in some territories. My partner on that one was a man named Fred Sandy, whose son, Jerry Sandy, was the AIP distributor in Washington, D.C. Fred was a very close friend of that cigar-chomping lout, Sam Arkoff, who ran AIP. He wanted to show off for Arkoff by making a deal to have AIP distribute *She-Devils*, which is a very playable picture by the way, even today. It was the first-ever female motorcycle gang movie. And the girls in it were not fake. They could really ride those big Harleys, Nortons, and BMWs. We decided to let AIP distribute the picture in some territories, and in others we went with states' rights. AIP paired it with a picture called *Born Losers*, the picture that introduced the character of Billy Jack to the screen, on a fifty-fifty deal. Turned out, we made far more money in areas where AIP was *not* the distributor. So, I said to Fred the only way we can make a permanent deal with AIP is if they give us a negative guarantee, which, of course, they wouldn't, and didn't.

Q: Over your long career, you made quite a variety of exploitation pictures, not just horror-gore films.

HGL: That's right. I did not want to be just a one-string fiddle.

Q: One of your more interesting concepts was the nudie lesbian Western *Linda and Abilene* [1969], which I believe you shot at the Spahn Movie Ranch, the domain of the infamous Charles Manson family.

HGL: Yes, they were living there at the time. We knew they were goofy—we saw them all over the place always half stoned—but we didn't know how goofy. Everybody there was either broken or crippled. There was Randy somebody, "the world-famous cowboy stuntman," who had taken so many falls over the years that he could barely walk. His ancient horse had to be thirty-five years old at least. The owner of the place, George Spahn, was blind. It was a *very* strange place. It was also a lousy place to shoot movies because they had all these telephone wires going into the ranch, so it was hard to say this was a ranch from the nineteenth century. But it was a place to shoot, and the price was right.

Q: Another of your more obscure films, *Blast-Off Girls* [1967], has gotten some favorable press of late as one of your most polished productions. Comparisons have even been made between it and the Beatles film *A Hard Day's Night* [1964].

HGL: Well, the only real similarity is that they're both about the '60s rock music scene. *Blast-Off*

Two vacationing college girls, lost in the Southern backwoods, meet their gruesome end in Lewis's *This Stuff'll Kill Ya!* (1971). *(Courtesy Daniel Krogh)*

Girls is about the rise and fall of an unscrupulous rock music producer, and it's not a bad picture at all. I have fond memories of it. I think it's still playable today.

Q: It and another later film, *Year of the Yahoo!* [1972], even have a degree of social commentary in them.

HGL: Indeed they do. *Yahoo!*, which takes its title from Jonathan Swift's *Gulliver's Travels*, was about a country-and-western singer who runs for U.S. senator. In fact, a Robert Redford picture called *The Candidate* came out not long after which in my opinion was a direct lift—except for the music—from *Year of the Yahoo!*

Q: The plot description also resembles the 1992 Tim Robbins film *Bob Roberts*.

HGL: Yes, it does.

Q: After that, you made only a couple more pictures and then got out of the business. Why?

HGL: I got tired of dealing with so many flimflam distributors. The fun had gone out of it. You see, I had no position. I couldn't say to a distributor, if you play this picture, I'll also give you this one. Universal can say, if you play this picture I'll give you *Jurassic Park* second run. So I had no carrots to dangle in front of the jackasses. Beyond this, there were just so many other pitfalls. For example, the producer gets last count. Let me explain. Let's suppose a theater in Joplin, Missouri, is playing my picture. How do I know how much money is coming into the box office? Now today, the chains prevent much of that just by the very nature of the bookkeeping they have to have. If I am part of some chain of theaters, the automation is such that cheating becomes almost impossible. They don't want their own managers cheating them; they in turn can't cheat the producer because it's all computer printout. It wasn't that way when I was in the business. Most theaters that we played in were individually owned. So you had to trust that whatever grosses might be reported were what they said they were. They were reported to the subdistributor, who had the second count. I as producer got third count. So Lord knows what the actual film rentals might have been. Yes, there were a handful of really honorable distributors. For example, Tom Dowd, who owned the Capri Theatre in Chicago where *Lucky Pierre* played for nine weeks. I shot five or six movies for him—*Alley Tramp* [1966] and *Linda and Abilene* were some.

Q: How did you lose the rights to your films?

HGL: I had bought a piece of a car rental

business, and my equity was guaranteed by the movies. The bank accepted them as equity—much to my astonishment because I thought they were burned-out, old, not commercial anymore. Anyway, the car rental business went under and the bank grabbed the movies and sold them. I didn't even care that much to tell you the truth. I figured what the heck, they're not really worth anything anymore, which goes to show you just how cloudy my crystal ball can be.

Q: Yes, they've come back in a big, big way, and are now making tons of money for other people.

HGL: The schlock that wouldn't die. Maybe we should make a sci-fi picture with that title.

Q: Since you and your films have become sort of a miniphenomenon have you ever thought of doing another film?

Year of the Yahoo! (1972), Lewis's satiric look at the tumultuous campaign of a conservative country-and-western singer running for U.S. senator, predated Tim Robbins's film on a similar theme by twenty years. *(Courtesy Daniel Krogh)*

HERSCHELL GORDON LEWIS

I'LL TAKE YOU ON-ALL OF YOU!

New Strange Pleasures
Of An Unrestrained Love Affair

ALLEY TRAMP

Starring
ANETTE COURSET · JEAN LAMEE

released by
United Pictures Organization

The new, strange
desires and erotic
pleasures of an
incestuous love affair
that had no restraints.

She gave French lessons
that the books blush at.

THE SLEAZE MERCHANTS

WILL SEXY GIRLS OVERRUN THE COUNTRY?

HOW TO MAKE A DOLL

In Eye-Popping COLOR

PRODUCTION-LINE INSTANT WOMEN WHO DO THINGS EVEN CASANOVA NEVER DARED HOPE FOR!

HGL: Dave Friedman and I have talked about doing a *Blood Feast II*. We have a movie called *Herschell Gordon Lewis' Grim Fairy Tales* totally scripted. But I'm not going to put my money into it. I'm perfectly willing to show up to direct a picture or do the campaign or just be elder statesman or whatever. But this time it's got to be with what they call O.P.M.—Other People's Money. I don't know why the offers haven't been forthcoming, either. I don't understand it because videos of the ancient movies are doing such a rip-roaring business that if nothing else the automatic following would account for recoupment of the negative costs. But it's not mine to say.

Q: What do you think of the phenomenon by the way? There's even a rock group calling themselves 10,000 Maniacs.

HGL: The dynasty continues! I appear at conventions when I'm invited and the deal makes sense, and I have a *wonderful* time. I really enjoy it. The most enjoyable thing is to sit there and have *2000 Maniacs* playing and half the people in the audience know the theme music, which I wrote, by heart. That to me is extraordinarily enjoyable. Some people come up to me with stuff to sign—stills, posters, et cetera—stuff I haven't seen for years and years. Where on earth did they get them? That is truly heartwarming.

People will remark on episodes I've long since forgotten. Who wouldn't respond to that sort of treatment?

Q: To what do you attribute it?

HGL: I guess I was more of a pioneer than I realized at the time. The other aspect might be because what I do bring to this arena is total irreverence. And I'm at the point now where I'm secure enough and enough out of it that I can say exactly what I think—which many people at these conventions can't do because they're always selling something, themselves or whatever. I don't sell a doggone thing. As Popeye used to say, "I yam what I yam and dat's all dat I yam."

Q: Is that your epitaph?

HGL: No, because it also applies to many other people. My epitaph? How about this: "He seen somethin' different. And he *done* it."

SELECTED FILMOGRAPHY

1960: The Prime Time, Living Venus; **1961:** The Adventures of Lucky Pierre; **1962:** Daughter of the Sun, Nature's Playmates; **1963:** BOIN-N-G!, Blood Feast, Goldilocks and the Three Bares (a.k.a. Goldilocks' Three Chicks), Bell, Bare and Beautiful, Scum of the Earth (a.k.a. Devil's Camera); **1964:** 2000 Maniacs, Moonshine Mountain; **1965:** Color Me Blood Red, Monster a Go-Go (a.k.a. Terror at Halfday), Sin, Suffer and Repent; **1966:** Jimmy, the Boy Wonder, Alley Tramp, An Eye for an Eye; **1967:** Santa Visits the Magic Land of Mother Goose, Suburban Roulette, Something Weird, A Taste of Blood, The Gruesome Twosome, The Girl, the Body and the Pill, Blast-Off Girls; **1968:** She-Devils on Wheels, Just for the Hell of It, How to Make a Doll (a.k.a. How to Love a Doll), The Psychic (a.k.a. Copenhagen's Psychic Loves); **1969:** The Ecstasies of Women, Linda and Abilene; **1970:** Miss Nymphet's Zap-In, The Wizard of Gore; **1972:** This Stuff'll Kill Ya!, Year of the Yahoo!, Black Love, The Gore-Gore Girls.

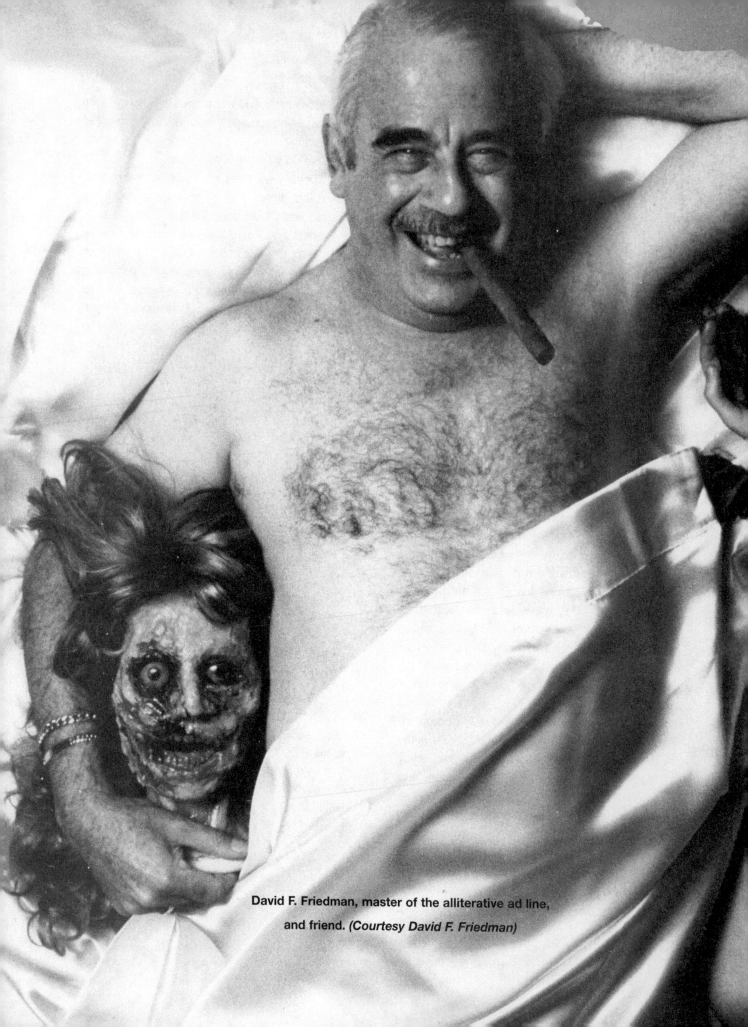

David F. Friedman, master of the alliterative ad line, and friend. (*Courtesy David F. Friedman*)

David F. Friedman

BY JOHN McCARTY

In most chronicles of exploitation film, the name David F. Friedman is overshadowed by that of his more famous former partner, Herschell Gordon Lewis. But Friedman continued to work in the field long after Lewis got out of the business, and his body of work as a trash-film producer, director, writer, soundman, and promoter looms even larger.

Now retired and living in Alabama—though he still maintains an office in Hollywood—Dave Friedman is also a virtual walking encyclopedia on the history of the American exploitation film. He has authored two volumes of memoirs recounting his hilarious adventures and misadventures in the trade, the first of which *A Youth in Babylon—Confessions of a Trash Film King* (Prometheus Books, 1990), concludes in 1963 when he and Lewis ended their partnership after changing the face of screen horror forever with their ground-breaking gore trilogy of *Blood Feast* (1963), *2000 Maniacs* (1964), and *Color Me Blood Red* (1965). Volume Two, *Kings of Babylon*, picks up where the first book leaves off, focusing on Friedman's more than twenty-year solo career as a sleaze merchant in Hollywood. Together, the two volumes form the ultimate chronicle of the heyday of exploitation film (the 1950s through the 1980s).

Like many of his compatriots in the exploitation film field, Dave is a former carny man with a lifelong interest in all things related to the gaudy, hucksterish world of the circus. Like Russ Meyer, he developed his filmmaking skills as a member of the U.S. Army Signal Corps during World War II. After the war, he worked as a carnival press agent and owner, then as a press agent for Paramount Pictures in Chicago. In the early '50s, he officially launched his career as a "circulating salesman of cinema sleaze" when he got a job as assistant to legendary "birth of a baby" film mogul Kroger Babb, whose last film, an Italian-made version of *Uncle Tom's Cabin,** Friedman considers to be one of the unintentionally funniest exploitation films ever made.

"The picture looked like *Gone With the Wind*," he says. "But the production company had redubbed the soundtrack using second-rate Italian actors who could barely speak English. So, you had things like Uncle Tom saying, 'Hey, please-uh, donna whippa me no more!' And Simon Legree retorting, 'I'm a gonna whippa you ass!' It was Kroger's last hurrah."

Friedman later bought out Babb's share in their distribution company, Modern Film, and struck out on his own. It was at this time that a young man named Herschell Gordon Lewis walked into his Chicago office and said he had some money to make a picture and needed a distributor. The two hit it off and cranked out a sexy tale of "youth, love, life, and the violent plunge into adulthood" titled *The Prime Time* (1960). The duo then turned to sexier stuff with a comic bent, a

* actually West German with Yugoslavian and Italian participation

55

Claire Brennan as the title character in *She Freak* (1967), Friedman's remake of Tod Browning's *Freaks* (1932). *(Courtesy David F. Friedman)*

genre known as "nudie cuties," the first of which, *The Adventures of Lucky Pierre* (1961), a "spicy dish of adult cinema fare filmed in cutie color and skinamascope," returned between $150,000 and $200,000 on their modest $7,500 investment.

"That was a lot of money back then," Friedman says. "So, we made several more. But then we started getting tired of them and started kicking around other exploitable ideas. The idea of blood, guts, and gore arose out of those discussions. We went to one of our investors, an exhibitor named Stan Kohlberg, and told him our idea, and he gave us $24,500 to shoot *Blood Feast* in Florida." The film was a big hit on the drive-in circuit, especially in the South, so Kohlberg told the duo to get busy making another, and another.

Following a disagreement, Friedman and Lewis decided to split up and go their separate ways. Lewis remained in Chicago but Friedman headed for California where he spent the next two decades writing, producing, and/or distributing a host of soft-X, sexploitation fare. He and Lewis have remained friends, however, and have the highest regard for each other. Friedman still calls Lewis "The smartest guy I ever met. He could watch a brain surgeon at work, and then do it himself the next day."

Q: Since you and so many of your fellow exploiteers are former carny and circus men, I was wondering if you think there's a relationship between the two.

FRIEDMAN: Oh, yes. Originally, all the exploiteers, including myself, were carnies. If they weren't working on road-showing a movie, they were out working with a circus or carnival. The early days of exploitation, what we call road-showing—a combination stage and screen show presentation—were definitely the transition period from the carnival to the movie theater. Road-showing involved a lot more than just showing a movie. There was a lecture onstage, a live appearance à la *Mom and Dad*, the sale of books, and a host of things that had their roots in carny. Let's take the career of Lewis Sonney, for example, who,

after capturing the bankrobber Roy Gardner and becoming the most famous cop in America, went on the stage as "Officer Sonney." He'd take out a .38 revolver, put a bulletproof vest on a kid from the audience, shoot him, and then say, "See, he's okay. He's not hurt." A live demonstration in other words. You could do things like that in the good old days before everybody starting suing everybody. Sonney then framed his own "Crime Doesn't Pay" show, and started showing a movie along with it, a Clara Bow picture he'd picked up called *Crime and Punishment* that he took from town to town. In the lobby of each theater where he was road-showing the picture, he'd set up a fake electric chair that the suckers could sit in, and he'd give them a blast from a Ford spark coil. He had a simulated jail cell where he'd install the town tramp dressed in a convict's uniform, and so on. So, you see, it was more than just showing a picture. Dwain Esper, who bought *Freaks* [1932] from Mrs. Tod Browning and took it on the road as *Nature's Mistakes*, brought a whole company of freaks with him that he'd set up in the lobbies of the theater à la a sideshow. Road-showing was really carny under a roof. That kind of thing—live appearances along with the show—ended with *Mom and Dad* [1947], one of the birth of a baby or sex hygiene pictures. After that, exploitation became ballyhooing the picture alone—a good example of which is Mike Rapps's picture *Poor White Trash* [1957]. Mike had a drive-in down in Mobile, and he made a picture to show there and at other drive-ins in the South called *Bayou*. United Artists distributed the picture for seven years, but did nothing with it. Finally, Mike got the picture back, retitled it *Poor White Trash*, and came up with a campaign: "Due to the abnormal nature of this picture, no one under eighteen will be admitted unless accompanied by an adult; uniformed guards will check admittance" and so on. His trailer for the film was just a back shot of him sitting in a chair, just talking about the abnormal content of the picture, the theme of which was incest. Nothing graphic was shown in

the film, of course; in fact, the picture today would probably get a G rating. Mike's whole thing was "If you want to see a movie, you can watch one on television. I give you a *show*." Of course, you saw the show before you ever got into the theater. That's exploitation.

Q: Is that your definition of an exploitation film?

FRIEDMAN: Any non-major film that is a little out of taste could be called an exploitation film. The secret back in the early days of exploitation was that the exploiteers could touch on subjects that were forbidden to the majors—drugs, incest, et cetera. The major companies, due to the code, couldn't make pictures about those subjects.

Q: But now they can. Have exploitation films today been co-opted by the majors?

FRIEDMAN: Of course. *All* film has been co-opted by the majors today, just as all theaters have been co-opted by the major theater circuits. There are no more independent theaters, or very few, no more drive-ins, and those drive-ins that are left are playing major company product, playing day and date with hardtop theaters. In the 1950s, when you had five thousand drive-ins in this country, exploitation was made to order for them because you could do things in a lot that you couldn't do inside a theater. You could bring in a circus if you wanted to, or shoot off fireworks. And you could bring in pictures the downtown theaters wouldn't play—pictures with a little skin, or whatever.

Friedman ballyhooed *The Lustful Turk* (1968) as "a picture in the tradition of *Lawrence of Arabia* . . . but with girls!" *(Courtesy David F. Friedman)*

DAVID F. FRIEDMAN

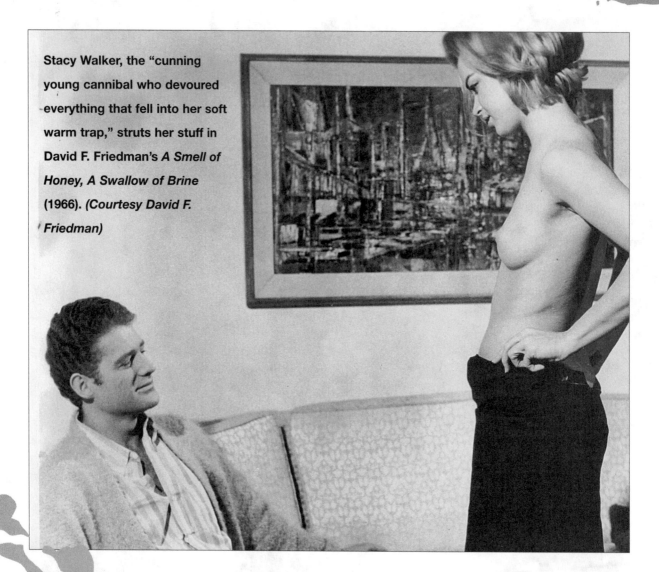

Stacy Walker, the "cunning young cannibal who devoured everything that fell into her soft warm trap," struts her stuff in David F. Friedman's *A Smell of Honey, A Swallow of Brine* (1966). *(Courtesy David F. Friedman)*

Another element of exploitation films is that they were cheaply made, very shoddily made if you will, and made well outside the Hollywood mainstream. Sam Katzman, for example, was the absolute master of exploitation. All Sam did was read newspapers every day, and the minute something bizarre appeared in the newspapers, Sam had a picture in production about it two days later. But exploitation as we used to know it is something whose time came and then passed. Today's exploitation pictures—the *Friday the 13th*s, the Freddy Krueger films, the action films, and so on are all in the mainstream. I think that's why there's such an interest today in the old-style exploitation pictures. It was a form of American theatrical history that has never been documented fully. Maybe four thousand or five thousand exploitation pictures were made, starting right in the silent era, where exploitation pictures dealt with such "forbidden" subjects as labor strikes and the immigrant experience—subjects the majors, on the whole, wouldn't touch with a twenty-foot pole.

Q: Whose idea was *Blood Feast*? Yours or Herschell's?

FRIEDMAN: We're equally guilty. Herschell and I sketched the story, and Allison Louise Downe, who worked for both of us, wrote the script. Connie Mason was my idea. Herschell wasn't very keen on her. She was a terrible actress. But I insisted on using her both on *Blood Feast* and *2000 Maniacs* because, being a former Playboy centerfold and Playmate of the Year, she was not only a very beautiful girl, but had some make pictures on my own. The first one I did after migrating to California was what we call a "roughie" titled *The Defilers*, which I wrote after reading John Fowles's novel *The Collector* about a kidnapping. I rehashed it into a story about two young rich punks out for kicks who kidnap this young girl who's just arrived in Hollywood and rape her. The picture had all the elements—nudity, violence, street language, kids smoking dope, you name it—although today it would probably get an R, certainly no worse than that. Lee Frost directed it, and I produced, photographed, and did the sound. My assistant, Billy Castleman, did a music score that was gangbusters. And it turned out to be a really well-made little picture. In fact, a couple of critics have called it the definitive black-and-white exploitation picture of the early '60s. After that a fellow named Pete Perry and his partner, Dan Sonney, Lewis Sonney's son, wanted to make a costume picture in color called *The Notorious Daughter of Fanny Hill*, and they hired me to be the producer. We shot it entirely in a studio in about four and a half days—Laszlo Kovacs, who went on to have a major Hollywood career, was the cameraman. The film was beautiful looking. In terms of production value, acting, and its overall presentation it was far and away better than any picture Herschell and I had made together. It made a ton of money, too. I did a string of costume pictures after that—*Headmistress*, based on a *Decameron* story, a Western called *Brand of Shame*, and *The Lustful Turk*, which was based on another old piece of pornography similar to Cleland's *Fanny Hill*, that I ballyhooed as "a picture in the tradition of *Lawrence of Arabia* . . . but with girls!"

Q: What was the average cost of these pictures?

FRIEDMAN: About twenty-five thousand dollars. And with the exception of *The Defilers* and another one I made after that called *A Smell of Honey, A Swallow of Brine*, they were all costume pictures, soft-X pictures, in color. The great thing about soft-X films was that you could advertise in *Daily Variety* and *The Hollywood Reporter* for casts, and you would get some of

the most beautiful-looking girls, who wanted to be actresses, to come in and test. You told them there would be nudity involved, but no sex, and

Their contract with the madman was only an oral agreement

THE SUCKERS

FILMED IN COLOR EXPLICITLY ADULT!!

that was no problem with them. You weren't always looking over your shoulder waiting for the L.A.P.D. to show up, as was the case with hardcore. Soft-X was a bona fide industry, a *big* industry, in L.A. at the time. And you could get fairly decent actresses and actors for these things. People who could actually read a line of dialogue. For a picture I made in about 1969 called *Starlet,* I gave one of these young girls three pages of dialogue to read for a scene that I'd cribbed from Portia's speech from Shakespeare's *The Merchant of Venice*, and she brought it off beautifully. We did crane shots, a real Hollywoodstyle set piece. When the shot was done, she came to me and said, "Gee, Mr. Friedman, that was such beautiful writing." And I said, "Well, thanks. But I did have a little help."

Q: Since you'd been so successful with the three gore films you'd made with Herschell, why did you go back to soft-X or nudie cutie pictures after you struck out on your own?

FRIEDMAN: After *BOIN-N-G!* [1963], Herschell and I decided we were getting a little tired of doing nudie cuties. We also thought that type of picture had about run its course, which was the one thing that Herschell and I figured wrong. There were only about two hundred houses in the United States playing X pictures at the time, when I got to California in 1964, the market expanded tremendously, and there were about seven hundred-plus theaters in the country playing them. Soft-X films played these same theaters, although they escaped the onus that fell on X films because they were not hard-core. And because they weren't hard-core, they could play in general release theaters and drive-ins,

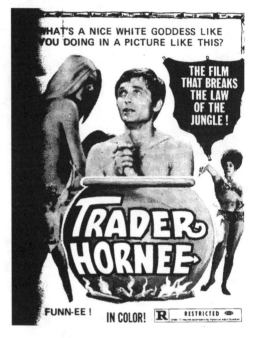

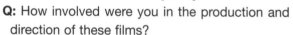

too, so there were a lot of outlets for them. Newspapers and the trades used to review these films, which they did not do with hard-core stuff. I remember I opened *Trader Hornee* at the Hippodrome in Buffalo, and the *Buffalo Evening News* called it the funniest jungle picture they'd ever seen. "Dave Friedman is a honky-tonk genius!" I'll never forget that quote. There was no stigma attached to these films, and we kept making better-quality ones all the time. We shot *The Erotic Adventures of Zorro* at the old Selznick Studios, where the presidio set from *Duel in the Sun* [1946] was still standing. We repainted it and it became downtown Los Angeles for *Zorro*. There were about a hundred people in that picture. It cost $76,000 and looked like a $2 million picture. And it was funny, too. We portrayed Don Diego as a gay when he wasn't being Zorro, an idea George Hamilton stole completely for his Zorro, *The Gay Blade* [1981].

Q: How involved were you in the production and direction of these films?

FRIEDMAN: I always took a very active hand in production. I wrote all these things and was on the set every day. If I had a suggestion for the director, he listened to me because normally it was the right suggestion. Byron Mabe directed several of these things. Byron wanted to be an actor and finally landed the lead in *The Doberman Gang* [1972] where he was upstaged by the dogs. Anyway, on *Space Thing*, he'd hired some young lady as costume designer—can you imagine? A costume designer for a nudie?—and she showed me some of her sketches of these long, flowing gowns and so on, and I said "What's this?" "This is what the girls are going to wear in the film," she said. "Uh-uh, they're going to wear the tightest crotch suits with the most exposure," I told her. "But this is what the director had in mind," she said. And I said, "Well this is not what the producer has in mind, or the distributor." So I had to let Mabe go and I finished the picture myself. It makes *Plan 9 from Outer Space* [1956] look like *Citizen Kane* [1941]! It's sold five thousand copies on video, though. Amazing!

Q: You were involved in a couple of major studio films too, weren't you?

FRIEDMAN: Yes, Fox needed some footage for a picture called *Marriage of a Young Stockbroker* [1971] with Richard Benjamin, who at one point in the picture is supposed to go to a nudie theater. They needed nudie footage for the picture being shown in the theater and they asked me to shoot it. Then a picture called *First Monday in October* [1981] came along, a Paramount Picture with Walter Matthau about an obscenity case. Paramount called me in to shoot the sequences for the dirty movie the Supreme Court justices are screening, and I made that for them. Funny thing—the day we shot the footage in my house all the top brass at Paramount showed up to watch. Meanwhile on the soundstages at Paramount they're shooting this big scene at the Supreme Court, which they've re-created at great cost with 250 extras and Walter Matthau and Jill Clayburgh acting up a storm, and we've got this whole contingent of Paramount brass over at my house watching us shoot footage of a couple of little naked girls. There's a message in there somewhere.

Q: Why did they come to you for this material?

FRIEDMAN: As I said, there was no stigma attached to shooting soft-X pictures in Hollywood at that time, as there was with hard-core. I wasn't famous—or infamous—but I was fairly well known in the industry. I knew everybody at Paramount because I worked there in my early career as a press agent. My name was in the trades quite often. I was invited to all the industry functions. I was a member of the Variety Club and various other organizations—I hobnobbed with industry people all the time. Went to

Cannes every year. That's why they came to me. Lee Frost, Russ Meyer, and I were the three guys who from time to time worked with the majors. Lee came up with an idea for a Peter Fonda and Warren Oates picture called *Race With the Devil* [1975]—

Q: One of my favorite drive-in movies!

FRIEDMAN: Lee had written that with Wes Bishop and Fox sent them down to Texas to shoot it. Being from the exploitation school of filmmaking, Lee edited in the camera. With a major company picture you're lucky to average two minutes a day of finished film. The first day, Lee sent back six minutes of film and it was all usable. And the studio said "This is excellent, but where are your outtakes?" And Lee said "What outtakes—there's just a couple of hundred feet, what do you need to see that for?" They told him they wanted to see the total footage he shot that day. "How much did you shoot?" they asked. Lee told them about eighteen hundred feet, half of which was usable, and they said "No! You're supposed to shoot eight thousand to ten thousand feet a day, no matter how much is usable!" Lee asked why, and they replaced him with Jack Starrett, who couldn't carry Lee Frost's bags. But that's how the majors think. Wes stayed on as producer, but that was Lee's big chance at the majors and it was through their stupidity that it didn't work out. Russ had two shots—*Beyond the Valley of the Dolls* [1970] and *The Seven Minutes* [1971]—but he said "Never again!" Russ is like I am. We're both fiercely independent. One of the reasons I walked away from Paramount was that it got to the point that everything was being decided by a committee. Russ and I did our own thing, used our own money, made pictures the way we wanted to make them, and if the public was pleased, we could thank God, but we didn't have to answer to anyone else.

Q: So you never harbored any real aspirations to work for the majors?

FRIEDMAN: No, because I knew I would never have the freedom that I had working for myself. But I brushed up against them now and again.

Q: Did you ever make a film you eventually decided to disassociate yourself from?

FRIEDMAN: Yes, *Ilsa—She Wolf of the SS* [1974]. That was one of the few times I was working as a paid mercenary. These people from Canada, André Link and John Dunning who ran a company called Cinepix, came down to Los Angeles to be producers and they asked me for help because I was licensed to do business in California, had all the necessary paperwork, could do a payroll, et cetera. I had an entrée they didn't have, so they hired me to produce *Ilsa* here in California. I knew the old "Hogan's Heroes" set was still standing, but it was on property that had been sold for development and was slated for demolition. They let me use it for *Ilsa* because we intended to burn it down at the end of the film and that saved them the expense of doing it. But Cinepix constantly played a money game with me. They had this script that was as thick as an encyclopedia with scenes with the Allies attacking two thousand German soldiers, storming the camp, and so on. And the budget was only $150,000! I said for that money there would be no two thousand soliders—just *one* soldier running into the camp shouting "The Allies are coming!"—and we'd shoot off some firecrackers, and that's it! At any rate, I dug up some equipment and rolling stock—German half-tracks and so on from a private collector I knew, assigned Don Edmonds to direct, and sent him and Billy Castleman up to

Space Thing (1968), "the picture that makes *Plan 9 from Outer Space* look like *Citizen Kane*." (Courtesy David F. Friedman)

Canada to close the deal. Cinepix sent us ten thousand dollars to get rolling, and then the cash flow dried up, and I was left with a bunch of bills and people to pay. They kept telling me the money was delayed because it was being routed through Panama and Luxembourg. I told them I didn't care how it was being routed, just to get it to me fast or I was going to shut the production down, send all the people to the state labor board, and Cinepix would never be able to set foot in L.A. again. And they said, "Could you lend us fifty thousand dollars for a few days?" I said, "Hey, I'm working for you guys, I'm not your partner!" Well, about an hour later, they wired me the fifty thousand dollars from the Bank of Nova Scotia. But this went on and on. When we completed the picture, we put together a rough assembly and sent it up to Canada, and they wired back a bunch of absurd editing instructions—cut three frames here, four there, and so on—as if I'd given them a fine cut. They didn't know what they had, or what they were doing, and it was all such a big headache by this time that I just bundled the whole thing up—music cues and everything—and sent it up there for them to work with a Canadian editor snipping frames as they wished. I washed my hands of it completely, even had my name removed from the credits. By the way, originally I'd cast Phyllis Davis to play Ilsa, but when she read the script and saw this scene where she would have to wee-wee on this general, she walked. I'd known Dyanne Thorne in Vegas where she'd been a showgirl, and she

You Don't Have to Assault a Groupie... You Just Have to Ask..!

A DAVID F. FRIEDMAN WILLIAM ALLEN CASTLEMAN PRODUCTION

BUMMER!

A FAR OUT TRIP THRU A HARD ROCK TUNNEL

in COLOR from EVI   R RESTRICTED

Starring KIPP WHITMAN • DENNIS BURKLEY • CONNIE STRICKLAND
CAROL SPEED • DIANE LEE HART • DAVID ANKRUM • DAVID BUCHANAN
Produced by David F. Friedman & William Allen Castleman • • • • Directed by William Allen Castleman
Distributed by Entertainment Ventures, Inc.

MAT 401

made a great Ilsa. But overall the film was a major headache. They sent this guy down named Don Carmody, an accountant, to watch the purse strings. What could I steal? There was never any money! When it came time to do the second *Ilsa* movie, they asked me to get involved, but I declined. I just didn't want any part of it.

Q: What's the picture you're proudest of, the one you consider to be your best?

FRIEDMAN: Well, one of my favorites is *Johnny Firecloud* [1975], a modern-day Western we shot in CinemaScope. It was about a young Indian who gets out of the army and returns home to find his tribe being victimized by a white rancher played by Ralph Meeker. Victor Mohica, a Puerto Rican actor, played the part of the Indian, Johnny Firecloud. David Canary, who was added to the Cartwright household after Pernell Roberts left "Bonanza," played the sheriff and Frank De Kova played the tribal chief. Sacheen Littlefeather, the woman who refused the Oscar for Brando, was in it too. She plays an Indian schoolteacher who triggers Johnny's revenge spree when she's raped and killed by several of Meeker's toughs. We did very well with that picture. We had 150 prints made up, which was unheard of for an exploitation film. Fox distributed it overseas. It was the most expensive movie I ever made. It cost about two hundred thousand dollars, and it made that much back in TV syndication alone. I did another little picture called *Bummer—A Trip Through a Hard Rock Tunnel* that's also a favorite of mine. But I guess

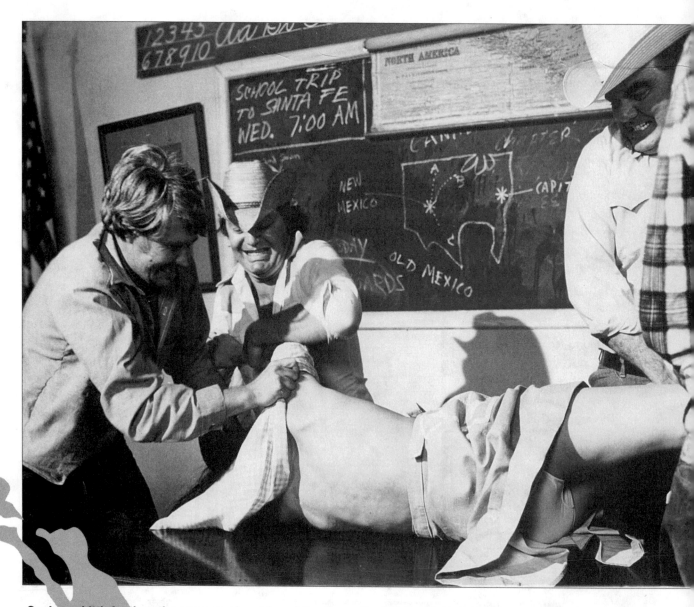

Sacheen Littlefeather, the woman who refused the Oscar for Marlon Brando, gets more than she bargained for in *Johnny Firecloud* **(1975), a modern-day Western shot in CinemaScope and one of Friedman's personal favorites.** *(Courtesy David F. Friedman)*

my all-time favorite is *She Freak* [1967]. Byron Mabe directed that one. He'd gone to the Pasadena Playhouse acting school, and most of the cast consisted of his fellow classmates. One of them was a kid named Bill McKinney who'd been working as a tree surgeon but wanted to be an actor. He was cast as the owner of the sideshow who marries the bad girl and gets killed and she inherits the sideshow. After that,

Bill was in *Deliverance* [1972], where he played the mountain man who rapes Ned Beatty. He's done well for himself. Worked constantly.

Q: Was *She Freak* intended as a deliberate rip-off of Tod Browning's *Freaks*?

FRIEDMAN: It was an outright remake of *Freaks*, which I first saw in Birmingham in the early '30s. Children were not admitted, but my uncle ran the theater, so I watched it from the booth, and it made a big impression on me. The next time I saw it was after Dwain Esper acquired it, and I've probably seen it twenty times since. No picture's ever made a more lasting impression on me. Not because of the freaks, either, but because of the circus elements and the carny atmosphere, which Browning, an old carny man himself, captured perfectly. The problem when I made *She Freak* was that I had to resort to makeup tricks instead of using real freaks. When Browning made the original, there were a number of human oddities traveling around in circuses and carnivals that he was able to use in the film. But by 1966 when we made *She Freak,* that sort of exploitation was frowned upon. As a matter of fact, in California there was even a law against it. So, except for the dwarf character and a couple of others, all the human oddities in the film were fakes.

Q: What do you consider your worst film?

FRIEDMAN: Take your pick! No, actually, it was probably *Space Thing*.

Q: Why did you get out of the business?

FRIEDMAN: Because there wasn't any more business for me to be in. When the industry went hardcore, I said this is going to be the end of a long and glorious business. Don't get me wrong. I didn't have any moral compunctions against hard-core. I just didn't like doing it for one basic reason: It was bad show business. The whole secret to exploitation and our successful little racket was the carnival tease: Boy, we didn't see it this week, but next week they're really going to show it to us. With hard-core, they give away the third act the minute the curtain is raised; and after you've seen the guy ejaculate and the girl fellate him, what else can you do? In addition, X-rated video put X-rated theaters out of business. There are practically none left. So, those two things together killed the market for my type of film—which sells the sizzle not the steak. Hard-core sells the steak.

SELECTED FILMOGRAPHY

1960: The Prime Time, Living Venus; **1961:** The Adventures of Lucky Pierre; **1962:** Daughter of the Sun, Nature's Playmates; **1963:** BOIN-N-G!, Goldilocks and the Three Bares (a.k.a. Goldilocks' Three Chicks), Scum of the Earth (a.k.a. Devil's Camera), Blood Feast, Bell, Bare and Beautiful; **1964:** 2000 Maniacs; **1965:** Color Me Blood Red, The Defilers, A Sweet Sickness, The Casting Couch*, The Poker Party*; **1966:** The Notorious Daughter of Fanny Hill, A Smell of Honey, A Swallow of Brine, But Charlie, I Never Played Volleyball*; **1967:** She Freak, The Pickup, The Brick Dollhouse, The Acid Eaters, The Head Mistress; **1968:** The Lustful Turk, Brand of Shame, Space Thing, The Big Snatch, Thar She Blows, The Ribald Tales of Robin Hood; **1969:** Starlet, Love Camp 7, The Ramrodder, The Suckers, Joys of Jezebel; **1970:** Trader Hornee, The Masterpiece, Love Thy Neighbor & His Wife, Red, White & Blue; **1971:** The Hitchhikers, The Erotic Adventures of Zorro, Come One, Come All, The Long Swift Sword of Siegfried, Marriage of a Young Stockbroker; **1972:** Bummer—A Trip Through a Hard Rock Tunnel, The Adult Version of Jekyll & Hyde; **1973:** The Flesh and Blood Show; **1974:** Ilsa—She Wolf of the SS, Marriage and Other Four-Letter Words; **1975:** Johnny Firecloud, The Journey of O; **1977:** Seven into Snowy; **1978:** Chorus Call, The Erotic Cartoon Festival, The Invitation to Ruin; **1980:** The Budding of Brie; **1981:** First Monday in October, Alexandra; **1984:** Matinee Idol; **1985:** Blonde Heat; **1990:** Sex and Buttered Popcorn; **1993:** Do You Think I'm Sexy?**

*Short film

**MTV video

Some of the carnage in Milligan's *The Ghastly Ones* (1968) was gruesome enough to have reportedly offended even Stephen King.
(Courtesy Eric Caidin)

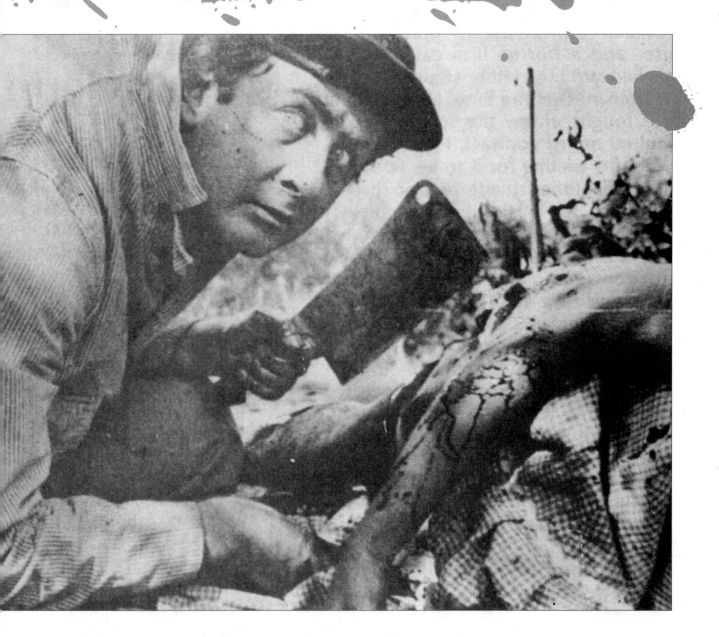

killing his rivals to obtain a coveted throne. A period picture, the film is fatally undone by the cast's anachronistic Brooklyn accents, the use of modern settings and props, and the recurring noise of passing automobiles on the soundtrack. In an effort to make sure these gaffes wouldn't interfere with the film's box-office chances, Milligan compensated by laying on the carnage and carnality with a vengeance.

Following this film, Milligan entered the notorious "British phase" of his career when he tucked his handy Auricon sound-on-film camera under his arm and set sail for England to crank out a series of "high-toned" period shockers for producer

Greedy relatives gather on a remote estate to claim an inheritance at any price in Milligan's *The Ghastly Ones* (1968), the film that set the stage for Andy's career. *(Courtesy Eric Caidin)*

Mishkin. Little is known about the first of these outings, *Nightbirds* (production/release date unknown), except that it earned an X rating, was shot in black-and-white in the same section of London once prowled by Jack the Ripper, and starred the rough-featured (and -talented) Berwick Kaler, who became a fixture in Milligan films from then on.

Anachronistic props, modern buildings, and the sound of passing autos on the soundtrack marred Milligan's medieval opus *Torture Dungeon* (1969), filmed on Staten Island.
(Courtesy Eric Caidin)

True to his contrary nature, Milligan followed up *Nightbirds*, one of his most obscure features, with his most notorious film ever: *Bloodthirsty Butchers* (1970), an extremely gruesome version of the oft-filmed tale of Sweeney Todd, the demon barber of Fleet Street. In Milligan's version, not one, but three maniacs set to work keeping Victorian London's population under control by murderous means. There's Todd himself (John Miranda), who slaughters and robs his customers, baker Jane Hilary, to whom he turns over the cadavers, and butcher Berwick Kaler, who chops up the meat for pies that are sold to unsuspecting customers in the neighborhood ("special parts" are also pastried for a select clientele of ghouls).

Angular-faced Miranda is especially enjoyable, spouting such choice lines as "Thieves, beggars, prostitutes—scum of the earth! We did a good thing getting rid of them; you notice they don't hang around *here* anymore!" Hilary and Kaler acquit themselves nicely as well. But the gore's the thing in this Milligan sleazefest, and the director dishes it out quite liberally. Highlights include: throat and wrist slitting; hand amputation; abdominal stabbing; corpse butchery; a breast in a meat pie; and murder by meat cleaver (Milligan's favorite screen weapon). In the film's original cut, Kaler scoops out the bowels of a freshly hacked victim (confirming the scene was shot, a photo of it was lovingly reproduced in several horror/ exploitation film fanzines a few years back), but Mishkin, who was either too grossed out by the scene or too worried it would cause rating problems, insisted that it be removed—much to the dismay of Milligan and gorehounds everywhere.

Mishkin had an even more profound influence on Milligan's next British-made period piece (and most infamous picture), *Curse of the Full Moon*, a talky yet compact seventy-five-minute werewolf tale. Mishkin saw the film as an opportunity to cash in on the success of a recent mainstream film about murderous rodents, *Willard* (1971), and he ordered Milligan to shoot additional scenes involving killer rats; the film was released as *The Rats Are Coming! The Werewolves Are Here!* (1971). This new footage provided an excellent showcase for frequent Milligan movie villainess Hope Stansbury to strut her stuff torturing rats with knives and fire. The rat footage bloats the film to more than ninety minutes—too much time for too little material—but it made the movie one of Milligan's most enduring box-office winners. It continued to play the drive-in circuit long after most other Milligan films had faded from the scene, and is still one of his most popular films on video.

The last of the Mishkin-produced, Milligan British horrors was *Dr. Jekyll and Mr. Blood* (1971), a film that suffers from even grainier photography than most of Milligan's other 16-mm (blown up to 35-mm) shockers, but which also boasts some of the best acting in the Milligan pantheon. Milligan stalwart Berwick Kaler was cast against type as the good guy, and Denis

A Milligan double bill to die for (or from): The top-billed feature, *Bloodthirsty Butchers* (1970), which went on to become Milligan's most notorious film ever, was the director's gory take on the familiar tale of Sweeney Todd, the demon barber of Fleet Street.

DeMarne was given the dual role of the well-intentioned doctor who mutates into a sadistic, whore-hopping psychopath.

Milligan loaded the picture with scenes of brain surgery, limb lopping, bondage, whippings, and disembowelments, but ads for the film bore (and continue to bear) a PG rating! Once again hoping to cash in on the success of some other films (in this case *The Thing with Two Heads*, and *The Incredible Two-Headed Transplant*, both 1971), Mishkin retitled the film *The Man with Two Heads*, thereby shortchanging what remains one of Milligan's most original and entertaining films.

Another of Milligan's best is *The Body Beneath* (1970), featuring Gavin Reed as the foppish Reverend Ford, a vampire masquerading as a minister in order to ensnare victims and continue the family bloodline. Milligan set the film in modern times to cut production costs by not having to shell out bucks for period costumes for all his actors. But he still managed to indulge his passion for bygone fashions by having his vampires anachronistically dressed in Victorian costumes during the gruesome cannibal feast scene that concludes the film. Otherwise, this scene, tinted red and involving several eerie tracking shots, stands as one of the most striking passages Milligan ever filmed (as well as one of the sickest). Newspaper ads for *The Body Beneath* touted "sexually rampant ghouls, depraved souls, and blood-red roses."

There are still plenty of blood-red roses, but the advertised sexual rampages apparently wound up on the cutting room floor.

The Body Beneath played the drive-in circuit with another noteworthy Milligan entry called *Guru the Mad Monk* (1970). Set in the 1400s and filmed in a Manhattan church, it stars Neil Flanagan (who looks suspiciously like Lynn Flanagan, the transvestite wonder of Milligan's *Fleshpot on 42nd Street*) in the title role, an insane jailer-priest who tortures prisoners in his religious sanctuary, then executes them in his private dungeon. In between killings and schizophrenic ravings, he tries to keep his vampire mistress in line and the mother church off his back, while also abusing his pet hunchback, Igor.

This was Milligan's first feature shot in 35 mm, a definite step up in that it eliminated the grainy photography characteristic of his previous work. But the film still contained the requisite number of gaffes, a favorite being the scene where a gushing disciple tells Flanagan/Guru "I walked all the way from Catania to see you." (That's some trick considering Guru lives on an island!)

The movie also contains one of Milligan's most revolting set pieces: After three victims have been graphically butchered on the same chopping block, Guru's girlfriend sashays in to lick up the blood. Yecchhh!

Milligan's offering for 1974, *Blood*, made at a whopping cost of twenty thousand dollars, was his most polished production up to that time. It starred Allan Berendt as Larry Talbot, Jr., the lycanthropic husband of Dracula's daughter (a perfectly cast Hope Stansbury). Along with the requisite red stuff, Ms. Drac also requires a special serum to keep her from shriveling up and dying. This elixir is derived from some man-eating plants tended by a dwarf and another man with cancerous growths on his leg. Blood is tapped from a hapless girl who has been shanghaied from an orphanage specifically for this purpose. On hand also is a creepy old lady who tends the local graveyard with fingernails the length of Max Schreck's in the classic F. W. Murnau film, *Nosferatu* (1922). Nobody could pack so many horror

icons into sixty minutes like good ol' Andy! Or so much gore, as one intruder after another is done in by shovels and cleavers and fed either to Stansbury or her pet plants.

In 1978, Milligan remade *The Ghastly Ones* as *Legacy of Blood*. Surprisingly bloodless, humorless, and totally lackluster, this one is wholeheartedly recommended for insomniacs only.

Having gotten that one out of his system, Milligan proceeded to make (in his words) the most ambitious film of his career, a Milligan-styled version of *Gone With the Wind* (1939) called *The House of the Seven Belles* (production date unknown). Milligan once boasted to an interviewer that the film cost *in excess of* twenty thousand dollars to produce and that it ran more than two and a half hours. To date, however, this epic remains unreleased (and possibly unfinished as well).

Milligan returned to familiar territory—the horror flick—and to the Mishkin family fold for financing with his next film, *Carnage* (1983), arguably his best movie. The film opens with the murder/suicide of two newlyweds. Later, another pair of lovebirds picks up the dead couple's New York City mansion for a song (that should have told them something right there, but you know how oblivious horror film protagonists can be), and strange things predictably begin happening to them. A phonograph plays the "Wedding March" from *Lohengrin*, the lady of the house has her hand cut open by a knife that unaccountably falls from a shelf; later she's almost brained by a flying flowerpot. In response, the couple invite their friends over for a get-together. While this may fly in the face of logic, it does provide Milligan with plenty of victims to dispose of during the remainder of the picture. Radios fall into bathtubs, electrocuting people; and sharp instruments fly through the air with the greatest of ease. When the homicidal haunts run out of houseguests, they set their sights on a meddlesome priest and a pair of burglars who are summarily cut to pieces.

William Mishkin's son Lewis produced the film, and, judging from the comparatively slick look of it, he was looser with the purse strings than his

The Man with Two Heads (1971, a.k.a. *Dr. Jekyll and Mr. Blood*), the last of Milligan's British-made horrors, boasted some of the best acting in a Milligan picture.

SADISTIC SUSPENSE!
SPINE-CHILLING!

MAN-EATING RATS
and
BLOOD-SUCKING WEREWOLVES!

THE RATS ARE COMING!
THE WEREWOLVES ARE HERE!

IN BLOOD-DRIPPING COLOR

HOPE with JACKIE
STANSBURY SKARVELLIS
and THE RATS
of MOONEY MANOR

Distributed by
William Mishkin Motion Pictures Inc.

IF YOU DON'T HAVE THE GUTS
—STAY AWAY!

GP PARENTAL GUIDANCE SUGGESTED
All Ages Admitted

• This film contains material which
may not be suitable for pre-teenagers.

Milligan added some additional footage involving killer rats to his werewolf opus *Curse of the Full Moon* and launched it on the drive-in circuit, where it played for years under the title *The Rats Are Coming! The Werewolves Are Here!* (1971).

tightfisted old man ever was. And the result is a must-see for sleaze fans.

As America marched into the Reagan era, Milligan suddenly decided to pack up his bags and migrated to the West Coast, where he moved into a Sunset Boulevard studio that was reputed to be haunted (even *before* Andy arrived), and ground out the final pictures of his career: *Menage* (date unknown), which sounds like more sexploitation fare; *Surgikill* (date unknown), which was initially planned as a horror comedy; *The Weirdo* (1990); and the appropriately titled *Monstrosity* (date unknown). *The Weirdo* is the only one of these that has been released.

The titular pariah of *The Weirdo* is a dull-witted youth (well played by Steve Burlington) who's persecuted by scummy social workers, evil parent/authority figures, and a gang of local bullyboys who look like strays from a Troma flick or one of S. Clay Wilson's biker comics. The one bright spot in the boy's tormented life is a similarly put-upon girl who wears a leg brace. The angst goes on for an

hour before the film finally gets in gear and starts delivering the gross-out goodies as Burlington flips out and strikes back against his oppressors. If much of the ensuing mayhem—pitchfork impalement, head and hand lopping—looks more convincing than usual, it's because Milligan finally hired a professional, Rodd Matsui, to handle the FX instead of doing them himself. According to Matsui, the title character of *The Weirdo* represents "*all* outcasts, all artists, everyone who isn't accepted by mainstream society. [The film] does have some meaning, and feeling." As a result, *The Weirdo* may be the closest Milligan (a known homosexual) ever came to making an artistic statement, or revealing whatever outsider anguish he may have felt about himself and his work on film. Matsui agrees, saying, "I'm sure it was cathartic for Andy."

With Matsui by his side, Milligan then made his final film, *Monstrosity*, the title of which can't be accused of misrepresentation. In the opening scenes, a young woman is raped and mutilated (Milligan wanted to use beef tripe and chicken gizzards for her disembowelment, but Matsui insisted on rubber "guts" instead). Three medical students, acting more like kindergarten rejects, decide to avenge this outrage by building their own golem and siccing it on the perpetrators of the deed. Unlike the clay titan of Jewish folklore, however, this golem is made of spare human parts, with the left arm of a gorilla thrown in for good measure (the resultant critter is played by Haal Borske, who had previously appeared in Milligan's *The Ghastly Ones* and *Torture Dungeon*). The med students inadvertently overfill the golem with blood, however, and it tends to leak crimson whenever it gets angry or horny. A babbling geek wearing an aviator cap serves as the golem's guardian angel and engages it in numerous rambling discourses that round out the fun. Suffering from AIDS at the time, Milligan deserves a lot of credit for continuing to work. Nevertheless, *Monstrosity* remains a poor book-end to his career.

Insiders who worked on Milligan's last pictures have described him as a benevolent, thinner version of Wilford Brimley with "a rather grandfather-like personality." Though he frequently scared Rodd Matsui and other collaborators with his penchant for dragging electrical cables through lightning and rainstorms, he seemed invincible, and destined to be a thorn in the side of normal filmmaking for many, many years to come. In 1992, however, the ravages of AIDS finally caught up with him, and the *Bloodthirsty Butcher* man died at the age of sixty-two. His work continues to live on, however. And to amaze.

SELECTED FILMOGRAPHY

1963: Liz (a.k.a. The Promiscuous Sex); **1964:** The Naked Witch (a.k.a. The Naked Temptress); **1965:** Vapors; **1967:** The Degenerates, The Depraved; **1968:** The Filthy Five, The Ghastly Ones, Kiss Me, Kiss Me, Kiss Me, Seeds, Tricks of the Trade; **1969:** Gutter Trash, Torture Dungeon; **1970:** Bloodthirsty Butchers, The Body Beneath, Guru the Mad Monk; **1971:** Fleshpot on 42nd Street, The Man with Two Heads (a.k.a. Dr. Jekyll and Mr. Blood), The Rats Are Coming! The Werewolves Are Here! (a.k.a. Curse of the Full Moon); **1974:** Blood; **1978:** Legacy of Blood; **1983:** Carnage; **1990:** The Weirdo.

Unfinished/unreleased (production date unknown): Nightbirds; The House of the Seven Belles; Menage; Surgikill; Monstrosity.

THE
Honorable Practitioners

From stage magician to filmmaker: the prodigious
Ted V. Mikels. *(Courtesy Eric Caidin)*

Ted V. Mikels

BY ERIC J. CAIDIN AND JOHN McCARTY

Oregon native Ted V. Mikels began his career in show business on the stage as a magician. Gravitating to film in the early 1950s as he entered his twenties, he packed his bags and moved to California, where he found work as a film and sound editor, stuntman, music composer, and cinematographer at many of Hollywood's major and most of its minor studios.

Mikels directed his first low-budget exploitation feature, *Strike Me Deadly*, in 1963. Three years later, he formed his own independent production and distribution company, Cinema Features Inc., which was responsible for some of the most outrageous, inexpensive, and successful exploitation horror and action films of the late '60s through the mid-'70s. These included: *The Black Klansman* (1966), a saga of racial intolerance and violence in which a light-skinned black man passes for white to infiltrate the Klan and revenge himself on the rednecks who killed his daughter in a church bombing; *The Astro-Zombies* (1969), a cartoonlike mixture of espionage and

A light-skinned black man infiltrates the Klan to revenge himself on the rednecks who killed his daughter in Mikels's timely *The Black Klansman* (1966).

evisceration cowritten and coproduced by actor Wayne Rogers (of TV's "M*A*S*H*" fame); *Blood Orgy of the She-Devils* (1973), the sex-cum-violence story of a beautiful witch (Lila Zaborin) and her bevy of gorgeous disciples who ritualistically torture and torch men as sacrifices to their cult; and *The Doll Squad* (1974), a spy thriller Mikels maintains was the inspiration for the TV series "Charlie's Angels," which deals with an all-girl army of assassins.

But Mikels's most notorious—and most successful—film of this period was *The Corpse Grinders*, the splattery tale of a couple of Burke and Hare-like entrepreneurs who use the chopped-up flesh of their murder victims as prime ingredients for their successful brand of cat food. Released in 1971 and subsequently rereleased on a triple bill with two similarly themed exploitation items, *The Undertaker and His Pals* and *The Embalmer*, *The Corpse Grinders*, made for a pittance, earned back millions. Fans have been clamoring for a sequel to it ever since.

Now living in semiretirement in Las Vegas, the seventy-plus-year-old Mikels recently set up a new production facility, and is awaiting financing to film that sequel.

Q: How did you get interested in making films?

TVM: I grew up in the theater and the stage. Probably the earliest memories I have are performing onstage. From the time I was fifteen, I had a two-and-a half-hour magic show with ventriloquism, accordion solos, getting out of a straitjacket, and all that. When I was seventeen, I said to myself, "What a shame that after putting on a two-and-a-half-hour show we had no record of it afterwards. Why couldn't we film it?" I learned very quickly, however, that filmmaking was a much more complex job than just turning a camera on the stage and recording the performance. To make the performance come alive on film, you needed to move the camera around, switch angles, get close-ups of the magic as it was unfolding, and so on. At first I used a little 8-mm camera, but that was no good, so I went to 16 mm, which was easier to edit. And it was with the process of learning how to edit that my real fascination with film began. By the time I was twenty, I was well dug in and making film projects with stories and stop-motion animation, which is an extension of magic. And things just progressed from there. I was a director of community theater in my hometown at that time, so I had lots of recruits to help me out with my little films. On Sunday, I'd start out with however many people showed up

The Astro-Zombies (1969) was written and coproduced by Wayne Rogers (later of TV's "M*A*S*H*".)

and scribble an outline of a story on an envelope— just the key words like "man robs bank," "police chase man," "chase ends in volcanic rock area"—and we'd shoot. I had some contractors who took part just for fun and for a scene one Sunday, with their help, we blew up a whole half of a mountain with twenty-five sticks of dynamite. Almost got hit by a flying boulder, but we got a great shot. That was maybe forty to forty-five years ago.

Q: So, you were pretty much self-taught as a filmmaker.

TVM: Completely self-taught. Never went to film school or anything. My feeling anyway is that you can only learn from doing. In a short period of time I found that many people teaching in film schools were people that I once taught with my own self-taught knowledge. Many of them went into the business, too. Bob Maxwell, an old protégé who used to pull cables for me, went on to become one of Hollywood's best cameramen. He had a deep love of the camera.

Q: How and when did you move from amateur to professional film work?

TVM: In the late '40s to mid-'50s, while I was still living in Oregon, I would try to get on the set of some of the major studio productions when they came to film on location in my neck of the woods. I would write to the production offices and offer to be of any help I could if they'd just let me on the set. I didn't want any money, even offered to pay my own way for food and everything. But they always turned me down flat, which is why, later on, whenever anyone asked to come by my sets and watch I always said yes. Anyway, I started out making these little story films. It was real backbreaking work, but I learned enough to become a cinematographer, started doing documentaries and industrial films, and became a member of NABET and IATSE. So, I moved to California to practice my trade. I got some work doing stunts and things on Westerns like *Tonka* [1958] and *Day of the Outlaw* [1959], got to see directors like André de Toth and Andrew V. McLaglen in action, and in the early '60s made my own first film as an independent writer-producer-director-editor and co-cameraman called *Strike Me Deadly*. It took me a while to get it done. I had to keep mortgaging my house to get to the next step, to keep things going, to pay for the master sound mix, and so on. To keep costs down I shot it back in Oregon using some of my old community theater pals. I only brought four people from Hollywood. To this day, a lot of my friends say it's still my best movie. That's probably because my heart and soul went into making it. I wasn't motivated by the demands of an audience, a theater owner, or a distributor to include certain elements, like sex scenes and whatnot. It was my story, told the way I wanted to. And it's a good outdoor action-adventure film, about the forest service. Played in theaters here and abroad and on television for years. But I never saw a dime. I did a lot of contract pictures, mainly for producer Joe Solomon, after that. Things like *The Doctors* and *Suburban Affair*.

Q: A lot of your early films are turning up on video through companies like Something Weird Video and Sinister Cinema. Did you lose the rights to them?

TVM: No, I retained the rights to all my films. But nobody pays attention to such things. They just take 'em and what can you do? If MGM with their billions can't do anything to stop it, what can I do? Video was the beginning of the end for the independent filmmaker.

Q: How so? I would think there would be even more opportunity now for independent filmmakers like yourself because of video.

Lila Zaborin as the sexy, evil ringleader of the man-killing witches in *Blood Orgy of the She-Devils* (1973).

TED V. MIKELS

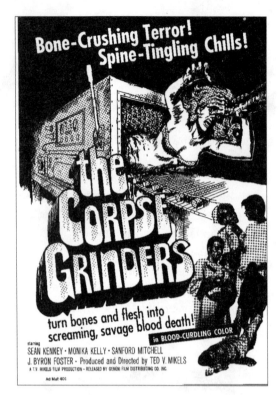

Bone-Crushing Terror!
Spine-Tingling Chills!

the CORPSE GRINDERS

turn bones and flesh into screaming, savage blood death!

in BLOOD-CURDLING COLOR

starring
SEAN KENNEY • MONIKA KELLY • SANFORD MITCHELL
J. BYRON FOSTER • Produced and Directed by TED V. MIKELS
A T.V. MIKELS FILM PRODUCTION • RELEASED BY GENENI FILM DISTRIBUTING CO. INC.

Ad Mat 401

TVM: I think it's an admission of the industry's failure. It represents the closing down rather than the opening up of opportunity for the independent producer as far as theatrical distribution is concerned. My greatest joy in life, apart from raising my family, has been making motion pictures. But today you cannot market a 35-mm motion picture to theaters unless you own the theater or have a direct pipeline into a major theater chain. Theaters only want major studio product, and most of them are run by chains, so you'll just never get your money back if you try to go theatrical. It all started to get bad in the late 1970s when you had to start paying anywhere from $1,600 to $1,800 for each print of your film, plus shipping costs of about $150 per print to a subdistributor in, say, Milwaukee, who'd charge you 25 percent

Mikels followed his smash hit *The Corpse Grinders* (1972) with the almost as successful *Blood Orgy of the She-Devils* (1973), the story of a coven of beautiful witches who tantalize and torture men as ritual sacrifices.

of the gate for booking your film. On top of this you'd have to split the cost of promoting the film with each theater. Most of the time you'd wind up getting stuck with a bill at the end of the run rather than making a profit. That type of situation spelled the destruction of the business for independents like me.

Q: But video at least allows you to stay in the game, doesn't it?

TVM: There are thousands of video stores out there renting movies, but try to get one penny from any participation on the video. Even the majors discovered that. And going direct to video is, to my way of thinking, a sad admission of failure. All you can expect to get is a certain amount of ego satisfaction from seeing your film is out there *somewhere.* Nothing else. The future for people like me, as I see it, is doing commercials, music videos, and projects for other people, not trying to finance and distribute your films yourself.

Q: Who are some of the people you've enjoyed working with over the years?

TVM: Rafael Campos, Bill Bagdad, Tony Pace, Leslie McCrea, people like that. They had great attitudes. They were always willing to work for the love of just being involved in a film. They'd go from one picture to another with me, and were willing to work under heavy circumstances—like *no* money. I think I spent 90 percent of my life looking for money for films, and most of the films I made were for no money. But I managed a film or two a

A TERRIFYING, SCREAMING PLUNGE TO THE DEPTHS OF HELL!

TED V. MIKELS presents

BLOOD ORGY of the SHE-DEVILS

MARA, QUEEN OF THE BLACK WITCHES AND HER WOLF-PACK OF VOLUPTUOUS VIRGINS INVADE SATAN'S TORTURED REALM OF THE UNKNOWN!

Mikels claims his buxom spy thriller *The Doll Squad* (1974) inspired the success hit TV series "Charlie's Angels."

year, using short ends—twenty to fifty feet—of raw stock that I bought from the major studios for a penny a foot. Some of these short ends were so short that you had to reload the camera after every take. It was very demanding on your patience. People just don't know how hard it was putting a film together this way. They talk about low budgets as seven thousand dollars—if I'd had seven thousand dollars for some of my films I could have made a spectacular!

Q: *The Corpse Grinders* was your most successful film. How did it come about?

TVM: *Corpse Grinders* cost forty-seven thousand dollars and made three million dollars! We'd open the picture in a city day and date across the street from a big first-run motion picture, and we'd outgross it every time. It generated so much money that the profits didn't all get lost from shipping costs, print costs, and all those other expenses I told you about. We later rereleased it with *The Undertaker and His Pals* and it did just as well. We had one hundred prints of that film moving around at one time. Typically, on the independent level, you opened six to ten theaters at one time, never more than that because

you had only so many dollars available for your ad campaign.

Q: Rumor has it that you're planning a sequel to it.

TVM: I get calls from magazines in New York every once in a while asking when *Corpse Grinders II* is coming. All I can say is that we're working on it. We keep revising the outline to bring it up-to-date; we're taking it into outer space with people on Earth looking for food for the planet. I won't do a script until I have some cash to start it, but I do have outlines of things I want in it. It will have to be campy to be marketable. The only way I can see to make *Corpse Grinders II* is either with a lot of money and a few big stars in the hopes of getting in on the tail end of what little is left of independent theatrical activity, or on video. Right now if I could show to any potential investor any positive way that he was going to get his money back on his investment, I could probably find the money. But I will not mislead just to get financing. I don't just *want* money because that brings with it the obligation to return that money. I would accept money on a joint venture deal where everyone knows they may never see a penny back. But that's the only way I'll do it.

Q: Why don't the majors turn to guys like you when it's obvious you know how to handle a budget and spend the cash wisely?

TVM: Because they're not interested in spending cash wisely. In the early '60s I knew an attorney at Twentieth Century–Fox. I'd just done *really* big business on *Corpse Grinders*, so I went to him and asked for $150,000 from Fox to do a film. He talked to the board and came back to me and said Fox—in fact, *all* the majors—were more interested in putting $40 million into a movie that might flop and make back only $40,000 than they were in putting $40,000 into a picture that

Lip-smackin' good! Director, cowriter, and star Herb Robins chows down in the Mikels-produced horror-comedy *The Worm Eaters*, filmed in 1975 but not released until 1978.

probably didn't stand a chance of making $40 million. It was the beginning of the blockbuster mentality, which is where it's at today, although it results in very few blockbusters.

Q: Why and when did you leave Hollywood for Vegas?

TVM: In 1985. I was given great encouragement by a man who did a lot of international business to move here and start a studio to make films. He promised to finance both the studio and the pictures, and said I'd get a check for six hundred thousand dollars the day I finished moving here to get the studio started. But, of course, nothing came of it. The guy meant well. He was a mover and a shaker, but he couldn't put it together.

Q: How much filmmaking activity was and is there in Vegas?

TVM: Not much. In Los Angeles, there were so many people I had started in film—maybe two or three

thousand—that there was always something going on. Somebody always needed your help, either with directing, producing, shooting, renting your equipment for a decent price—I had all my own trucks and editing rooms. Here the only activity occurs when someone comes into town to shoot something, and when they do they bring with them everything and everyone they need. I have managed to put a studio here together, though, with broadcast quality cameras, all my film equipment and so on. I'm pretty much self-contained.

Q: What's your favorite of all your films, *Corpse Grinders*?

TVM: Each of my films averaged a year to make, so none of them was really soul-satisfying to me. From the time I started the film to the time I got it finished and out onto the screen my desires for the film had taken me well beyond where the finished film itself could possibly go. By the time I managed to get the thing finished, it was old hat to me. I was sick of it.

Q: Nonetheless, your films do have a lot of fans and you do attend a lot of exploitation film festivals and conventions. What do you think of your cult status? How do you feel about it?

TVM: If the cult following is paying regard to somebody—like myself—who has made films under twenty impossible obstacles, but was able to do it and put together something out of nothing due to their sheer, driving will, then I'm really pleased with it. But I do not like to be included in admirations of trash films. I dislike that completely because I don't consider my films trash, and neither do the people who have actually *seen* them, which I find many of the people who have written about them clearly have not. If anyone looks at any five of my films—*Black Klansman, Girl in Gold Boots, The Doll Squad,* et cetera—and just *views* them objectively, they would never in a million years associate them with what you might call trash cult films.

Q: What's in store for the future?

TVM: I'm waiting for the first indication that there is a market for a film made on video, employing the same techniques involved in filmmaking—in other words a video that looks more like a film than a video. As soon as I find that there's a market for that, I will soon begin making films again, day in and day out.

Q: Hope that day comes soon.

TVM: Me too!

SELECTED FILMOGRAPHY

1963: Strike Me Deadly; **1964:** One Shocking Moment; **1965:** Day of the Nightmare; **1966:** The Black Klansman (a.k.a. I Crossed the Color Line), The Hostage, Agent for H.A.R.M.; **1967:** Cataline Caper; **1968:** Girl in Gold Boots, Up Your Teddy Bear; **1969:** The Astro-Zombies; **1972:** The Corpse Grinders; **1973:** Blood Orgy of the She-Devils; **1974:** The Doll Squad (a.k.a. Hustler Squad); **1975:** The Worm Eaters; **1982:** Ten Violent Women; **1985:** Space Angels; **1986:** Naked Vengeance; **1987:** Angel of Vengeance. Production/release dates unknown: Fool's Prospects; The Doctors; Suburban Affair; Mission: Kill Fast. Plus hundreds of television shows, documentaries, industrial films, and commercials.

Vampires, astronauts, warring cavemen,
and oversized lizards highlighted Adamson's
Horror of the Blood Monsters (1970), another
of Weird Al's marvelous paste-up jobs.

its running time, an Adamson trademark for most of his subsequent career. More representative of the Adamson style is 1971's *Blood of Ghastly Horror,* a hodgepodge consisting of old footage borrowed from an unfinished Adamson opus called *Psycho-a-Go-Go* combined with new footage of former Disney stalwart Tommy Kirk getting understandably nauseated when someone sends him a severed head in a gift box, and other cinematic delights, forming a patchwork geek show that's amusing for all the wrong reasons.

Released the year before, Independent-International's *Horror of the Blood Monsters* was another of Weird Al's marvelous paste-up jobs. It opens with a vampire attack that's fairly intense, an attack, we're soon informed, that was spawned by a vampire plague that originated in outer space. Astronauts Robert Dix and Vicki Volante and scientist John Carradine ascend into the cosmos to check out the situation, and land on a planet populated by warring cavemen, oversized lizards, mutated crayfish-critters, and more. The atmosphere on the planet shifts between bilious shades of red, yellow, and green, which Adamson intersperses with black-and-white footage culled from one of Sherman's Filipino shockers that is also tinted, a process the film's advertising ballyhooed as "Spectrum X." The film pops up frequently on video shelves under various other titles— *Creatures of the Prehistoric Planet; Horror Creatures of the Prehistoric Planet; Space Mission of the Lost Planet;* and, best of all, *Vampire Men of the Lost Planet*—so keep a sharp eye out.

In *Blood of Dracula's Castle* (1967), the name of former screen Dracula John Carradine was played up in the lurid ad campaign, but when patrons got to the drive-in to see the film, they were in for an unexpected surprise, for Carradine played the butler not the title character. In the film, the Draculas (Alex d'Arcy, Paula Raymond) have settled in the Mojave Desert under an assumed name. Gentleman's gentleman Carradine siphons blood out of girls chained in the cellar for his employers' frequent cocktails. To keep things

Blood of Ghastly Horror (1971) combined old footage from an unfinished Adamson opus called Psycho-a-Go-Go with gruesome new footage to form a patchwork geek show that's amusing for all the wrong reasons.

hopping, Adamson added a moronic hunchback and a werewolf to the sanguinary stew as well.

One of Adamson's best-known Sherman-produced shockers is *Dracula Vs. Frankenstein*, which he made between 1969 and 1971, the date when it was finally released. To give the film a bit more production value than the usual Independent-International fare, Adamson and Sherman borrowed some leftover Kenneth Strickfaden–designed lab equipment previously seen in Universal's classic *Frankenstein* films.

The gist of the arguable plot involves Count Dracula (Zando Vorkov) coercing a wheelchair-bound Dr. Frankenstein (J. Carroll Naish) into reviving his creature (John Bloom) in order to start a reign of terror. Prior to the climactic monster duke-out (and a bloody one it is, complete with dismemberment and decapitation), we're treated to mute servant Lon Chaney, Jr., chasing women with an ax, dwarfish Angelo Rossitto dishing out and being subjected to much violent mistreatment, Russ Tamblyn appearing as yet another

biker, and Jim Davis (of TV's "Dallas" fame) embarrassing himself as a detective. At the risk of giving away an important plot twist, the hero (Anthony Eisely) is killed off early on—a twist necessitated by the fact that Adamson couldn't afford to pay Eisely to do any more scenes.

As Dracula, Vorkov suggests a chalk-faced male anorexic with an Afro. Big John Bloom's Frankenstein monster sports a mask that looks rather like a rotten summer squash. Chaney's part was played mute because, sadly, he was dying of throat cancer at the time. However, the elderly Naish, Sherman has said, played the part of Dr. Frankenstein in a wheelchair out of choice, not necessity.

Reflecting on the film and its troublesome on-again off-again production history, Sherman has termed *Dracula Vs. Frankenstein* the "*Heaven's Gate*" of Independent-International." What he neglects to mention is that unlike the Michael Cimino disaster, *Dracula Vs. Frankenstein* was a box-office success. It's also nowhere near as boring. In fact, in its own patchwork way, it's a real hoot!

John Carradine surprised audiences by playing
the butler and not the title character in
Adamson's *Blood of Dracula's Castle* (1967).

AL ADAMSON

95

Adamson and the Filipino monster movie industry intersected in 1972 with *Brain of Blood*, wherein mad scientist Kent Taylor transplants the brain of a dying Middle Eastern(!) tyrant (Reed Hadley) into the body of a deformed half-wit in order to seize control of the despot's nation. (At one point, the Islamic ruler is shown emoting beneath an emblem that looks like a Celtic symbol, but that's how things go in the cinematic world of Denver Dixon's most famous son.) John Bloom was once again trotted out to play the monster, this time in makeup suggesting a spoiled melon rather than a rotten squash. Pint-sized Angelo Rossitto was also on hand as a lab assistant, albeit one who proves totally useless since he can't quite see over the operating table. In Adamson's hand-me-down tradition, the entire music score was lifted from another Filipino shocker, *The Mad Doctor of Blood Island* (1969), directed by Eddie Romero.

In the early 1970s, Al paused from full-time sleazemeistering to go legit by producing the Emmy Award–winning telefilm "Cry Rape," and semilegit by producing the Fred Williamson boxing melodrama *Hammer* (both 1972). Thereafter, he devoted the remainder of his moviemaking career to turning out a variety of exploitation fare not just horror films.

His versatility in this regard was apparent early on, for the same year he made his notorious biker film *Satan's Sadists*, he directed *The Female Bunch* (a.k.a. *A Time to Run*), another nasty little item with tongue firmly planted in cheek (I think) in an altogether different genre. Released by Burbank International, this film deals with a gang of misanthropic women living on a desert ranch (in actuality the notorious Spahn Movie Ranch, lair of the infamous Charles Manson and his family). The only man these gals have any use for is hired hand Lon Chaney, Jr., who pushes a few controlled substances in between odd jobs. The violent vixens—Jennifer Bishop and ol' reliable Regina Carroll among 'em—have their hands full when suave Russ Tamblyn shows up, and some ensuing bullwhipping and strategically thrust pitchfork activity push the violence quotient up to an R-rated level.

Not content with grinding out horror flicks, biker pictures, and an occasional entry in the Feral Female genre, Al also did considerable damage to the Western with his 1969 sagebrush sleazefest, *Five Bloody Graves*. An Independent-International cutie scripted by Adamson regular Robert Dix, *Graves* strives for allegory by having star Gene Raymond (as Death) narrate the sordid proceedings with Dix himself acting the part of Death's Messenger. But whatever traces of art and allegory survived the film's raunchy ad campaign ("Lust-Mad Men and Lawless Women in a Vicious and Sensuous Orgy of Slaughter!") quickly vanished in the film's savage storm of ferocious Indian assaults, shooting, rape, torture, and assorted other mayhem. Not to slight alleged Apache tradition, Adamson also treats us to the sight of one poor dude staked out on an anthill.

In addition to Raymond and Dix, the film's cast boasts such Adamson stalwarts as John Carradine (playing a voyeuristic preacher), Scott Brady, John "Bud" Cardos, Jim Davis, Paula Raymond, and Vicki Volante. The high-tone photography was provided by Vilmos Zsigmond, who went on to lens *Deliverance* (1972) and many other A features. Variously known as *Lonely Man* and *The Gun Riders*, *Five Bloody Graves* is a doozy under any title.

Back in 1967, Adamson "inherited" (from the late, lamented Rex Carlton) a crime/action film variously known as *The Fakers* and *Operation M*. Turning to his stock company of players—Scott Brady, Kent Taylor, and John Carradine, and bringing in Broderick Crawford and Colonel Sanders of Kentucky Fried Chicken fame, 1967 *Playboy* Playmate Anne Randall, as well as members of an actual motorcycle gang called The Hessians for extra box-office clout—Adamson spiced up the film by adding new footage, including stock shots of Adolf Hitler (never let it be said he limited his patchwork methods exclusively to horror films), and released the film through Independent-International in 1970 as *Hell's Bloody Devils*.

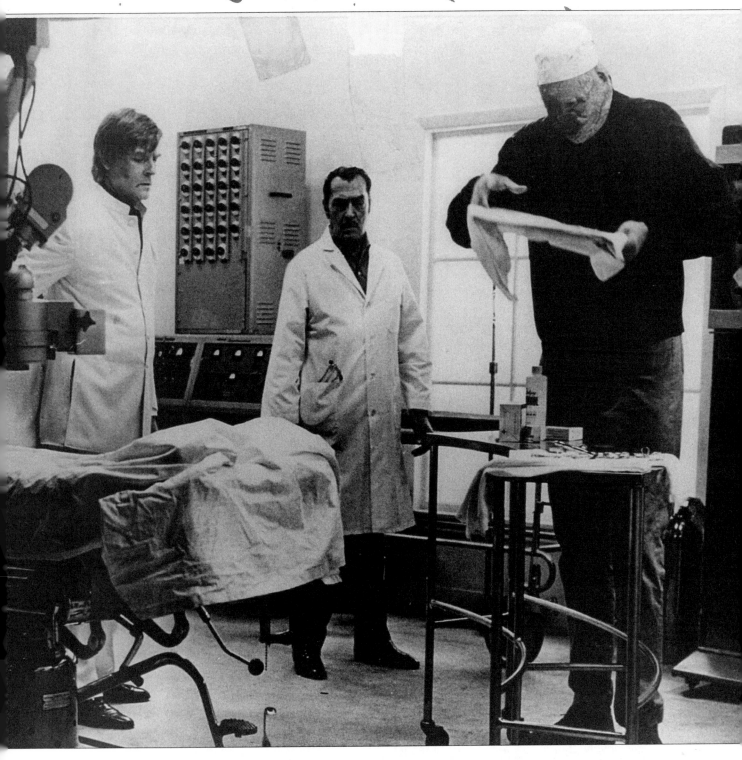

Adamson and the Filipino monster movie industry finally intersected in 1972's *Brain of Blood.*

The violent vixens take out their wrath on a male victim in *The Female Bunch* (1969), Adamson's take on the Feral Female genre.

Under that title, this bizarre hodgepodge dealing with a triumvirate of bikers, Mafiosi, and Nazi war criminals involved in a counterfeit money racket, kicked ass at the box office. So, quite naturally, Al zoomed into production with another biker mélange with the boffo title *Screaming Angels* (1972). Independent-International and Adamson milked two exploitation cash cows with this one by having the bikers, the film's sympathetic char-

acters, lock horns with a murderous cult patterned after the Manson gang. (In fact, this film, too, was shot at the Spahn Movie Ranch, and even featured some Manson Family hangers-on in the cast!)

But then the audience for biker films that had exploded with *Easy Rider* suddenly vanished. The film might have been deemed "unmarketable" and shelved by anyone else, but not Sam Sherman. Noting the recent success of New World's Feral Female picture *The Big Doll House* (1971), Sherman and Adamson flew into action, changed the title of *Screaming Angels* to *Angels' Wild Women* (1972), shot additional footage and trans- formed the film into a tale of female bikers (though the biker aspect was toned down in the ad campaign), who whip and chain their way through every cliché left over from the 1960s, including Satan worship and communal living. According to Sherman, this initially doomed feature, which Adamson produced, directed, and wrote under the pseudonym "D. Dixon, Jr.," went on to make "a bloody fortune."

No regular drive-in patron of the mid-1970s could possibly have escaped the popular wave of R-rated nurse/teacher/stewardess nudie flicks which, for a while, were hitting outdoor movie screens on a regular basis. And even if you didn't attend the pictures, you still got a dose of the cleavage and thighs-for-miles elements they contained from the cheesy trailers and posters accompanying them. Sam and Al got into the act early on with a project of their own called *The Naughty Stewardesses* (1975), the tale of a rich, dirty old man who gets involved with the titular airborne temptresses. Sherman pal Bob Livingston, a former star of Republic Pictures Westerns, was brought in to play the male lead. At first, Adamson balked at the idea of doing a nudie, thinking it too close to pornography, a field he disdained. But Sherman prevailed on him to do it by convincing him that in their hands *The Naughty Stewardesses* could be the crème de

la crème of stewardess films. While not exactly that, it was a big hit, but its follow-up was even more successful, and, over the years, has achieved cult film status.

They called their follow-up *Blazing Stewardesses* (1975) and set it on a dude ranch, thus giving themselves the opportunity to pay tribute to (or lampoon) the old Westerns cranked out by Republic Pictures, as well as a certain Mel Brooks film that also had the word *Blazing* in its title. Bob Livingston returned to star, along with another old cowboy movie hero, Don "Red" Barry. Attempts were made to get Rita Hayworth to appear in the film, but that deal fell through and Yvonne De Carlo was hired in her stead. Material was also written for The Three Stooges, but that grand plan collapsed due to the ill health of Larry and Moe. Two of the surviving Ritz Brothers, Harry and Jimmy, were brought in to replace them. Connie Hoffman, T. A. King, and Regina Carroll (busting out all over, as usual) showcased the cheesecake elements as the "stewardesses." The film was a smash and has a big following to this day.

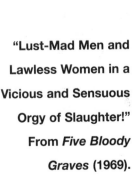

"Lust-Mad Men and Lawless Women in a Vicious and Sensuous Orgy of Slaughter!" From *Five Bloody Graves* (1969).

AL ADAMSON

Despite his aversion to porn filmmaking, Al subsequently got himself involved with a little number called *Girls for Rent* (1975), which, while not hard-core, boasts a truly scummy-porno atmosphere and mentality. Porn star Georgina Spelvin stars as a mob hitwoman, who, with black cohort Rosalind Miles, is hot (in more ways than one) on the trail of an informant. Apart from the sleazy—but, again, not especially graphic—sex, the film's most offensive scene (indeed, the scene that marks the nadir—or apex, depending on your point of view—of Adamson's career) shows Spelvin raping a retarded guy then blasting him away with a pistol at the climactic moment. When the film was released on tape, the title was changed to *I Spit on Your Corpse* to cash in on the controversy stirred up by the Meir Zarchi sex-and-bloodbath *I Spit on Your Grave* (1980) and a clip from the offending scene adorned the video box.

America's bicentennial year was a busy one for Al. It saw the release of *The Kill Factor* (a.k.a. *Death Dogs*), a flick starring George Lazenby, who had previously excelled as James Bond in *On Her Majesty's Secret Service* (1969) before becoming an instant trivia question. But Adamson's crowning achievement of the year was a cheap rip-off of the Raquel Welch Western, *Hannie Caulder* (1972), called *Jessie's Girls*. In it, Mormon wife Sondra Currie hits the old vengeance trail after a trio of outlaws named Rufe, Slime, and Moose rape her and kill her husband. Jessie gets gunfighter training from a scruffy old hermit who's a poor substitute for *Caulder*'s Christopher Lee. Her "girls" are a bunch of floozies, one of them played by Regina Carroll, whom she rescues from jail. The film drags a bit after the opening gang bang, then shifts into higher gear with lots of hilarious name-calling, furious gunplay, and a rousing "catfight" between Carroll land one of Jessie's other girls.

Unlike most Adamson sleazefests, *Jessie's Girls* doesn't appear to have been patched together with fragments and leftover footage from other Adamson films. In fact, the smoothness of its continuity suggests that it was probably shot in a single week. It does boast some anachronisms, however: for example, obvious silicone boobs on

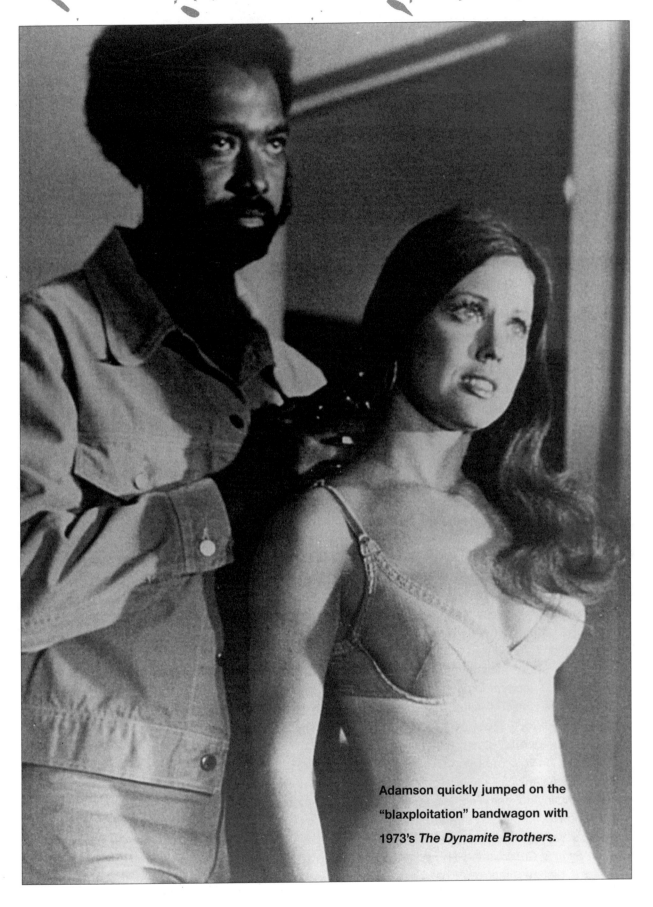

Adamson quickly jumped on the "blaxploitation" bandwagon with 1973's *The Dynamite Brothers*.

AL ADAMSON

the heroine. So, *High Noon* (1952) it ain't. But for
collectors of junk Westerns, it's a must.

Nineteen seventy-eight marked the appearance of Adamson's last major film as of this writing, *Nurse Sherri*, although the film's long
out-of-fashion hipster dialogue suggests it may
have been filmed much earlier. Cute-as-a-cup-
cake Jill Jacobsen stars in the title role, that of a
nurse possessed by the vengeful ghost of a religious nut who expired during surgery. Of course,
the spirit uses Jill to wipe out the medical person-
nel who failed to save him. Along the way she gets
to speak in a man's voice *Exorcist*-style and
whack people with cleavers and pitchforks Andy
Milligan–style, while treating the viewer to some
welcome T & A as well.

Though far from perfect, *Nurse Sherri* moves
at a fast clip and makes the most of its low budget, providing gore and sleaze fans with more
than their money's worth. It's certainly miles
ahead of Evan Lee's similarly plotted *Hollywood
Meatcleaver Massacre* released the previous year,
and deserved a better fate than being released to
home video on the "World's Worst Movies" label.
Also known as *Beyond the Living* and *Hospital of
Terror*, it's an above-average terror flick—and for
Adamson, a damned good one.

Just as Al Adamson seemed to be hitting some
sort of stride in his career, he abruptly departed
the film scene and took up another line of work,
real estate (Can you blame him? A steady income
is a wonderful thing!), and left members of his
stock company to carry on the fight. Greydon
Clark, who played the part of a biker named Acid
in *Satan's Sadists*, had already directed the successful *Satan's Cheerleaders* (1976), then graduated to B pictures such as *Final Justice* (1986)

Meet SHERRI.....
for an evening of
PLEASURE and TERROR

NURSE SHERRI

Starring
JILL JACOBSON • GEOFFREY LAND • MARILYN JOI
with Mary Kay Pass • Prentiss Moulden • Clayton Foster
Screenplay by Michael Bockman & Gregg Tittinger
Special effects by — Optical Systems Unlimited
Directed by AL ADAMSON • Produced by MARK SHERWOOD
in Eastman Color R RESTRICTED
an INDEPENDENT-INTERNATIONAL release

boasting bigger names and international locales.
And Adamson acolyte Kent Osborne turned his
hand to the sleazy Western with considerable success with a truly sick little Civil War–era vengeance
opus called *Cain's Way* (a.k.a. *The Blood Seekers*
and *Cain's Cutthroats*, 1970), featuring Adamson
regulars Scott Brady, John Carradine, and Robert
Dix. So, the tradition lives on.

Adamson himself turned out only two obscuri-
ties during the 1980s, *Carnival Magic*, which was
barely released in the U.S., and a G-rated film
about a young girl who runs away from her step-
father, *Lost* (also known as *Skipper*). Tragedy
struck the Adamson fold in recent years when his
longtime wife and leading lady, Regina Carroll,
succumbed to cancer in 1992.

But Adamson appears to be bouncing back at last, to the great joy of his many fans who haven't forgotten him. As of this writing, he has allegedly finished filming two UFO movies entitled *Beyond this Earth* and *From Other Worlds*; we certainly hope these rumors are true. As flawed as many of Adamson's films may be, in terms of entertainment value, they're miles ahead of just about any big-budget exploitation snoozer coming out of Hollywood these days.

SELECTED FILMOGRAPHY

1964: Two Tickets to Terror; **1967:** Blood of Dracula's Castle; **1969:** The Female Bunch (a.k.a. A Time to Run), Five Bloody Graves; **1970:** Satan's Sadists, Hell's Bloody Devils, Horror of the Blood Monsters (a.k.a. Creatures of the Prehistoric Planet; Horror Creatures of the Prehistoric Planet; Space Mission of the Lost Planet; Vampire Men of the Lost Planet); **1971:** Blood of Ghastly Horror, Last of the Comancheros, Dracula Vs. Frankenstein; **1972:** Brain of Blood, Angels' Wild Women (a.k.a. Screaming Angels), "Cry Rape," Hammer; **1973:** The Dynamite Brothers; **1975:** Girls for Rent (a.k.a. I Spit on Your Corpse), The Naughty Stewardesses, Stud Brown, Blazing Stewardesses; **1976:** The Kill Factor (a.k.a. Death Dogs), Jessie's Girls, Black Heat, The Murder Gang (a.k.a. Girls Hotel and U.S. Vice).; **1977:** Cinderella 2000, Black Samurai; **1978:** Sunset Cove, Death Dimension, Nurse Sherri (a.k.a. Beyond the Living and Hospital of Terror). **1981:** Carnival Magic; **1984:** Lost (a.k.a. Skipper); **Forthcoming:** Beyond This Earth; From Other Worlds.

Christopher Lee played the title role of *Count Dracula* (1969), Franco's erratic, but faithful version of Bram Stoker's novel.

Jess Franco

BY WALTER L. GAY

Born in 1930, Spain's Jesus Franco Manera—better known as Jess Franco—is a truly prodigious director in the exploitation film arena. Some sources credit him with an amazing 150 films, while others claim his body of work goes as high as 200 films—or more! Since many of his films have been heavily censored for one market and padded with hard-core inserts for another, an exact total may never be agreed upon. No one can deny, however, that Jess Franco is *the* most prolific sleaze merchant of all time.

Franco once worked for Orson Welles (as an assistant on the 1966 Shakespearean film *Chimes at Midnight*) and is an avowed admirer of such polar extremes as directors Ken Russell and Richard Donner. However, little seems to have rubbed off on Franco in the association. Franco flicks as a whole are darkly lit, poorly paced, and filled with enough technical gaffes to give bargain-basement sleazemeister Jerry Warren a run for his money. (Much has been written about Franco's love affair with the zoom lens, though he's not the only director to have overused this cost-cutting device, especially in the early 1970s.)

His works tend to be either soporific or unintentionally funny; some of his movies manage to be both at once. Misogynist themes run throughout his films with obsessive regularity; some show screaming females broken and bleeding while others portray them as domineering vampire/bitches. Many of his films were financed by a combination of British, French, and German investors and shot outside his native Spain, possibly to escape the repression of another Franco who, presumably, was no relation. His films are populated by a regular repertory company of European actors who never seem to work for anyone else. Franco-philes routinely spout off about Britt Nichols, Maria Rohm, Howard Vernon, and Lina Romay in the way Clint Eastwood fans discuss Sondra Locke, John Quade, and Geoffrey Lewis. But sometimes, Franco managed to rope in some bigger names like Christopher Lee, Caroline Munro, Herbert Lom, Fernando Rey, and the immortal Klaus Kinski as well. The gore content of his films vary, but bloody or not the average Franco-fest boasts enough sadism and perversity to astound the most hardened of sleaze-hounds.

In 1959 Georges Franju's poetically atmospheric *Eyes Without a Face* (a.k.a. *Horror Chamber of Dr. Faustus*) elevated the "plastic surgery" subgenre of the horror film to an art form. More concerned with raking in money than matching Franju's high standard, a horde of filmmakers oozed out of the woodwork with tawdry imitations. Leading the pack was Señor Jess with *The Awful Dr. Orloff* (1961), one of his earliest films.

As in Franju's film, Orloff (played by Franco stalwart Howard Vernon) tries to restore his daughter's ravaged face via skin grafts. European prints of this flick feature extended surgery sequences and touches of necrophilia (courtesy

Franco entered the "plastic surgery" subgenre of the horror film with 1961's *The Awful Dr. Orloff,* which was shorn of much of Señor Jess's characteristic rough stuff for its U.S. release.

of Orloff's hunchbacked assistant) that would be repeated, more graphically, in Franco's later work. Shorn of some rough stuff, *Orloff* played in the United States with the Italian film *The Horrible Dr. Hitchcock*—a double bill not approved by the AMA. In many quarters, *Orloff* is considered to be Franco's best and slickest production. It also kicked off a series of Orloff films that continued for nearly two decades. In the meantime, Franco tapped nearly every other exploitation vein as well, and bled them dry.

The Bloody Judge, set in the reign of England's James II, had Christopher Lee's witch-finding Lord Chancellor Jeffries presiding over numerous witch trials and routinely sentencing defendants to death by hanging, decapitation, or torture. He extends the same courtesy to pro–William of Orange insurrectionists. Along the way, he devel-

ops a serious rail-on for Maria Rohm and tries to have her lover done away with in a plot reminiscent of the cult Michael Reeves film *Witchfinder General* (a.k.a. *The Conqueror Worm*) released the previous year. His downfall comes with the return of William, and his eventual end, which though nowhere near as bloody as that of Vincent Price in the Reeves film, is pure poetic justice.

Despite some unpolished technical aspects (oh, that delirium-causing zoom lens!), this Harry Allan Towers production is entertaining, multidimensional and, dare it be said, somewhat intelligent. It benefits immensely from Lee's manic performance and supporting players Leo Genn and Maria Schell. Upper-crust Franco or not, it still contains the wet, red stuff that made witch-killer movies such a draw at the drive-ins during this period. Sexual extortion and attempted rape are present, along with some well-staged battle scenes and a few torture dungeon numbers. The latter were reportedly shot after Lee departed the production, and the ever-present Howard Vernon was assigned the job of mutilating the hapless victims. These scenes were removed by the film's suddenly bashful American distributor, American-International Pictures, when the film was released in the United States in 1970 as *Night of the Blood Monster.*

Another of Jess's historical horrors is *The Demons* (1972), also featuring the character of Lord Jeffries, who, along with his associates, is cursed by a witch and burned at the stake himself this time around. The witch's daughters (Ann Libert, Britt Nichols) hide out in a local convent, and the nuns there become possessed, committing all manner of sins of the flesh. The presence of Lord Jeffries as the head bastard is the only element the two films have in common. Abandoning all intelligence—and all but the most rudi-mentary attempts at storytelling—Franco went right for the groin this time—hirsute female groins in particular. His camera lingers so repeatedly on the nuns' bare rear ends and pubic bushes that one begins to wonder if Jess isn't a frustrated gynecologist. The film's explicit lesbianism and masturbation scenes involving the nuns guarantee Franco a permanent failing grade with the Catholic Legion of Decency. As Jeffries, John Foster is a poor substitute for his predecessor, Christopher Lee; his idea of acting villainous is to suck in his cheeks and glower at everything in sight. An anachronistic jazz score further sends the film into the toilet (although the score may have been imposed on Jess, and its presence may not be his fault).

Maria Rohm (left) and Maria Schell in Franco's entertaining, multidimensional and, dare it be said, intelligent *Night of the Blood Monster* (a.k.a. *The Bloody Judge*).

JESS FRANCO

109

The fact that the works of the Marquis de Sade are practically unfilmmable did not deter Jess and his producer, Harry Allan Towers, from trying to bring de Sade's *Justine* (1968) to the screen, and falling flat on their butts in the process.

Justine opens with Klaus Kinski, well cast as the marquis, making one of his many trips to prison. In his cell, he begins having hideous visions of naked women being restrained, humiliated, bled, and tortured. One sweet brunette in particular dominates his dark and bloody fantasies. De Sade names her Justine and takes quill in hand to scrawl his famous masterpiece about her and her sister, Juliette, two orphans who go their separate ways, the latter practicing vice and prospering while the former, Justine, pursues the path of righteousness and virtue and is exploited by, among others, a horny innkeeper played by Akim Tamiroff and a convicted murderess (Mercedes MacCambridge). She also encounters a fringe fraternity (Howard Vernon, Jack Palance) that practices arcane rituals in a remote monastery. At one point, Palance hoists a wine goblet and proceeds to blow off at the mouth for nigh on five minutes of screen time. His dialogue isn't dubbed, either. (Too bad this footage wasn't played before the Best Supporting Actor was announced a couple of Oscar nights ago.)

Romina Power is quite affecting in the title role, while cold Maria Rohm makes a good Juliette. MacCambridge plays her part to the hilt; likewise Sylvia Koscina, who plays a countess who ensnares our heroine in a murder plot. Other assets include a great Bruno Nicolai score and generally lavish photography devoid of the nau-seous color schemes so prevalent in other Franco films. Still, as Sadean cinema, *Justine* falls far short of its source. Unfilmed, or cut from American prints (which go under the title *Deadly Sanctuary*), are episodes involving a count with a decapitation fetish and a nobleman who quaffs gushing blood from his wife's punctured veins. Such restraint is distinctly out of character for Franco.

Jess then went on to film another classic for exploitation producer Harry's "Towers of London" company. The result—1969's *Count Dracula*—has vampire movie fans talking to this day.

The film's plot sticks fairly closely to the Bram Stoker original. Christopher Lee plays the title role as Stoker described him—an aging nobleman at the outset who grows younger and more vital the more blood he consumes. Herbert Lom is merely adequate as Van Helsing, but crazy Klaus Kinski makes possibly the screen's best Renfield. And as Mina, Maria Rohm has never been more gorgeous than she is here. The Bruno Nicolai score is also outstanding. However, *Count Dracula* suffers abominably from having Mediterranean architecture stand in none too convincingly for Victorian London. (One can't help but wonder why Britisher

Towers, who intended the film to be the definitive screen version of the Stoker story, didn't opt to shoot it in his native country.) There's also an embarrassing sequence in which two vampire hunters are menaced by obviously stuffed wildlife.

Striving for the respectability of other *Dracula* films, Franco makes his version far too sedate for its own good, while trying to have it both ways by throwing in snippets of sadism as well, as when a mental patient takes a two-story dive onto a stone wall. The ending also chickens out on Stoker's grisly finale. While the film isn't the total loss some say it is, it's no *Horror of Dracula* (1958), either.

Many directors have resorted to the old "monster rally" gambit of cramming as many creatures and weirdos as possible into one movie after another for more box-office appeal. So it should come as no surprise that Franco has pulled this stunt several times as well. His *Dracula Contra Frankenstein* (1972) opens with Dr. Seward impaling Dracula (Howard Vernon) on a silver stake, after which the vampire mutates into a dead bat. Somehow, the stake becomes a wooden one by the time Dr. Frankenstein (Dennis Price) comes upon the count's corpse. Apparently, the good doctor feels that his giant, moronic, homicidal monster isn't enough to contend with, so he brings Dracula back from the dead with the intention of enslaving him. This is accomplished by placing the impaled bat into a beaker and filling it with blood. The film then alternates between frenzied action and endless, pace-dragging footage of silhouetted characters walking languidly in front of windows. Viewers will be kept awake, however, by a number of Franco outrages such as a scene where Frankenstein's servant fondles a girl's

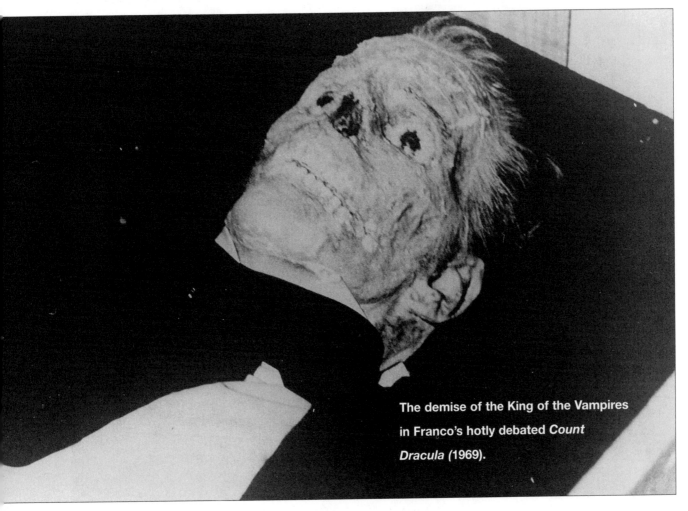

The demise of the King of the Vampires in Franco's hotly debated *Count Dracula* (1969).

JESS FRANCO

corpse before shoving it into an oven. A crazed gypsy woman and a werewolf drop into this "monster rally" just in time to participate in its thoroughly nonsensical ending. American viewers who *must see* this freakish free-for-all will have to content themselves, however, with a poorly dubbed, bowdlerized video version available under the title *The Screaming Dead.*

Franco's even more risible follow-up, *The Erotic Rites of Frankenstein* (1972) again featured Dennis Price as the title character, who is mortally wounded in the opening reels by a vulture woman. She's in league with a sorcerer (Howard Vernon) who wants to use the Frankenstein monster to abduct nubile young girls for his satanic rituals. Hero Alberto Dalbes periodically brings Frankenstein back to life so the doc will give him some pointers on how to deal with the sorcerer and the monster. A shot of the silver-skinned Frankenstein monster preparing to mount a female victim was featured in *Playboy* magazine's annual survey of "Sex in Cinema," probably swelling Franco's head, but how much actual sex is actually on view in the film depends on where you see it since, like many of Franco's wonderworks, it has different running times in various territories.

Lesbian vampire movies were a hot item with filmmakers and audiences in the 1970s; leave it to Franco to have at least three of them on his résumé. The title of his German-made *Vampyros Lesbos* (1970) is self-explanatory and the German-language version lives up to its name. *La Fille de Dracula* was made fast and cheap in 1972, featuring many of the same people who appeared in *Dracula Contra Frankenstein*. One of the film's few novelties altered the manner in which vampires are destroyed—Franco has them staked in the

Franco directed and played the title role in *The Sadist of Notre Dame* (1979). (Courtesy Mike Accomando)

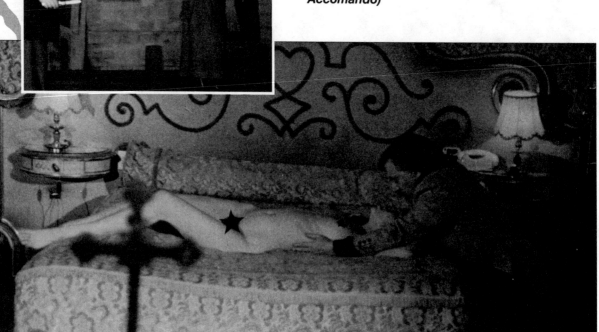

EL SADICO DE NOTRE DAME

NADINE PASCAL · JESS FRANK · LINA ROMAY
DIRECTOR JESS FRANCO TECHNICOLOR
EXCLUSIVAMENTE MAYORES DE 18 AÑOS

JESS FRANCO

head rather than the heart. The most famous of the trilogy, *The Bare-Breasted Countess*, in which Lina Romay stars as a bisexual vampire who kills her victims via oral sex, followed in 1973, and exists in a number of different versions, two of which have made it to U.S. shores on video.

The Force Video version, titled *Erotikill*, is considerably less explicit in the sex department, but features all the film's horror set pieces, which include various throat-rippings and so on. The Private Screenings release, which goes under the title *The Loves of Irina*, is another story, however, boasting a number of hard-core inserts such as a doctor thrusting his hand into a female corpse's vagina and Lina Romay performing fellatio with a zeal that makes Linda Lovelace pale by comparison. (Her obvious talent in this department may explain why the seemingly misogynistic Franco ultimately married her.) Because of the porn inserts, most video stores are forced to shelve it in their adult video sections—so, seek it there and ye shall probably find.

Expecting Jess Franco to avoid the lucrative and often lowbrow slasher genre would be like asking a starving weasel to stay out of the henhouse. In fact, it's surprising that Jolly Jess hasn't cranked out more stalk 'n' slash films than he has. In 1980 *Bloody Moon* combined nudity, a woman immolated in her wheelchair, and a mounting heap of corpses. In 1974 Franco shot the infamous *Exorcisme et Messes Noires*, which he later revised and rereleased in 1979 as *The Sadist of Notre Dame*. He himself plays the title character, a scuzzy religious fanatic who tortures and murders sexy young women, then heads to the confessional in between slayings to spill his guts to the priest. Today, this chiller exists in at least three different versions, each containing various amounts of hard-core violence, and, in one case, hard-core sex. It often goes under the title *Demoniac*.

In Franco's German-made *Jack the Ripper* (1976), a crazed doctor, unable to cope with the fact that his mother was a whore, slices and dices his way through the prostitute population of a distinctly Teutonic-looking London. The Ripper at one point simultaneously rapes and gut-stabs a harlot; he also mastectomizes Lina Romay in a truly harrowing scene. One of Franco's grisly set pieces in this film will please gore-hounds and gaffe-spotters alike: The Ripper takes the knife to a petite dancer, but when the police show up the mutilated girl's severed breasts have somehow grown to Dolly Partonesque proportions.

The redoubtable Klaus Kinski acquits himself well as the mad doctor, even with somebody else's voice dubbed in. But Franco's contribution to Ripper cinema blatantly disregards virtually all the documented facts of the case as much as the director himself flouts the laws of good moviemaking. Along with Paul Naschy's *Jack El Destripador de Londres* (1971), this ranks as one of the sloppiest "Saucy Jack" films ever made.

Franco's excursions into zombie country have also yielded less than classic results. He was slated to direct *Zombie Lake* (1979), which he coscripted, before being dismissed in favor of the French sleazemeister, Jean Rollin. And there is some debate as to whether the infamous *Oasis of the Zombies* (a.k.a. *Bloodsucking Nazi Zombies*, 1982) is his work or not. The film is credited to one "A. M. Franck," which, along with the film's snail-like pace, a Franco-foolish scene where the heroes pour gasoline onto the desert sand and light it to ward off the undead, and gut-ripping final reels, would seem to be a dead giveaway. Many reference books claim this gem was helmed by one Daniel or Marius Lesoeur; if so, he seems to have picked up quite a few of Jess's habits along the way.

Franco's name *is* stamped across all eighty-eight minutes of *A Virgin Among the Living Dead* (1971). Christina Von Blanc plays the title character. Traveling to a remote island for the reading of her father's will, she stops at an inn to ask directions and gets the sort of response from the locals usually accorded those inquiring about the location of Castle Dracula. (Say what you will about him, but Jess is no coward when it comes to clichés.) Along the way, she also spouts obscure, art-film voice-overs concerning "Bird of prey . . . that

Misogynistic themes run throughout Franco films like *Succubus* with obsessive regularity. (Courtesy Mike Accomando)

"WEIRD AND WAY-OUT, EROTIC-SEXY!"
Bob Salmaggi

Because of the unusual nature of the title, we suggest you call ███████████ for the full meaning so that you will not be surprised by the sophisticated subject matter of this film.

succubus
THE sensual experience of '69

This motion picture is rated X adults only, naturally.

"SUCCUBUS" Starring JANINE REYNAUD · JACK TAYLOR
Produced by   Directed by   Screenplay by
ADRIAN HOVEN · JESS FRANCO · PIER A. CAMINNECI
A PIER A CAMINNECI / ADRIAN HOVEN Color Film Production   In COLOR
of The AQUILA FILM ENTERPRISES, BERLIN   A TRANS AMERICAN FILMS RELEASE

©1969 **Trans American Films**

don't live in valleys" and "Flowers … with dull colors." (Why should the flowers differ from the rest of the movie?) She's also plagued by that hoariest of all horror movie devices, dream sequences, which are fairly abundant, but lack the entrail-gulping elements *Living Dead* audiences expect and demand from such fare. Instead, pasty-faced zombies emerge from the ground and surround her, mugging and gyrating like recruits from the local drunk tanks or psycho wards. Interspersed are scenes of geekish, inbred villagers ogling a skinny-dipping maiden, a "surprise" appearance by the dead father, and extended scenes of conversation boasting the worst dubbing imaginable. The ending is one of those "Is it a dream or reality?" twists that should have been mothballed sixty years ago.

Like most Franco films, *Virgin* was cut for its American theatrical release and trimmed even further for distribution to television, where it goes under the title *Among the Living Dead*. European prints are allegedly longer, more coherent, and free of post-induced "fogging" aimed at obscuring the film's more graphic elements—something for Franco-buffs to remember on their next jaunt to France, Spain, or Germany.

Franco has also flirted with the zombie movie's sick twin, the cannibal movie. His most important contribution to this tasty subgenre is 1979's *Mondo Cannibale*, in which flesh-eating natives jump aboard a boat cruising along the Amazon

River and lay waste to a family of travelers. Mama is gruesomely butchered. Papa's arm is lopped off. And their blond daughter is kidnapped by the natives and taken into the jungle. Years later, the father—looking not one day older and with his "severed" arm obviously tied behind his back—returns to the scene of the carnage to locate his daughter and finds the cannibal tribe is now ruled by a golden-haired goddess (guess who?). The ending is characteristically lame, the cannibal munch-outs look like inserts from some other film, and many observant gaffe-spotters have noticed wedding rings, wristwatches and even tan lines on the all too European-looking "natives." Jess himself puts in an appearance playing an (ahem!) opportunistic soldier of fortune.

Video City released this corker as *White Cannibal Queen*, proudly crowing that it was made a few years before John Boorman's similarly-themed *The Emerald Forest* (1985)—although

The agony and the ecstasy in Franco's sexy murder mystery *Venus in Furs* (1969).

comparing Franco's film to Boorman's is the same as likening tinfoil to Toledo steel.

Today, Franco's name and the genre known as women-in-prison pictures are often mentioned in the same breath. Franco neither invented the genre nor improved upon it, but he's certainly cranked out more movies of this type than any director alive (or dead). What he has managed to do is to elevate this inherently mean-spirited breed of film to new levels of cruelty.

In his first outing, *99 Women* (1968), Mercedes MacCambridge plays the superintendent of a West Indies prison beset by a high rate of "accidental" deaths. The island is ruled by Herbert Lom, a governor with a "thing" for the girls. Enter compassionate new warden Maria Schell (whose eternally troubled expression practically invites viewers to chime in with a chorus of "I See That Worried Look Upon Your Face"). Female prisoners break into fights, stage soft-core lesbian scenes for Lom's titillation, and tell sob stories to one another that provide the director with plenty of opportunities to indulge in flashbacks involving rape and others forms of violence. To have Schell kicked off the island, MacCambridge fabricates an affair between her and inmate Maria Rohm

(whose name is misspelled in the credits). In the meantime, we see a bunch of escaped prisoners hacking and slashing with plastic knives at a jungle snake that placidly slithers away. The big prison revolt hinted at throughout the movie consists of the put-upon women running around and squawking like chickens.

The unintentional humor of the film apparently eluded the M.P.A.A., who socked *99 Women* with an X rating. Shocking as the film is, however, it was small time compared with other Franco atrocities in the genre to come. Less than a decade later, Jess was at it again with two more entries shot back-to-back, which are calculated to churn the stomachs of the most jaded fans everywhere.

The first, *Barbed Wire Dolls* (1975), features humiliation, starvation, Lina Romay bound to an electrified bed frame, and a woman exciting herself with a lit cigarette. (Since this is a Franco flick, we should be grateful she uses the filter end.) Monocled Monica Swinn as the warden struts around in an open shirt and panties, though she'd look more appealing fully clothed. A prison break-out foiled in the downbeat finale is somewhat undone as well by the most lackluster firefight in movie history; soldiers are hosed by machine-gun fire and fall without even a tear in their uniforms. Most horrible of all, Franco plays an incestuous rapist in one of the film's innumerable flashbacks.

Apparently, Jess decided this movie wasn't gross enough for his tastes, so he strived to outdo himself with *Greta the Mad Butcher* (1977) in which heroine Tania Busselier gets herself thrown into a South American "rehab center" to locate her missing sister. There she finds herself caught in a ménage à trois between Sadean dyke Dyanne Thorne, who runs the place, and twisted top inmate Lina Romay.

Franco's ladling on of degradation, flogging, branding, and other outrages in this film have since become legend. Thorne sticks pins in Romay's belly and breasts and thrusts them in prior to indulging in lesbian sex. This does little for Romay's disposition judging from a subsequent scene where she forces Busselier to substitute her tongue for toilet paper. In yet another highlight, Thorne douches our heroine with a hypo full of acid. Then, to push the sleaze factor completely through the stratosphere, Thorne and her bullyboys film gang rapes and murders for fun and profit, intending to sell the flicks to snuff film fanatics. The ending, however, is that rarest of animals in the Franco oeuvre— violent and hard-hitting with the guilty actually paying for their sins. Jess turns in another cameo appearance as a helpful doctor,

Franco elevated the women-in-prison picture to new levels of cruelty in such outings as *99 Women* and *Sadomania*.

although with typical Franconian logic some of the doc's extended voice-over narration is in the first person despite the fact the character is killed early on.

Greta was incongruously reissued as *Wanda the Wicked Warden*, then disappeared altogether, except for heavily censored copies that occasionally surfaced on the bootleg market. It might have stayed in limbo had not Thorne starred in another, more popular women-in-prison series where she played *Ilsa—SheWolf of the SS* (1974) and *Ilsa— Harem Keeper of the Oil Sheiks* (1976). Capitalizing on these two films, an enterprising video outfit resurrected *Greta* in 1987, fiddled about with the dialogue track, and rereleased it as *Ilsa the Wicked Warden*. Thus did one of Franco's scuzziest movies return to delight us all.

Franco has continued to turn out exploitation pix with unbridled energy, each of them growing more explicit (and more deranged) with the pass-

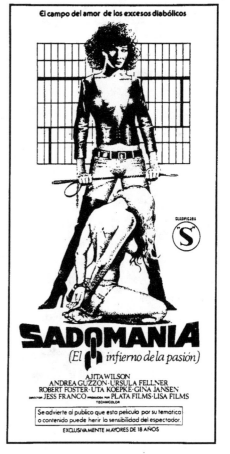

ing years. *Manhunter* (1980), another zombie-in-the-jungle film, featured *Playboy*'s Miss October of 1979, Ursula Buchfellner, in the title role, although she understandably hid behind an alias. A subsequent thriller, *Neurosis* (1982), featured a high-octane power-drill murder that was cut from the U.S. release when the film hit the videocassette market under the title *Revenge in the House of Usher*. And Franco has frequently returned to the type of material that first put him on the exploitation filmmaking map—the mad doctor movie.

Faceless (1988) falls back on the basic plot of one of Franco's entrées into the business. The sister of plastic surgeon Helmut Berger has her face seared by acid, and it's up to Berger to make her beautiful again. He consults other surgeons for help—including venerable movie bad guy Anton Diffring, and even Howard Vernon, who puts in a guest appearance as Dr. Orloff! Between them, they help Sis put on a happy face, many murders and unwilling donors later.

Despite its hoary plot, *Faceless* is well written and evenly paced with none of the sluggish passages so characteristic of Franco's past efforts. The cast, which, in addition to the above-mentioned, includes Chris Mitchum, Telly Savalas, Caroline Munro, and former Euro-porn star Brigitte Lahaie, is good and the sensational bits—gruesome surgeries, power-tool slayings and rapes committed by Berger's acromegalic servant—are both powerful and convincing.

By any standards, *Faceless* is a bloody-good little exploitation picture. Does this herald a new direction for Franco? Now in his early sixties, an age when most directors seem inclined toward retirement, Señor Jess remains as tireless as ever. Will he continue to turn out good product like *Faceless* or go back to his old hit-or-miss (mostly miss) style? Time will tell. But no matter what happens, his position as Europe's number-one sleaze merchant will forever be assured.

Selected Filmography

In view of the immensity of Franco's output and the fact that his films have undergone so many title changes, what follows is just a partial listing of his corpse of work.

1957: Arbol de España (O'Olivier); **1958:** L'Exil du Cid; **1959:** Tenemos Dieciocho Años; **1960:** Labios Rojos (Operation Lèvres Rouges), Reina del Tabarin (La Belle de Tabarin); **1961:** The Awful Dr. Orloff; **1962:** La Muerte Silba un Blue (a.k.a. 007 Operation Sexy), Vampiressa 1930 (Certains l'Aiment Noire); **1963:** Rififi en la Ciudad (Chasse à la Mafia), La Mano de un Hombre Muerte (Le Sadique Baron von Klaus), El Llanero (Le Jaguar); **1964:** Dr. Orloff's Monster (a.k.a. El Secreto del Doctor Orloff); **1965:** The Diabolical (a.k.a. Miss Muerte); **1966:** Cartas Boca Arriba (Cartes sur Table); **1967:** Residencia para Espias, Lucky el Intrepido, El case de las Dos Bellezas (a.k.a. Sadisterotica); Kiss Me Monster (a.k.a. Castle of the Doomed, Besame, Monstruo); Necronomicon—Getraumte Sunden (a.k.a. Succubus, Delirium); **1968:** Castle of Fu Manchu, Blood of Fu Manchu (a.k.a. Kiss and Kill, The Death Kiss of Fu Manchu), Sumuru, 99 Mujeres (99 Women), Justine; **1969:** Black Angel (a.k.a. Paroximus, Venus in Furs), De Sade '70, Count Dracula (a.k.a. El Conde Dracula), Il Trono di Fuoco, X 312 Flug zur Holle, Fierno Tuya Es la Victoria; **1970:** Las Vampiras (a.k.a. Die Erbin des Dracula, Vampyros Lesbos, Sexualité Speciale), Eugenie de Sade, Der Teufel Kam aus Akasawa, Dr. M. Schlagt zu (a.k.a. El Doctor Mabuse, Mabuse '70), Les Yeux de la Nuit, Sex Charade, Sie Totete in Ekstase (Mrs. Hyde, Night of the Blood Monster, [a.k.a. The Bloody Judge]), Der Todesracher von Soho (a.k.a. El Muerto Hace las Malestas); **1971:** 3 Filles Nues dans l'Ile de Robinson, Christina, Princesse de l'Érotisme (Une Vierge Chez les Morts-Vivants, A Virgin Among the Living Dead), Jungfrauen Report; **1972:** Dracula Contra Frankenstein (a.k.a. Dracula Prisonnier de Frankenstein and The Screaming Dead), A Filha de Dracula (La Fille de Dracula), La Maledición de Frankenstein (Les Expériences Érotiques de Frankenstein, The Erotic Rites of Frankenstein), Los Demonios (Les Démons), Un Capitaine de Quinze Ans, Les Ébranlées (La Maison du Vice), Le Journal Intime d'une Nymphomane, El Misterio del Castillo Rojo, Un Silencio de Tomba; **1973:** Los Ojos Siniestros del Doctor Orloff (Los Ojos del Doctor Orloff), Relax Baby, Plaisir à 3, La Comtesse Perverse, Al Oltro Lado del Espejo (Le Miroir Obscene), Les Amazones de la Luxure (Maciste Contre la Reine des Amazones), Les Exploits Érotiques de Maciste dans l'Atlantide, La Noche de los Assesinos, Le Chemin Solitaire (Frissons sous la Peau), Sexy Blues, Les Nuits Brûlantes de Linda (a.k.a. Le Plaisir Solitaire), Los Amantes del Isla del Diablo (Violences Érotiques dans une Prison de Femmes), Les Avaleuses (a.k.a. La Comtesse aux Seins Nus, The Bare Breasted Countess, Erotikill, The Loves of Irina); **1974:** Exorcisme et Messes Noires (Sexorcisme), Celestine, Bonne à Tout Faire, Lorna . . . L'Exorciste (Les Possédées du Diable), Les Chatouilleuses (Les Nonnes en Folie), Le Jouisseur (L'Homme le Plus Sexy du Monde), Les Emmerdeuses (Les Grandes Emmerdeuses); **1975:** De Sade's Juliette, Shining Sex (Le Sexe Brilliant), Midnight Party, Frauengefangnis, Down Town, Lèvres Rouges et Bottes Noires, Barbed Wire Dolls; **1976:** Jack the Ripper, Dirty Dracula (a.k.a. Ejaculations, Le Portrait de Doriana Gray), Lettre d'Amour d'une Nonne Portugaise; **1977:** Greta, Haus Ohne Männer (Greta the Mad Butcher [a.k.a. Ilsa or Wanda the Wicked Warden]), DasFrauenhaus, Frauen ohne Unschuld, Frauen für Zellen Block 9, Die Teuflischen Schwestern (La Cabaret des Filles Perverses!), Die Sklavinnen, Camp Érotique, Passions et Voluptés Vaudoués (Le gri d'Amour de la Déesse Blonde, Ruf de Blonden Gottin; **1978:** Cocktail Special, Elles Font Tout, Je Brûle de Partout, Symphonie Érotique; **1979:** El Escarbajo de Oro, Mondo Cannibale (a.k.a. White Cannibal Queen), The Sadist of Notre Dame (a.k.a. Demoniac); **1980:** Le Corps et le Fouet (Il Cacciatore di Uomini); Les Bourgeoises et l'Amour (Die Nichten der Frau Oberst), Sadomania, Bloody Moon, Linda, Gefangene Frauen, Manhunter; **1981:** Eugenie—Historia de una Perversione (De Sade 2000), Orgía de Ninfomanas, LasChicas de Copacabana, Aberraciones Sexuales de una Mujer Casada, La Chica de las Bragas Transparentes, Girl Pick Up, El Sexo Esta Logo, El Lago de las Vergines, La Tumba de los Muertos Vivientes; **1982:** Porno Dama (Lady Porno), El Siniestro Dr. Orloff, Nevrose (Neurosis, Revenge in the House of Usher, El Hundimiento de la Casa Usher), Botas Negras, Latigo de Cuero, Confesiones Intimas de una Exhibicionista, El Hotel de los Liques, Historia Sexual de O (The Story of O), La Casa de las Mujeres Perdidas, La Mansión de los Muertos Vivientes, Germidos de Placer, La Noche de los Sexos Abiertos, Las Orgías Inconfesables de Emmanuelle, Macumba Sexual; **1983:** Sangre en los Zapatos, Los Monstruous de Fiske Manor, El Tesoro de la Diosa Blanca (a.k.a. TheTreasure of the White Goddess); **1985:** Viaje a Bangkok, Ataúd Incluido (a.k.a. Trip to Bangkok, Coffin Included); **1986:** Sida, la Peste del Siglo XX, Angel of Death; **1987:** El Ojete de Lulu, El Chupete de Lulu; **1988:** Predateurs de la Nuit (a.k.a. Faceless).

Writer, director, and producer John ("To me, bad taste is what entertainment is all about") Waters. *(Photo by Henny Garfunkel/Copyright © 1989 Universal City Studios, Inc./Courtesy Eric Caidin)*

John Waters

BY KEN HANKE

If, as he claims, it is necessary to have *good* taste in order to understand *bad* taste, then John Waters must have the best taste ever known to civilization.

Unlike many filmmakers who spend large chunks of their careers wandering through low-budget pictures and the world of exploitation in the hopes of making so-called legit films some-day, Waters set out upon this path willingly and deliberately. In his autobiography, *Shock Value* (Delta, 1981), he states his artistic credo in the very first line: "To me," he writes, "bad taste is what entertainment is all about." Fair enough. And whether right or wrong in his definition, Waters has produced a substantial body of work that more than backs up his unique vision.

Born in Baltimore in 1946, John Waters, like many filmmakers of his generation, began making home movies as a teenager. Unlike most, however, he did not attempt overambitious retreads of films he'd seen and admired as a child. Rather, he immediately staked claim to his own outré spe-ciality with a fifteen-minute debut film called *Hag in a Black Leather Jacket* (1964) that chronicled the wedding of a black man and a white girl in a ceremony performed by a Ku Klux Klansman. He admits the film was terrible—improperly exposed and with every inch of film shot appearing in the final cut—but where most of his contemporaries would have been content showing such an early effort only to their parents and friends, Waters went a step further and "premiered" it at a coffee-house in his native Baltimore, apparently garnering the approval of the audience and a profit of thirty dollars. According to Waters, the film now resides in his closet "where it belongs." Even so, it's abun-dantly clear from the film's synopsis that Waters's artistic sensibilities—sleaze with attitude—were already fully formed.

Enter into this already-skewed vision of the world the perfect girl next door. Except that in Waters's case the girl next door was a cross-dresser named Glenn Milstead, whom he quickly rechristened "Divine." It was through Divine that Waters met David Lochary and his girlfriend, Roxanne, all of whom would have a major impact on Waters's filmmaking desires and aspirations. Without realizing it—and against all laws of logic, reality, and normalcy—Waters was forming a stock company of appropriately extreme individuals to help him realize his wildest cinematic fantasies.

An almost complete immersion into the drug world and a brief stint at NYU (where Waters quickly fled film classes in favor of watching movies at underground theaters to get his cine-matic education) followed. When he was kicked out of school, Uncle Sam called. The image of John Waters, P.F.C., is not a comfortable one under the best of circumstances; he managed to wiggle out of the situation, however, by claiming to be "an alcoholic drug addict bed-wetting homosexual." Somehow all this led back to film-

What De Niro is to Scorsese, the late Divine was to John Waters. *(Courtesy Eric Caidin)*

making and a movie called *Roman Candles* (1965), shot on stolen movie film with a borrowed 8-mm camera. Typically, Waters stuffed the film with ideas and images designed to outrage the sensibilities of his audience—sex, drugs, perversion, and a distinctly irreligious tone in scenes involving a nun and a priest making love intercut with stock footage of the pope. As he'd hoped, *Roman Candles* succeeded in scandalizing the audience at the premiere he held for it in, of all places, a church hall!

Waters's next film, *Eat Your Makeup* (1968), was his first on 16 mm. According to Waters, it was "technically too fucked-up and arty." What he sought for the film was a "trashy" look to match and even enhance his bizarre subject matter. This he found in his next film, *Mondo Trasho* (1969), which Waters terms a "gutter film" (based mostly

on its array of unpleasant locations, he says). The story line presents Divine as a kind of ultra-cheap Jayne Mansfield type, who runs down a young woman (Mary Vivian Pearce), after which visions of a miracle in a launderette land them in a mental institution where they undergo the insidious experiments of one Dr. Coat Hanger (David Lochary), and eventually expire in a pigpen. *Mondo Trasho* got Waters noticed, garnered some favorable reviews, and made his name familiar in film circles even if his films themselves were not.

Flushed by this success, Waters talked his father out of five thousand dollars to make a "talkie," *Multiple Maniacs* (1970), which, by his own admission, was intended as an antidote to the Woodstock generation attitude, glorifying violence as a laughing matter in the face of a generation preaching peace and love. He describes the film as a personal favorite because of its "meanness and harsh documentary look." Maybe so, but it's also important to note that this was also his "breakthrough" film—not just because it was the first of his films to boast a synchronized soundtrack but because it was also the first to adhere fully to the principle of trash for its own sake without any concessions to an art film sensibility. And what could ultimately be more trashy than a film that trades on the Manson murders for its inspiration?

The plot is both convoluted and absurdly simple —with ample room left over for Waters's growing penchant for the twisted digression. In this instance Divine and boyfriend David Lochary are the owners of a traveling sideshow, the Carnival of Perversion, which features such delights as a bicycle seat fetishist and a fellow called the "puke eater." The show itself is merely a front for Divine's larcenous and murderous activities, providing her with victims who come to gawk at the weird performers. When Lochary takes up with another woman (Mary Vivian Pearce), Divine happens upon a "religious pervert" played by Mink Stole, who seduces her in a church with the charms of a "rosary job." The duo engineer the murder of Lochary and his lover, after which Divine loses her mind and imagines herself raped by a giant lobster. Completely around the bend, she is shot down in the street.

Without a doubt, however, *Pink Flamingos* (1972) is the film that comes to mind when most people think of John Waters. This insane tale of Divine and her family (comprised of a degenerate son named Crackers [Danny Mills], the egg-obsessed Mama Edie [Edith Massey] and her sleazy friend, Cotton [Mary Vivian Pearce]) vying with the Marbles (David Lochary and Mink Stole) for the right to lay claim to the title of "the filthiest

Divine is raped by a giant lobster in *Multiple Maniacs* (1970), Waters's Manson family–inspired antidote to the Woodstock generation's attitude of peace and love. (Copyright © 1970 New Line Cinema/Courtesy Eric Caidin)

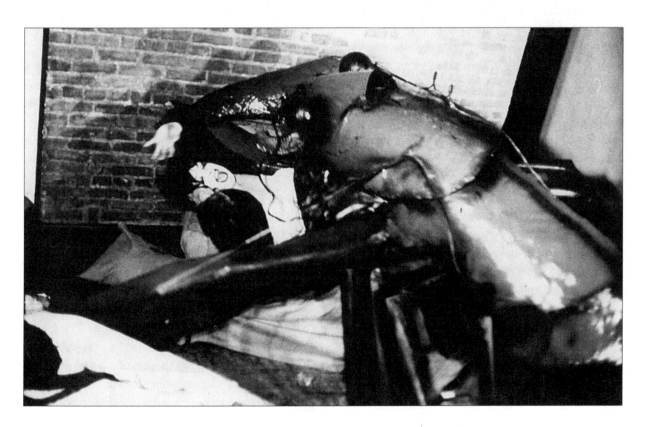

JOHN WATERS

123

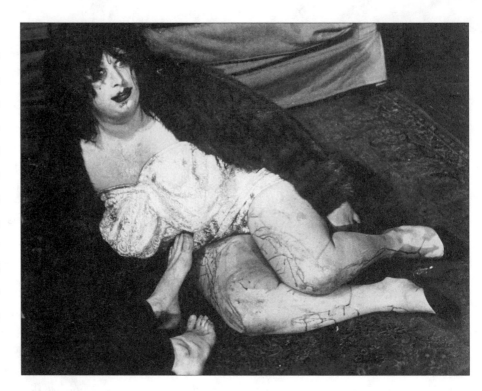

The aftermath of the lobster rape from *Multiple Maniacs* (1970), the break-through film that launched Waters's midnight-movie reputation as the "Prince of Puke." *(Copyright © 1970 New Line Cinema/ Courtesy Eric Caidin)*

people alive" struck a nerve with early '70s audiences, who (A) thought they'd seen it all, and (B) were starting to find a little cynicism creeping into their '60s sensibilities.

Regardless of whether this "trash epic" is anything more than an oddity, it can probably lay claim to being the most singularly ugly-looking film ever made. Though shot on 16 mm and blown up to 35 mm, *Pink Flamingos* looks for all the world like it was filmed on inferior 8-mm equipment with outdated film. Yet this presumably is what Waters wanted—a final product with the look and feel of a peculiarly perverse home movie. That everything about the film is substandard is hardly surprising, since the budget was ten thousand dollars, but this may actually have been a benefit—the grungy, poverty-row feel of the movie perfectly matches its subject matter.

In that he couldn't have produced a slick film under the circumstances, Waters opted instead to "give the audience something no other studio could dare to give them," which meant a series of ever-increasingly twisted takes on American life. The questions arise: Is the film a satire, or is it the way Waters actually views contemporary American life? The answer to both questions is yes.

The catalogue of *Pink Flamingos*'s grotesqueries is almost staggering in its sheer volume. Buried within the film's ninety-minute running time are such jaw-dropping events as a sex scene with a live (well, it starts out live anyway) chicken sandwiched between the participants; a bit where imprisoned girls are "raped" via artificial insemination by a half-wit armed with a plastic syringe (the resulting babies are then sold to lesbian couples); Divine receiving a gift-wrapped turd in the mail ("My God! Someone has sent me a bowel movement!" she cries in perfect Bea Arthur tones); a sideshow/birthday party featuring—among other things—a naked contortionist with the most amazing sphincter control ever recorded on film; a bit of cannibalism; a sequence where Divine and her son get so worked up licking their enemies' furniture that mother goes down on son; and, of course, the infamous capper where Divine (without benefit of cuts or camera trickery) eats dog shit. Waters intended on giving the audience something they had never seen before. There's no denying that he succeeded.

"The world of the heterosexual is a sick and boring existence!" exclaims unique Waters's discovery Edith Massey in Waters's far more accomplished follow-up, *Female Trouble* (1974), as she tries to convince her straight hairdresser nephew how proud she would be if he'd "go nellie." Waters's claim that the film's theme is "crime is beautiful" actually does the picture a disservice, since what *Female Trouble* really does is take traditional values and inverts them to the point where the inversions seem *less* absurd than their traditional counterparts. As a result, *Female Trouble* is probably Waters's most delightfully subversive work, which neatly balances the technical crudity of his early films with the often too slick quality of his more recent efforts.

Female Trouble is far more structured than its predecessors, too, although, as might be suspected, Waters's idea of structure consists of grafting his vision of the world onto the most unrespectable of all film genres, the juvenile delinquency exploitation drama, and presenting a kind of "case history"— of career criminal Dawn Davenport (Divine, of course) from her high-school years to her death in the electric chair. It is also Waters's most outrageously funny film.

The insanity starts immediately with the film's deliberately tacky theme song (lyrics penned by Waters and sung by Divine) and even tackier credits —not to mention its dedication to Charles Manson henchman Charles Watson (whose prison-made toy helicopter can be seen in the dedication). Any film dedicated to a member of the Manson clan can't be too far along the path to normalcy and *Female Trouble* certainly isn't. We are at once propelled into Dawn's "youthful" period in school where we find her already on the road to delinquency and sociopathy as evidenced by her in-your-face hairstyle and almost fetishistic longing for "them cha-cha heels" as a Christmas present from her parents ("I asked and I better get!"), not to mention her singularly unacademic attitude toward school ("Fuck homework—I wanna quit right where I am after I get my Christmas presents"). Not surprisingly, Dawn doesn't get her cha-cha heels and all hell breaks loose on the homefront. Toppling the family's painfully artificial tree on her mother, Dawn takes her heated leave of home life declaring, "Fuck you! Fuck you both! You're not my parents! I hate you! I hate this house! I hate Christmas!"

David Lochary and Mink Stole prepare to torch a trailer in their quest to become known as the "filthiest people alive." From *Pink Flamingos* (1972). *(Photo by Lawrence Irvine/ Copyright © 1972 New Line Cinema/ Courtesy Eric Caidin)*

JOHN WATERS

123

Female Trouble (1974) chronicles the criminal career of Dawn Davenport (Divine) from her high-school to glamour queen years to her death in the electric chair. *(Copyright © 1974 New Line Cinema/Courtesy Eric Caidin)*

Edith Massey starred as underworld Queen Carlotta, who is eventually overthrown, cooked, and eaten by her minions in Waters's *Desperate Living* (1977). (Copyright © 1977 New Line Cinema/Courtesy Eric Caidin)

In keeping with this cozy spirit of Yuletide, Dawn soon finds herself being "raped" (not altogether unwillingly) by the driver of an Edsel station wagon named Earl Pearson (also played by Divine!), whose wallet she steals in the process. Finding herself pregnant, she gives birth to little "Taffy" on the sofa of her cheap room (biting the umbilical cord in two with her teeth), then tries her hand at waitressing and a stint as a go-go girl to support herself and her baby. Along the way, she falls into a life of prostitution and petty crime with her old high-school chums Concetta (Cookie Mueller) and Chiclet (Susan Walsh). In no time Taffy has turned into the ultimate monster child, who is restrained in manacles on her tiny bed in an attic room, while Dawn happily cuts up her jump rope ("It's the last time she's gonna jump with this goddamn thing!"). Encouraged by her friends to cheer herself up by treating herself to a trip to the Lipstick Beauty Salon, Dawn meets the owners, the Dashers (David Lochary and Mary Vivian Pearce), who are interested in the "truly appalling" and the abnormal (they throw one customer out because she works for the phone company). Of course, they decide to take Dawn under their wing. She meets the salon's only straight hairdresser, Gator (Michael Potter), and much to the chagrin of his aunt Ida (Edith Massey), he marries Dawn—in a ceremony featuring the bride dressed in a see-through gown and the groom in a tiger-striped dinner jacket.

Married life turns out to be far from blissful, since Gator is pathologically unfaithful; he even comes on to the now adolescent Taffy (played by a rapidly aging Mink Stole, who, it is pointed out by her mother, doesn't look "so good for fourteen"). Taffy, however, will have none of his advances ("I wouldn't suck your lousy dick if I was suffocating and there was oxygen in your balls!") and spends her time alternately blackmailing her mother, playing "car accident" by dragging pieces of cars into the living room and pouring ketchup on herself, and trying to find her "real father"—whose sexual advances prompt Taffy to stab him to death when she *does* find him.

When her marriage falls apart and Gator moves to Detroit ("to find happiness in the auto industry"), Dawn fully takes up with the Dashers, who seek to document her criminal activities on film to prove their notion that "crime enhances one's beauty." With this opportunity for a new career as a model, Dawn finds her true position in life.

The bulk of the film then follows Dawn's "modeling" career, which only takes off after Aunt Ida throws acid in her face in revenge for having caused Gator to leave. This results in the horribly disfigured Dawn being pronounced more beautiful than ever! The Dashers not only support Dawn's career, but remodel her home and present her with Ida in a cage for her amusement. Dawn's fortunes reach their pinnacle with a bizarre stage act in which she makes such outlandish claims as "I blew Richard Speck," jumps around on a trampoline, and finally murders several members of the audience. Arrested for her crimes, she finds the Dashers have turned on her and, despite her lawyer's indisputable assertion that she is insane, the jury brings in a guilty verdict with a recommendation for death. Still thinking she's a superstar, Dawn goes to the chair laughing.

Despite a tendency to meander, *Female Trouble*'s major failing lies in Waters's insistence that a tacky film about tacky people in a tacky story must also look as if it was made by an amateur. To some degree, he's right, if only because the amateurishness of his approach does much to defuse the film's overt nastiness. The tacky zoom shots, the tendency to let shots linger long beyond their worth, the flat lighting, the bad sound, the awkward "shock" inserts of Gator's private parts all make the film merely *look like* the bad-boy antics of a clever, but not accomplished, filmmaker. Slickly made, *Female Trouble* would have been threatening rather than sickly funny. It is no accident that Waters's better-made later films are also a lot less overtly warped.

Without Divine (whose cult status had suddenly engendered numerous other commitments), but with the added benefit of a behemoth black woman named Jean Hill and old standby Edith Massey, Waters next set out to make an X-rated movie without any sex or violence. The result was *Desperate Living* (1977), the first of his films to gain a broad release. A bigger budget ($65,000) than usual and a more fantasy-oriented plot made it at once a better-looking and more distanced film, which showed signs that Waters was clearly drifting toward the mainstream. However, its story, involving lesbianism, murder by such creative means as suffocation with the body of a four-hundred-pound maid (Jean Hill), and a city of criminals lorded over by Queen Carlotta (Edith Massey), who is eventually overthrown, cooked, and eaten by her citizenry, shows that he wasn't as yet straying too far afield from his roots. The film was taken with a surprising degree of seriousness by the more adventurous critics, and helped make Waters appear like a far more bankable commodity (albeit a rather questionable one) than Hollywood had ever guessed.

Seen today, *Desperate Living* is indeed slicker than its predecessors, but it's ultimately a little too much of the same thing. Also, its relative restraint does not especially suit its plot. In deliberately going after a more coherent approach to filmmaking, Waters lost some of the anarchic edge of his earlier *Pink Flamingos* and *Female Trouble*. This is not to say that the film is suitable viewing for one's grandmother, however; it just misses the mark as a truly great disgusting comedy—the type of comedy at which Waters is best.

Constantly told by less-charitable critics that his movies "smelled," Waters decided to deck out his first genuinely professional-looking film (if, indeed, a film in which microphones and lens shades are constantly making "guest appearances" can be called professional), *Polyester* (1981), shot in 35 mm, with a gimmick called "Odorama." The gimmick was nothing more than a scatch-and-sniff card viewers were supplied for use at key points in the film to enhance the cinemagoing experience. This William Castle–like gimmick is perhaps the least notable aspect of the film, but it's the one most people remember. What tends to be forgotten is that the film is actually one of Waters's most pointed jabs at the vapid sterility of suburbia—a place where mom is incarnated as a three-hundred-pound transvestite (Divine), success-oriented dad runs a porno theater ("Our current attraction is *My Burning Bush*"), daughter is an out-of-control slut, and son is a wigged-out foot fetishist (and part-time Peeping Tom), who is terrorizing the city as the "Baltimore Foot Stomper." The film often cleverly, but occasionally tediously, traces the decline and fall of this "ideal" family, along with the liberation of Divine from her suburban shackles.

Added into this already heady mix are such delights as the ever-popular Edith Massey (in her final performance) as Divine's best friend, Cuddles, a former cleaning lady who has come into a fortune and now believes herself to be a debutante; Waters regular Mink Stole (in black undies and stockings and a Bo Derek hairdo) as Divine's errant husband's girlfriend; a funny bit for Jean Hill as a terrifyingly overzealous vigilante-minded choir member; and Tab Hunter as the smarmy fortune hunter with whom Divine becomes involved

when her marriage falls apart. As if all this weren't enough, there's also a deft satire of a radical "pro-life" group, an hysterically nightmarish vision of life at a Catholic home for unwed mothers (where activities include midnight hayrides in the middle of thunderstorms); Divine's botched suicide attempt; the family dog's more successful suicide; Divine's mother's shooting at the hands of her granddaughter's psychopath boyfriend; and a wild ending with multiple deaths and plot twists all neatly wrapped up and glossed over with—what else?—air freshener! For sheer quantity of incident the only possible response to *Polyester* is an unqualified *"wow!"*

More shocking than his most extreme outrages was the emergence in 1988 of a PG-rated John Waters film, *Hairspray*, which, depending on one's outlook, is either the movie where Waters grew up, or finally sold out. In truth, it was a shrewd move, for Waters had taken gross-out and shock humor about as far as possible in his earlier films.

Hairspray **(1988), Waters's look back at the fads, fashions, and politics of the early 1960s, was the product of someone with a keen eye for satire and a shrewd sense of history. (Photo by Henny Garfunkel/Copyright © 1988 New Line Cinema/ Courtesy Eric Caidin)**

J O H N   W A T E R S

Kim McGuire, Darren E. Burrows, Johnny Depp, Ricki Lake (now a talk-show host), and Traci Lords in *Cry-Baby* (1990), a more overt attempt by Waters to tap into the mainstream. *(Photo by Henny Garfunkel/Copyright © 1989 Universal City Studios, Inc./Courtesy Eric Caidin)*

Hairspray is the product of someone with a keen eye for satire and a shrewd sense of history. Its plot is deceptively simple. It involves the rivalry between stuck-up society girl Amber Von Tussle (Colleen Fitzpatrick) and "upper-lower-class" newcomer Tracy Turnblad (Ricki Lake) on an afternoon TV dance show for teenagers, a rivalry played out against the backdrop of early racial integration. Waters's vision of the time is at once nostalgic and warm without being falsely sentimental. He knows full well that the early 1960s were no barrel of laughs and he presents the period as a seething hangover from the 1950s. He may love the cheerfully inane music, the fash-

ions, foibles, and, of course, hairdos of the period, but even as he celebrates these fond memories, he points his considerable gift for satire at the narrow-minded bigotry that also marked the era of *Hairspray*. Just as he had made "normalcy" seem patently ridiculous by standing it on its head in *Female Trouble*, here he makes his points against racism, bigotry, and snobbery by painting them in garishly ludicrous terms.

There is also something agreeably fitting in the fact that *Hairspray* was Divine's swan song for Waters. After years of playing tormented and tortured psychopaths and sociopaths for him, Divine was here given the most normal role of his/her career as Edna Turnblad, the loving (if a bit opportunistic) mother of the film's heroine, and dutiful wife to her joke-shop store owner husband (Jerry Stiller). She is the very picture of the typical suburban hausfrau, alternately bitchy ("I've got nothing but hampers of ironing to do—and my diet pill is wearing off!") and caring ("Don't run, Tracy, you'll hurt yourself! You're wearing heels!"), but ultimately—and aptly—a happy and even heroic figure who

THE SLEAZE MERCHANTS

does her bit for social justice and compassion for the "different." Divine made a career out of being different, so it's only right and proper that she should have ended up her career playing the heroine in what is, to date, Waters's greatest ode to the different. The rest of the cast is equally fine, especially Waters discovery Ricki Lake, a vibrant and vivacious performer and a real find.

While managing to retain its sense of bad taste, Hairspray was the first Waters film to display a firm grasp of filmmaking technique and not designed to jar and look ugly. The film is well-lit, always in focus, has logical shot breakdowns, and even boasts a degree of professional-looking camera work. Gone are the flat home-movie lighting and clumsily edited inserts. However, even when he does come up with a pleasing composition, Waters also undermines it with his own twist (as in a romantic shot of the moon reflected in a puddle of water that climaxes with a rat running through). In addition, whereas longtime Waters production designer Vincent Peranio's sets may be a little cleaner and more spacious than usual, they are certainly no more tasteful.

Like all Waters films, Hairspray is structured as a series of set pieces, the best of which are among the funniest and most genuinely creative of his career. Particularly outstanding is the hysterical sequence where the absurdly racist Prudence Pingleton (Jo Ann Havrilla) follows Tracy and Tracy's boyfriend into the black section of Baltimore and finds herself confronted by the most blandly innocuous occurences imaginable, which in her mind are transformed into terrifying life-threatening situations. For example, when a panhandler asks her for a quarter, she hands over all the money in her wallet ("Don't hurt me!") as the rest of the neighborhood convulses in laughter. By contrast, Divine, suddenly prone to incorporating Bob Dylan lyrics into her speech, and her husband are able to move with the times "that are a-changin'." Despite the fact that their adaptations tend toward the ridiculous—like joining the NAACP—their hearts are clearly in the right place. In fact, that might be the best assessment of the film itself: Its heart too is in the right place.

Waters's next film, Cry-Baby (1990), which is similar in theme to Hairspray, was an even more overt attempt at tapping into a mainstream audience—an audience whose tastes were already showing signs of willingness to meet the director halfway. John Waters was becoming, dare we say it, respectable at last! Despite a handful of engaging sequences, good performances from Johnny Depp, Ricki Lake, Polly Bergen, the ever-delightful (and underrated) Susan Tyrrell, and a couple of dynamite musical numbers staged and shot with a technical prowess one would not have expected of Waters, the film really doesn't work, however. The story line is at once too limited in its theme (class distinction) and too complicated in its relationships and contrivances without ever crossing over into Waters's trademark territory, outright lunacy. In other words, the film is too normal in its plotting. It is at its best in its digressions, especially a subplot involving former teen porn star Traci Lords and her goodie-goodie parents, who are played with an almost blasphemous relish by David Nelson and Patty Hearst! If nothing else, Cry-Baby is a monument to Waters's amusingly perverse sense of casting against type. But to know Waters by this film alone is not to know Waters at all.

Thankfully, Waters's most recent project as of this writing, Serial Mom, starring Kathleen Turner as an average suburban housewife with a not-so-average predilection for committing mass murder, harkens a welcome—albeit even more mainstream—return to form for the self-billed "Prince of Puke" and self-styled chronicler of his beloved city of Baltimore's high and low life.

SELECTED FILMOGRAPHY

1964: Hag in a Black Leather Jacket*; **1966:** Roman Candles*; **1968:** Eat Your Makeup*; **1969:** Mondo Trasho; **1970:** Multiple Maniacs; **1972:** Pink Flamingos; **1974:** Female Trouble; **1977:** Desperate Living; **1981:** Polyester; **1988:** Hairspray; **1990:** Cry-Baby; **1993:** Serial Mom.
*Short film

THE Young Turks

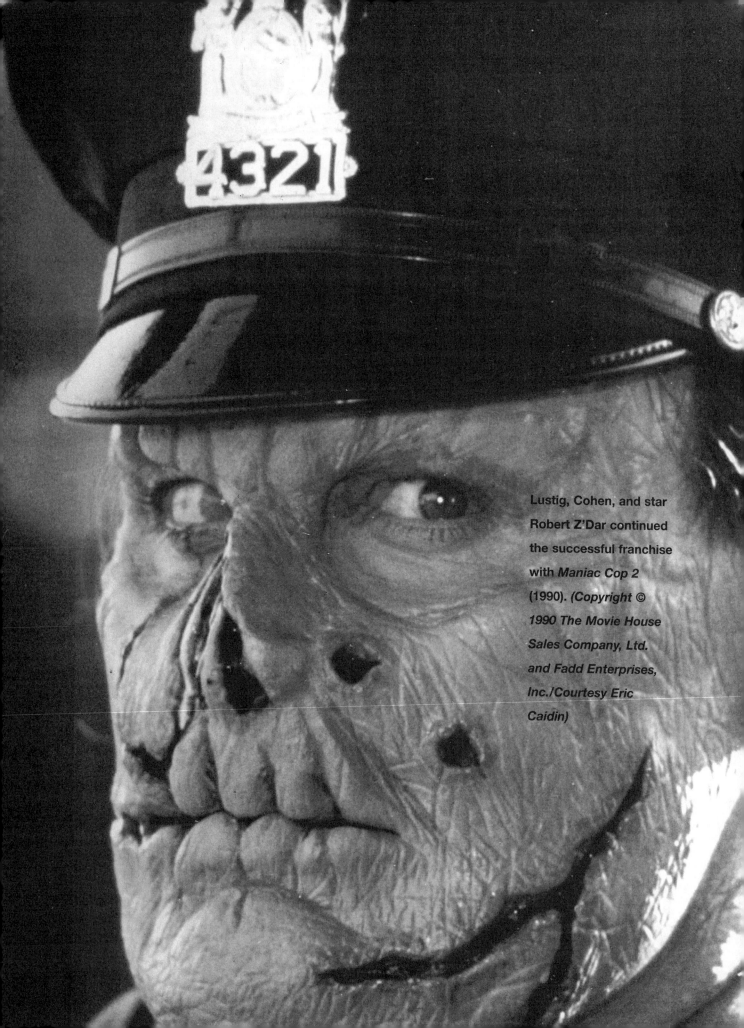

Lustig, Cohen, and star Robert Z'Dar continued the successful franchise with *Maniac Cop 2* (1990). *(Copyright © 1990 The Movie House Sales Company, Ltd. and Fadd Enterprises, Inc./Courtesy Eric Caidin)*

William Lustig

BY ERIC J. CAIDIN AND JOHN McCARTY

Born in New York City in 1955, William Lustig began his career working as a production assistant in the adult movie business while still in high school.

"I was sixteen years old," he says. "That made for kind of an interesting experience since, being under twenty-one, I was too young to get in to see any of these films in a theater."

In 1977 he transitioned full time to the director's chair and, under the pseudonym Billy Bagg, made his own first hard-core feature, *The Violation of Claudia*, which many adult film aficionados consider a classic of the triple-X genre.

A fan of low-budget horror films since his childhood, Lustig seized the opportunity presented by the success of *Friday the 13th* (1980) and its ilk to shift from graphic sex to graphic gore with *Maniac* in 1981. The story of a psycho (Joe Spinell) who murders and scalps his victims, this roller-coaster ride of pathology and splatter became a minor cause célèbre due to its controversial scenes of murder and mayhem (orchestrated by splatter FX maestro Tom Savini) and potent atmosphere of psychosexual depravity and 42nd Street sleaze. Though disavowed by Savini and by many exploitation film fans for being *too* ugly and depressing, the infamous *Maniac* has achieved cult status over the years and has even achieved a degree of respectability.

The success of that film and others have kept Lustig much in demand as one of the most reliable producer-directors in the low-budget film business. His career since then has alternated between graphic psychological horror shockers in the vein of *Maniac* and ultra-violent crime thrillers like *Vigilante* (1983)—sometimes mixing the two genres together as in the successful series of *Maniac Cop* films Lustig created in association with prodigious exploitation film writer-producer-director Larry Cohen.

Q: What made you want to pursue a movie career?

WL: I was addicted to movies! I used to cut school and go to 42nd Street and that area to see movie after movie. I fell in love with everything I saw, from the art pictures to the Harry Novak type of sexploitation pictures I used to sneak into. I was maybe thirteen or fourteen years old when I started thinking about movies seriously as a career.

Q: Did you have any formal training in filmmaking?

WL: I attended New York University for about two semesters, where I had the opportunity to work a little with 16-mm filmmaking. But in terms of formal training, it really started with adult movies. The majority of my training was on the job. Independent study, you might call it. I worked a lot with Jamie Gillis, Andrea True, who later became a pop singer, and a guy named Mark Stevens, who worked under the name Dave Longshlang—all the big names in the adult film

business. During the time I was working on adult films, I would get the opportunity to direct a scene here and there, but the first one I directed from beginning to end was *The Violation of Claudia*, which went out and became a big hit on the adult film circuit.

Q: Then you went "mainstream" with *Maniac*. How did that come about?

WL: I love horror films, and I'd wanted to do one even before I'd directed my first adult picture, but I couldn't raise the money. I had saved some of the money I'd made working on adult pictures —about thirty thousand dollars. A childhood friend of mine named Andy Garroni had about

twelve thousand dollars. And actor Joe Spinell, who had just finished co-starring in the Al Pacino film *Cruising* [1980], had about six thousand dollars. We put our money together, threw it into a bank account, and with the help of some other investors who came in later started making *Maniac*.

Q: Which went on to become a big hit.

WL: Yeah, it was quite remarkable. I used to say to Joe, who cowrote the script as well as starred in the film, that the only place this picture will ever play is 42nd Street and drive-ins. But it turned out to be quite a phenomenon. It was denounced by critics from coast to coast because of the graphic nature of some of the murder scenes. With a low-budget film that kind of bad press always packs in the crowds. In recent years I've gotten a good deal of positive criticism about the film, though, because some people have found it to be a very accurate depiction of a serial killer, a psychosexual killer. It's even been compared to *Henry: Portrait of a*

Serial Killer [1990], which it predated by almost a decade. So, it's been kind of interesting to see that film gain a certain amount of respectability that it certainly didn't have at the beginning.

Q: How did you meet Joe Spinell?

WL: I met Joe on the set of a movie called *The Seven-Ups* [1973] starring Roy Scheider; it was sort of a follow-up to *The French Connection* [1971] which Scheider had also been in. Joe had a bit part in the film and I was a member of the crew. In addition to working on adult movies, I also worked on legitimate movies as a production assistant, assistant editor, and whatnot. Films like *The Longest Yard, The Gambler, Death Wish* [all 1974] and others. I even worked on a compilation movie involving Our Gang—the Little Rascals—so I didn't just work on adult films. They just seem to stick out most in my mind because they were the ones that gave me the most hands-on experience—no pun intended. Anyway, I met Joe on *Seven-Ups*, we struck up a friendship, and vowed to make a film together someday, which we did.

Q: What immediate impact did *Maniac* have on your career?

WL: After *Maniac* I was declared a genius by everyone who had put money into the film. They'd made a lot of money back on their investment. So, flush with that success, we went out and did another picture called *Vigilante*, which was my answer to the *Death Wish*–type movies, although I actually envisioned it as kind of a Sergio Leone Western set in an urban environment. I designed the look and feel of the movie to be like the Leone films. Andy Galloni coproduced it with me. Joe Spinell was in that one too.

Q: Yes, and Robert Forster, Fred Williamson, Carol Lynley, Woody Strode—not exactly a no-name cast. In fact, you've always managed to get good actors for your films.

WL: Yes, I've been quite lucky in that regard. So many low-budget films are terribly acted, but I've been fortunate in that I've not only been able to get good actors to work for me but people I sought out because I've been a longtime fan—like Fred Williamson and Robert Forster. Forster wasn't the original star of *Vigilante*, Tony Musante was. We actually started production with him, but he flipped out. Then I learned from a mutual friend that Bob Forster was available, and I was thrilled when Bob agreed to step in. Frankly, I didn't think he would be accessible to me since he'd been in a lot of major Hollywood films. But he read the script, liked it, and came to New York City to have some fun.

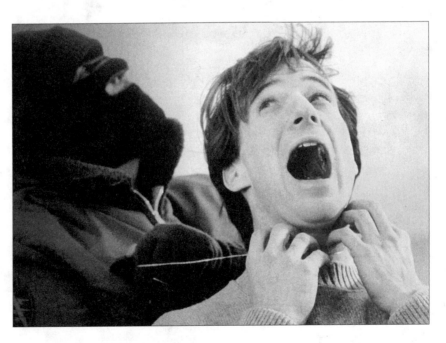

Though initially disavowed by many exploitation film fans for being too ugly and depressing, Lustig's infamous *Maniac* (1981) has today achieved cult status and a degree of respectability. (Copyright © 1981 Analysis Film Releasing Corp.)

WILLIAM LUSTIG

Lustig's *Maniac Cop* (1987),
produced and scripted by
Larry Cohen, mixed the horror
and action movie genres into
a successful stew. *(Copyright
© 1987 Glickenhaus Films,
Inc./Courtesy Eric Caidin)*

Q: You tend to use a lot of the same people from film to film behind the camera as well.

WL: Well, there was a block of films—about four or five—where I did use the same people, but now everybody's gone off in different directions, so I don't know if I'll have a lot of the same people available for the next one. I like working with the same people over and over because you develop a rapport and that leads to working smoothly. You begin to complement one another; you're all on the same wavelength. You become a team. I know there were two films of mine where the results of that kind of teamwork really showed: *Relentless* [1989] and *Maniac Cop 2* [1990].

Q: The *Maniac Cop* films have been quite successful. How did the series get started?

WL: I was in New York closing up my apartment when I got a call from Larry Cohen, who was staying at the Mayflower Hotel about a block away; he had just been fired from a movie, the title of which I forget, knew of me from *Maniac* and *Vigilante*, and wanted to know what I was up to. So we went and had lunch, kicked around horror stories about working in pictures, and he asked me why I had never done a sequel to *Maniac*. I didn't think there was a sequel in it and all of a sudden he came up with the idea for a film that would be sort of an unofficial sequel about an overzealous cop who seeks revenge against the city's authorities for sending him to prison where he'd been sliced up and almost killed by several of the cons he'd busted. A copy line, "You have the right to remain silent . . . forever!" grew out of that discussion, and we said we've got a movie, let's go make it. I immediately commissioned a script from Larry, and an ad campaign, and went to the American Film market to stir up financial interest. I got some but not enough to make the movie. About six months later, we got Shapiro-Glickenhaus to finance the movie to the tune of about $1.2 million. After we finished shooting, we made a product reel out of some of the footage to get presales on the movie before it was actually finished, which is a quite common practice. Shapiro-Glickenhaus presold the picture all over the world. After I'd completed the movie and screened it for them, however, they ran out of the screening room, and I thought they were mad at me for some reason. I caught up with them in the parking lot and said, "Guys, guys, what's wrong? Tell me!" And they looked at me and said, "How come you didn't tell us the finished movie was going to be that good?" And they started rattling off how much money they lost on each territory by preselling the film with a product reel instead of waiting until later when they had the finished film! The film was so successful that I immediately—and I mean *immediately*, about two weeks later—started pre-production on *Hit List* [1989] for CineTel Pictures, starring Jan-Michael Vincent, Lance Henriksen, and Rip Torn, which had a budget of about $1.3 million. My career has sort of alternated between horror and action thrillers ever since. I think the *Maniac Cop* series has done so well because they combine the two genres.

Q: You ran into some problems with your star on *Hit List*, didn't you?

WL: Yes. Jan-Michael Vincent had a substance abuse problem at the time. He had trouble standing up, slurred his words; we wound up having to post-sync about 120 of his lines afterwards when he was finally sober. All of that created a real morale problem—because when your star can't stand up or say his lines, it sort of casts a mood or pall over a picture, a prospect of doom, and it's hard for everybody to get worked up about doing their best if they feel the project is doomed. Basically, we just propped Jan-Michael up, did what we had to do with him, and worked around him as best we could. If you watch the film closely, you'll notice a lot of shots where Jan-Michael is completely isolated. The reason for that is I felt he was probably going to have to be replaced, and I didn't want to have to reshoot the whole movie, just the shots he was in. So, that's why I began isolating him in shots from the very beginning. In the middle of shooting the picture I had a blowup with the head of

The titular fiend goes to his watery grave (or does he?) in the exciting finale of Lustig's *Maniac Cop* (1987). *(Copyright © 1987 Glickenhaus Films, Inc./Courtesy Eric Caidin)*

CineTel at lunch and he fired me. I said, "Should I leave now?" And he said, "No, just finish out the day." I did and at the end of the day he rehired me. Then, when I finished the movie and it was screened for some executives at Warner Brothers, they stood up and overexaggerated, I think, but honestly said, "*Hit List* is a better action picture than Steven Seagal's *Above the Law* [1988]."

Q: It is.

WL: Well, I don't know about that. But anyway, they got all excited, so I went overnight from being a bum to being a king. When I went to Cannes to promote sales of the picture, CineTel didn't even hand me a bill for my hotel room afterwards. They picked it up!

Q: After that you moved back to psychological horror with *Relentless* [1989] starring Judd Nelson as a serial killer.

WL: That's right. On the strength of *Maniac Cop*, Lenny Shapiro of Shapiro-Glickenhaus wanted to do another picture with me and handed me a bunch of scripts that had been submitted to them. I came across one called *Sunset Slayer*

that I thought was especially good. It was written by Phil Alden Robinson, who had just written and directed *Field of Dreams* [1989], which hadn't come out yet. So, he was a big-time Hollywood name even then. But then Shapiro-Glickenhaus ran into some financial problems and couldn't bankroll the picture. So, on the heels of my success with *Hit List* I wound up making it for CineTel instead and changed the title to *Relentless*. That title, by the way, was the original title of Sam Raimi's *XYZ Murders* [released in 1985 as *Crimewave*]. I'd always liked that title and when Sam dropped it for his film, I called him up and asked him if I could use it. He said okay and that's why there's a special thanks to Sam at the end of the film's credits. After that I did *Maniac Cop 2* [1990], which was tough to get financing for.

Q: Why was that, considering the fact that the first film was such a big success?

WL: Because my goal was to make a better picture than the first. I wanted to take the elements that got people excited in the first film and amplify them—sort of what they did on *Lethal Weapon 2*

[1989], following the success of the first *Lethal Weapon* [1987] film. Unfortunately, a month after I finished the film, the company that financed it was falling into bankruptcy and they made a direct to video sale to bring in some fast cash rather than take the risk of going the theatrical route—although it was released theatrically overseas. It did well on video but no better than *Maniac Cop*, which was disappointing to me because it was a much bigger and better picture. It's one thing if a film bombs at the box office—at least you know it was given a fair shake. But just to bury it on video and never give it the chance to go out there and see how it performs is a real heartbreaker. It was treated as sort of a throwaway. Then, on top of that disappointment, I lost the chance to direct *True Romance* [1993], a script I'd nurtured for about a year.

Q: How did that happen?

WL: CineTel wanted me to do a *Relentless II** and had developed a script which I didn't like. I began looking around for a writer to work on it and Sam Raimi's partner, Scott Spiegel, introduced me to Quentin Tarantino, who went on to write and direct *Reservoir Dogs* [1992]. Quentin sent two scripts to my home via Federal Express collect—which I thought was kind of an interesting approach. One was *Natural Born Killers* and the other was *True Romance*. I started reading *Natural Born Killers* [subsequently directed by Oliver Stone] and while I liked the opening, I didn't like the rest of the script. But *True Romance* I fell in love with, although I felt it had certain prob-

* Two sequels subsequently were made without Lustig's involvement: *Dead On: Relentless II* (1992) and *Relentless III* (1993).

Crazed assassin Lance Henriksen goes to extreme lengths to fulfill his contract in Lustig's problem-plagued action thriller *Hit List* (1989). (Copyright © 1988 Hit List Productions, Inc./Courtesy Eric Caidin)

WILLIAM LUSTIG

lems like being too complicated in its structure. Nothing that couldn't be easily fixed, however. So, I approached Quentin about it and we struck a deal to do some work on it. The mistake I made was turning control of the project over to a company that said they would finance the movie—although it's quite normal to do things that way. The problem was they didn't have the ability to finance the movie—which had a budget of about $3.5 million—and shooting kept getting pushed back. Ultimately, they showed the script to director Tony Scott, and when he agreed to do it and Morgan Creek got involved, they sold the project to Morgan Creek out from under me and the film was made as a big-time twenty-million-dollar Hollywood production.

Q: It bombed, though, so maybe there's some justice after all.

WL: Well, if it had been made for its original budget, maybe it wouldn't have bombed. I was in production on *Maniac Cop 3* [1992] when the news came down about my loss of *True Romance*, so that threw me into a bit of a depression. About midway through, I just parted company with the producers, and *Maniac Cop 3* was finished by someone else [Joel Soisson], so I'm credited as codirector on the film in this country. Overseas my name alone appears on the film. I didn't really have anything to do with the script on that one—maybe one or two scenes.

Judd Nelson stars as a loner who accepts rejection almost as easily as he can commit murder in Lustig's gritty portrait of a serial killer, *Relentless* (1989). (Copyright © 1989 Out of the Dark Productions, Inc./Courtesy Eric Caidin)

Q: Would you be interested in doing a *Maniac Cop 4*?

WL: At the present moment I'm not too interested, and, frankly, to keep the momentum of the series going, the fourth installment should be done soon. If so, I would probably serve as producer, not director.

Q: There have been rumors of a possible *Maniac Cop* TV series. How would you feel about getting involved in something like that?

WL: I might be interested. The idea of a TV series has been talked about. Larry Cohen's gotten the rights back to the character and story, so it might happen. But it doesn't appeal to me right now. Andy Garroni, my childhood pal and coproducer on a number of my films, has formed a company called Axis Films that I've gotten involved with, and I'm more interested in seeing what develops with that. The idea is to produce a number of pictures by independent directors. I would be overseeing them but not directing any of the pictures myself. There are a lot of talented directors out here, and I think my experience in an overseeing capacity could help them avoid a lot of the unnecessary problems young directors often encounter trying to get their first films made.

Q: Is it getting more and more difficult for independents like yourself to get your films produced and released?

WL: The major problem for the most part is that most of the independent companies that produce and release low-budget films are here today, gone tomorrow. Historically, they never last very long, so it's very hard for a director to create any continuity with any one company. But as more and more major studio megabuck extravaganzas continue to bomb, maybe they'll start turning to us independent guys because we've learned how to do a lot with very little. That's happened before in movie history; maybe it'll happen again. I'm hoping with this new company Andy has formed that maybe we can improve on some of the things we've seen in the past, and make things more filmmaker-oriented.

Q: You're not giving up directing, though?

WL: No, no! I've got a number of projects in the works. For my next film I'm bouncing from horror back to the crime thriller. It'll be called *Brute Force;* I'll be shooting it in Ohio.

SELECTED FILMOGRAPHY

1977: The Violation of Claudia; **1981:** Maniac; **1983:** Vigilante; **1987:** Maniac Cop; **1989:** Hit List, Relentless; **1990:** Maniac Cop 2; **1992:** Maniac Cop 3; **1994:** Brute Force.

Fred Olen Ray with the cave
girls and The Great One on the
set of *Dinosaur Island* (1994).
(Courtesy Fred Olen Ray)

Fred Olen Ray

BY BRUCE G. HALLENBECK

ver the past two decades, Fred Olen Ray has ground out more low budget, schlock horror/ sf/action pictures and accumulated a more impressive list of directing and/or producing credits —at least in terms of quantity and variety—than any other living American filmmaker, exploitation or otherwise. So, if anyone has earned the title Roger Corman once held as the American exploitation cinema's reigning "King of the Bs" (or "Pope of Popular Pulp," a title Corman prefers), it must surely be Fred.

Born in West Virginia in 1954 and raised in Florida, Fred Olen Ray taught himself the craft of directing while a teenager by turning out one homemade monster movie after another with his family's regular 8-mm movie camera. After graduation, he took a job as an engineer at a Florida television station, while continuing to turn out more low-budget movies, this time in 16 mm, on the side. In the early, '80s, he emigrated to Hollywood to work full time in film production and distribution, and he has never looked back. His colorful array of titles—*Star Slammer* (1985), *Armed Response* (1985), *Hollywood Chainsaw Hookers* (1988), *Beverly Hills Vamp* (1989), *Evil Toons* (1991) and many, many others—have endeared him to sleaze film fans the world over.

Despite his reputation, Fred remains wholly unpretentious about his work, which, he will be the first to tell you, is completed quickly, and, to put it politely, inexpensively. About his shooting schedules, he comments flippantly: "Six days, no waiting." And despite the ruination of a number of his films at the hands of "the money people," he never anguishes over the end result, either. After all, he says dryly and with a shrug, "It's only a movie." We talked with him at his California office, where he had just finished taking a call from a hungry producer looking for an exploitation vehicle for defrocked televangelist Jim Bakker's former paramour, Jessica Hahn.

FOR: [laughing] I told him we'd sent him this sci-fi alien script with a strong female character in it, but he said, "No, no, no!"—he's an Israeli. "We need lots of schtumping! An erotic film!" I'm sure I've got something around here for him. That's the good thing about having scripts that you own. You just kind of thumb through those that have never been produced, and, sometimes it takes years, but they always get made. You just go, "I've got this script around here if you want to rewrite it," and the producer says, "Let's do it! Let's do it!" And they give you a million bucks! When you consider how hard it is these days to get films off the ground, it's nice to have enough of a reputation to get on the inside track with these people. It makes life a lot easier.

Q: I'm sure it does. You've come a long way since your Florida days.

FOR: Actually, I was born in West Virginia in a little place called Wellston, near the border. My family was basically from West Virginia. But we moved around a lot—to Florida, to Mississippi, to South Carolina at one point. But we always seemed to wind up back in Florida. Mostly in Sarasota and finally Fort Lauderdale.

Q: As I understand it, you made your first feature-length movie for the astonishing sum of $298!

FOR: That's right. But we won't let anyone see that one.

Q: I'd like to see it sometime.

FOR: I'd almost like to see it myself. But I haven't been able to bear watching it in almost fifteen years. It was called *The Brain Leeches*, and I made it probably somewhere in '77 or '78. My son was born in 1977, and he was a baby in diapers at the time. So, it must have been early '78.

Q: Was it made in 8 mm?

FOR: No, 16 mm, black and white.

Q: That's still a pretty amazing budget.

FOR: Well, I had everything going for me. You wouldn't say that if you saw the film, but I really did. At the time, the TV station where I worked had just retired their Auricon sound-on-film camera, and they were willing to let me have it for an extended period of time. And in the station refrigerator, there was some nine-years-out-of-date black-and-white film with a sound stripe along the edge. You had a microphone and an amp that attached to the camera and recorded the sound right on the edge of the film. So, you couldn't cut for dialogue; everything had to be a master shot. I edited it on the station's telecine. I had titles superimposed by video. I did all my sound work at the station, too. The music score consisted of an arrangement of *Pictures at an Exhibition*. I just played the album straight through. When I came to the end of the record, I just picked the needle up and plunked it down again. That was the score! Very embarrassing!

Q: At least you showed good taste by choosing classical music. Didn't you premiere the film in a bar?

FOR: Yes, we did—at the Racquet Club on Orange Blossom Trail, which was a tennis club. Right after that, we actually sold the distribution rights on that picture for about fifteen hundred dollars to a company out of Texas that managed a nightclub performer who appeared in the film. They wanted to show it in nightclubs where they'd booked him, so we sold it to them. I thought I was doing great!

Q: Was that when you decided you were going to do this for a living?

FOR: No, no. It took me a long time. It took a lot of films before I actually made enough money to go into business for myself and make a living at it. And distribution was what helped me go independent, not filmmaking. I made money out of distribution by buying films that were in people's closets.

Q: Let's backtrack a bit. Since so many of your films fall into the categories of horror and science fiction, it would seem you must have been a big fan of them when you were growing up.

FOR: Yeah, through denial.

Q: Denial?

FOR: Yeah, my folks wouldn't let me watch any of 'em. They wouldn't let me see any of the *Frankenstein* films, although they talked about them all the time. So, when they finally said it was okay and I got to start watching them, I guess I overdid it. And have been ever since.

Q: Who were your favorite directors when you were growing up?

FOR: You know, to tell you the truth, I read *Famous Monsters of Filmland* and all, but I don't believe I thought too much about the directors. I thought more about horror stars and makeup artists like Jack Pierce than about directors. But for some reason, I've always been fascinated with threadbare movies that were made on what might be called Hollywood's edge, or fringe. I've never been super bowled over by what the studios could do with unlimited resources. That's not to say I didn't enjoy those films, but they weren't the ones I would go back and watch over and over again. Take for example the Universal horror films. I love all of them. But the ones that are my favorites are not the big name ones, but stuff like *Captive Wild Woman* [1943],

Back then there was no film industry in Florida, so I called him and said, "Isn't there *anything* going on?" And he said, "Oh, nothing but that Peter Cushing/John Carradine movie they're making." I said, "Oh, my God!" These were two of my heroes! Doug had passed on the makeup job, but he intervened on my behalf and pleaded with the producer to give me work. And he agreed, provided I worked for free, which was okay with me. Because I had a regular job that I was on hiatus from, I couldn't stay for the whole show. Shooting took about five weeks, and I was there for two—but I was there the entire time Cushing and Carradine were there, and that was a real treat because no one else on the film was

The Mummy's Curse [1944], *The Mummy's Ghost* [1944] and *House of Dracula* [1945]. *Abbott and Costello Meet Frankenstein* [1948] is probably my all-time favorite film, next to *Frankenstein Meets the Wolfman* [1943]. Those movies didn't pretend to build up a solid story. The Wolf Man got trotted out in the first five minutes. They didn't spend thirty minutes on how the Mummy got to be—he already was and is and let's get on with it. That's what I liked about those films.

Q: Wasn't *Shock Waves* [a.k.a. *Death Corps*, 1975] the first professional film you worked on?

FOR: That's correct. It was shot in Florida. I was a still photographer, gofer, I did a lot of things. I did whatever I could to get on that film because I was so desperate to work on it. I found out about it from a makeup man named Doug Hobart.

FRED OLEN RAY

a real fan of those guys. The producers basically hired them because they were making a horror film and they knew those two guys were big horror film names.

Q: When did you move to California?

FOR: Around 1980, right after I'd made *The Alien Dead* [1979] and *The Halloween Planet* [1979]. *Alien Dead* did nothing for me because there wasn't as yet any home video market and it was too bad to go theatrical—I shot it in 16 mm. So I took a job doing the makeup on a Christmas TV special that came out with a soundtrack album, coloring books; Coleco Toys bought it for one year for two hundred thousand dollars. I thought that was incredible since the show was pretty pathetic, and said, "Hey, I can do better than this!" So, I made my own TV special called *The Halloween Planet*—a half-hour special with Kirk Alyn, the star of the old *Superman* serials, and Ernie Farino did some dinosaur effects for it. And I never made a dime. I spent six thousand dollars making this epic, and it's never been released. Even the station I worked for refused to run it. In fact, they seemed to hold it against me that I'd gone outside of what was supposed to be my niche as an engineer or technical director and, on my own, produced a movie, *The Brain Leeches*, outside the station and a TV special within. They thought I was an upstart and just wanted me to shut up and stay out of their hair. So, I got pissed off and decided to quit and go to Hollywood and become a movie director. My brother and I

packed up the car—I think we had about a thousand dollars between us—and we drove out there and went at it.

Q: Your breakthrough film was *The Tomb* [1985], wasn't it?

FOR: Yes, definitely. As I look back on it, the performances aren't great, but when you think how much we spent on it compared with how much we made, it was the most amazing thing. I'd already made *Biohazard* [1984], my first film in 35 mm; it had Aldo Ray and Angélique Pettyjohn in it, so I was feeling pretty fortunate. But I raised the money for that one and felt that I would never be able to call myself a director until someone stepped forward and said they would actually pay *me*. Anybody who raises money to publish his own fanzine can call himself an editor or a writer. But as Andy Griffith tells Jeff Bridges in *Hearts of the West* [1975]: "You're not a writer until someone else says you are." That was my situation. I never felt that I was really a director until someone else had enough faith in me to bankroll *me*, and that happened with *The Tomb*. I thought I'd fuckin' died and gone to heaven, you know what I mean? The film was made for $135,000 and it earned three and a half million! In fact, it saved the company that bankrolled it, Trans World Entertainment, from bankruptcy. They'd lost their shirt on a previous film called *Creature* [1985], and it saved them

Michelle Bauer in another scene cut from *The Tomb* (1985)—this one for being "too sexy." Ray later used the scene in *Beverly Hills Vamp* (1989). (Courtesy Fred Olen Ray)

what: I'll pay for a truck to move that set; I'll rent some studio space for a weekend, we'll put the set up on Friday, and you can have it for twelve hours a day Saturday and Sunday, and I'll take it from seven in the evening until seven in the morning." He agreed, I trashed out maybe thirty pages of script, and put together enough footage for a trailer for this thing called *The Tomb* over a couple of nights. My intention, you see, was to have something concrete to show that I was actually making a film called *The Tomb* so that New World would buy us off because of the title conflict. Then we'd take the footage and make a different film out of it some time later. But Trans World

from ruination. So, yeah, I think *The Tomb* was definitely my breakthrough.

Q: You had some quite elaborate sets in that.

FOR: Yeah, I'll tell you how that film came about. I was trying to lose some money, actually, and wound up making a film instead. Right as I was finishing *Biohazard*, Twentieth Century–Fox announced a film called "Biohazard" starring Sam Waterston and Yaphet Kotto. So, I sent them a letter saying, "Hey, look, I've got this title already. I already shot my film, I'm a week away from delivering it." They had an eleven-million-dollar budget. I told them that for 1 percent of their budget I would give up the title. And they offered me only five grand. I said it would cost me more than that to shoot the title over again, and told them to change their title instead. So, they wound up calling their film *Warning Sign* [1985]. But that whole episode got me to thinking. I got wind that New World Pictures were going to make a movie version of F. Paul Wilson's book *The Tomb*. I also knew there was a public domain H. P. Lovecraft story of the same title. I had a friend, Bob Tinnell, who was trying to put together a film at the time for Columbia. They'd given him studio space for eight hours a day for two days to shoot it, but he needed more time. He showed me this Egyptian set he'd borrowed from some Wrangler's jeans commercial that he had to move, and I said, "Bob, I'll tell you

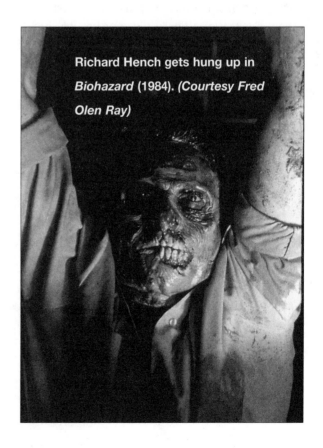

Richard Hench gets hung up in *Biohazard* (1984). *(Courtesy Fred Olen Ray)*

Angélique Pettyjohn played the part of a "space mentalist" in *Biohazard* (1984). *(Courtesy Fred Olen Ray)*

Entertainment loved the trailer the minute they saw it, and I wound up making the thing for them. New World finally did rear its ugly head, but it was way after I'd made the movie. They came in and threatened to sue! But I'd covered myself by having chosen a title that was also in the public domain. New World couldn't do a thing because in my contract with Trans World it read "Based on H. P. Lovecraft's *The Tomb*!"

Q: One of my favorite films of yours is *Star Slammer*. It looked like you had a good time making that.

FOR: We did have a good time, although it was unbearably hot. Everything but two days was done in a studio where it was 110 degrees, with no air-conditioning available. They fogged and smoked up the sets, which made it even worse. And it was shot over eighteen days. But it was fun; impoverished but fun. I think we had an initial budget of $175,000 and then when the producer, Jack Harris of *The Blob* [1958] fame, came in and saw what we had done, he fell in love with it and dumped in another thirty thousand dollars to do it up in stereo.

Q: Your next film, *Armed Response* [1985], was your first million-dollar movie. That was quite a step up.

FOR: It was. You learn a little bit as you go along, and you usually learn by getting burned. The people behind it had been partners with Trans World on *The Tomb*, and they approached me to make a film for them. They said the only thing *The Tomb* lacked was better actors and told me they were going to up my budget to $250,000 so I could hire better actors. I was given a fifteen thousand dollars salary to make the film, and I said that was fine. But after they got involved with RCA/Columbia on distribution, they got starrier-eyed, and came to me and said, "David Carradine would be good in this part." So, the budget would then go up. Then they'd say, "Lee Van Cleef would be great as Carradine's father," and the budget would go up again. Finally, by the time we got rolling, we were making a million-dollar movie that I was getting paid fifteen thousand dollars to direct. I think the production manager ended up making more on that one than I did.

Q: After all those low-budget films, did the million-dollar budget make things easier for you on *Armed Response*, or did the pressure of a bigger budget make things even more taxing?

FOR: I've always believed, especially after that picture, that the directing aspect never changes, no matter what the budget is and how many perks it makes available to you. Really, as a director, you never travel more than six feet from the camera. So all the fancy motor homes and honeywagons they bring in as perks because the budget allows for them are for nothing for the director because he never gets a chance to use them. I'll tell you a funny story that shows you how naive I was about the fact that I was finally working on a film that wasn't impoverished. I didn't even know that with a budget like that they could get permits and keep people from parking around where you were filming. So, I kept driving around trying to find a place to park and seeing signs that said, "Don't Park Here! Tow Away Zone!" I finally saw one of the crew and said, "Where the hell am I supposed to park? These signs say I can't park anywhere." And he said, "Oh, no, we permitted the whole area. Just pull up to the curb and get out!" I followed the cables leading from the generators to the location, and it was like stepping into a circus. There were lines of trailers and cops and

equipment and forty or fifty people instead of the fifteen I was used to. It was really mind-boggling. It was the first time, of all the movies I had made, that I ended up finishing the picture and not knowing the names of some of the people who worked for me. What I also learned from that experience was that, even if I didn't know what to do next, I had to say *something*. Because the minute you show any kind of weakness or uncertainty, an assistant director, the photographer, an actor, or whomever will want to step right in and tell you what your next shot is. So, if you want to control your own show, you'd better say something—right or wrong—or they'll just eat you up.

Q: Back in the mid-'80s, you shot a lot of generic footage of John Carradine over a weekend that you wound up using in four different movies. How did that come about?

FOR: Five different movies! I had offered John Carradine a role in *Star Slammer*, but his manager turned it down. Then, about six months later, he called back asking if I had anything for John. And I thought, "Well, shit, what a great opportunity!" At the time I wasn't making a film, but I had acquired a demented death farm massacre movie called *Shantytown Honeymoon*. I changed the title to *Death Farm* and nobody wanted it. They all laughed that I'd bought this movie for five grand—the negative, *everything*!—but no one would buy it from me. Then a company called Continental Video said they'd pay me fifteen thousand dollars if I put John Carradine in this movie. So, I looked at the film again and there was this preacher character in it. They kept cutting to him, but he never

Mako and two of his kidnap
victims in *Armed Response* (1985).
(Courtesy Fred Olen Ray)

FOR: Well, production-wise it probably was, but it didn't have the names. It didn't have the name value. If you took the David Carradine and Lee Van Cleef paychecks and added them to *Commando Squad* you would probably have the same budgeted movie. But it was a package deal with two unknowns, Kathy Shower and Brian Thompson, and there was no questioning that. So, I tried to fill out the cast with movie villains I had always admired—Russ Tamblyn, Bill Smith, Sid Haig, Ross Hagen, and I had Marie Windsor, whom I was very thrilled to work with. I just tried to have as much fun as I could on that show. I went from that to *Phantom Empire* [1987]. In fact, we used a lot of the same sets.

Q: Jeffrey Combs was in that. He tells me it was pretty amazing working on a seven-day shooting schedule.

interacted with anyone. So, I cut the guy's scenes out, filmed John Carradine doing the same scenes, and cut them in. And since I had John available and was paying him around $2,500 for a whole weekend's work—even though the *Death Farm* footage would only take about twenty minutes to shoot—I had him do a bunch of random scenes as well where he played a bunch of different characters—Judge Death, Dr. Frankenstein. I even recorded his voice doing some wild lines. And we wound up using all this stuff in other movies. I did the same thing with Cameron Mitchell. People used to call me up when they needed some bucks, and if I didn't have a film, and I liked them, I would shoot something anyway, knowing I could always use it a little bit later.

Q: After *Armed Response* you made *Commando Squad* [1987]. Did you have the same size budget?

Family portrait: Linnea, Gunnar, and Michelle Bauer in *Hollywood Chainsaw Hookers* (1988).
(Courtesy Fred Olen Ray)

Michelle Bauer, Toni Naples, and their cave-girl band in *Dinosaur Island* (1994). *(Courtesy Fred Olen Ray)*

Q: Your company also funded what is perhaps your most famous, or infamous, film: *Hollywood Chainsaw Hookers* [1988].

FOR: Yeah. We sold the video rights based on the title. Which was a mistake. It got us the twenty-five grand to do the movie with, but we didn't know what the movie would be like when we started it. It turned out to be worth a lot more than the twenty-five grand we'd sold it for. We should probably have gotten a hundred grand for it.

Q: That movie's a riot!

FOR: We're gonna do a comic book based on it, a *Hollywood Chainsaw Hookers* adult comic. We'll see how that goes.

Q: *Beverly Hills Vamp* [1989] was kind of a remake of that, wasn't it?

FOR: It was six! We started on a Monday and finished on a Saturday, although about four months later we added another day doing some pickup shots. It's not a very good picture, and I have to say I think the reason was that I was rather panicked at the prospect of going from a four-week-long movie to a one-week-long movie. I think I was just terrified, and it shows in the film because I didn't stop and take enough time to shoot enough coverage. I've done six-day and even five-day movies that were far superior to *Phantom Empire* technically. But I guess I panicked with that one because I was using my own money.

Q: *Phantom Empire* was financed by your own company?

FOR: Yes. I was watching other people make a mint off my films, and I was just getting a paycheck. And I kept saying "You know, if I owned the movie and got all the profits, what a wonderful idea that would be."

Antonia Dorian meets the (off-screen) Beast of the Haunted Cave in *Dinosaur Island* (1994). *(Courtesy Fred Olen Ray)*

FOR: Yeah. It was meant to have the same message—if you could consider that the film *had* a message! And it was much less violent. The foreign market was drying up because of censorship of sex and violence, and that kept us from selling a lot more rights to *Hollywood Chainsaw Hookers* overseas. So, we toned down *Vamp* because we wanted to sell it in more territories. Britt Ekland was the "name" in it. The film looked better than *Hookers*. Eddie Deezen was pretty funny, and Tim Conway, Jr. We made it in five or six days, I guess.

Q: *Haunting Fear* [1991] is a pretty good film, too.

FOR: Another six-day movie! It cost $115,000 and I wrote the script in three days. I just recently optioned the sequel rights to another company and they're developing story lines right now. I'd like to turn the film's main character (played by Brinke Stevens) into a franchise-type character. But we don't know. The only thing in the film that disappointed me was the whole Karen Black past life regression bullshit. That was put in just to eat up script space. And it stopped the movie cold in its tracks, I think. But, hey—I made a lot of money on it! Can't argue with that. The picture performed very well.

Q: There are certainly no pretensions about you!

FOR: Well, no, I mean I like the movie. If somebody wanted to screen one of my little films, that would be the one I'd choose. I like it because it's story-driven, not gimmick-driven. A lot of the movies I've made are gimmick-driven. We'd try to get a nice, snappy title and a kernel of an idea and build a film around it. *Haunting Fear* was actually built around a *plot*. It didn't rely on gimmicks. The only gimmick in it really was the casting of Jan-Michael Vincent because he was a

"name." He was the gimmick. I hired him for one day—one long, tortuous day; at the time he was in demand and that gave the film a glossier veneer and deluded people into thinking that I'd spent some money on it.

Q: Tell me a little about *Evil Toons* [1991].

FOR: That's a gimmick film, for sure. All I wanted to do was prove to people that I could actually combine cartoon animation with live action à la *Who Framed Roger Rabbit?* [1988] on a budget. Nobody would give me the money to do it, so we scraped together the money ourselves. The film

The Great One attacks the cave-girl village in *Dinosaur Island* (1994). *(Courtesy Fred Olen Ray)*

performed real well; I get checks on it every week. I've heard of people who have *Evil Toons* parties where they get together and drink beer and watch the movie. They have little T-shirts made from it, and all kinds of stuff. It was a good idea.

Q: *Inner Sanctum* [1992] is also an interesting little film.

FOR: It might have been more interesting if they'd allowed us to film the script we sold them. I've been all over the place in this town and worked for a lot of different people. You go in with a script that makes sense. And they buy it. But by

Brinke Stevens goes crazy and tries to kill her tormenter (Delia Shepard) in Fred Olen Ray's *Haunting Fear* (1991). *(Courtesy Fred Olen Ray)*

Q: You've collaborated with Jim Wynorski on several occasions, haven't you?

FOR: Yes, on *Hollywood Scream Queen Hot Tub Party* [1993] and *Dinosaur Island* [1994]. With *Dinosaur Island*, Roger Corman said, "Here's the money, go make it!" It was a negative pickup deal. It's a comic book story where five GIs crash-land on an island full of tribal cave girls and they're all threatened by dinosaurs, including a big tyrannosaurus called The Great One. It's funny and, of course, full of girls: Toni Naples, Michelle Bauer, Becky LeBeau. It turned out very well; Roger told

the time they're all done rewriting it, and the actors come in—like Tanya Roberts, whom they let rewrite a certain part of it—it doesn't make sense anymore. The picture looked beautiful, I thought. It was a very handsomely mounted little thriller that lost its focus toward the end. But you can't argue with success. A six-and-a-half-million-dollar picture that's the number-one most-rented video in the United States? On the top fifty for four months in a row! And it was a film that inspired maybe twenty other movies. One film even ripped off our ad campaign. A movie called *Secret Games* stole our ad campaign and duplicated it almost to the letter, which led to a big lawsuit. So many films we'd done were little films that had set out to emulate other genre successes. Then, all of a sudden, we created a genre success that led others to rip-off and imitate us! It was interesting for the shoe to be on the other foot!

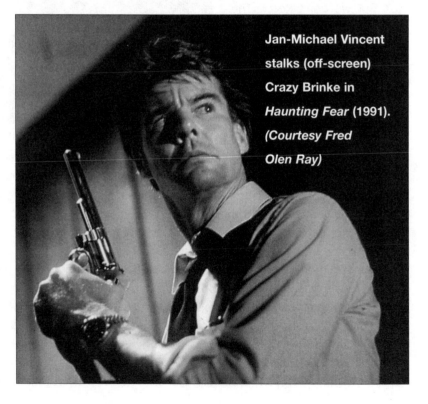

Jan-Michael Vincent stalks (off-screen) Crazy Brinke in *Haunting Fear* (1991). *(Courtesy Fred Olen Ray)*

us it will be the break-through picture of the year for his company. We were very flattered. I am assuming he doesn't give that kind of compliment to every picture that comes through. Especially one as low-budget as ours.

Q: *Hollywood Scream Queen Hot Tub Party* sounds like a winner, too. How did that one come about?

FOR: Jim and I realized that some of these video interviews done with scream queens were not very interesting to the audience.

Another shot of crazy Brinke in *Haunting Fear* (1991). (Courtesy Fred Olen Ray)

People who watch those things aren't interested in whether or not Michelle Bauer's husband lays Tarmac for a living, but if she's sitting there topless, you'll sell a lot of tapes. Jim and I were kidding around over dinner one night, and he said, "Let's do an interview tape of our own and call it *Scream Queen Revue*." I recalled a "Saturday Night Live" skit I'd liked with Eddie Murphy—the "James Brown Hot Tub Party" skit—so I countered with, "Let's call it *Hollywood Scream Queen Hot Tub Party*. I've got a hot tub in my house." So we called up the girls we wanted and shot a lot of footage of them running around naked, which we interspersed with film clips from movies they'd been in. We had Brinke Stevens showing you how to take the perfect movie shower and that sort of thing. In other words, we had what you wanted to see. We shot it all in one day and did the video distribution ourselves. We sold it to the U.K. and a couple of other foreign territories, and away we went.

Q: You've been quoted as saying that nudity is the cheapest—

FOR: Special effect! That's right, it is. It was probably Brian De Palma who gave me the idea. Apparently, he once made a movie where he

mounted a camera on the ceiling and photographed a nude girl sleeping. The only thing she did was roll over now and then, but the audience didn't complain, didn't get bored. And he said what he learned from that was that as long as you have a nude girl on the screen, everyone stays riveted. I really believe that, too. It's the best special effect you can have. It's fast, it's cheap, and people find it entertaining.

Q: You considered getting out of the business at one time, didn't you?

FOR: Yes, about a year or two ago, I just dropped out for a time. I'd just made a picture called *Little Devils* [1991], and I said, "That's it! I've had enough!" I just didn't think I could do anything more. I liked the picture a lot, but felt I'd plumb run out of ideas since this kind of movie had run its course, like the maniac movies and *Road Warrior* [1981] rip-offs. I was also tired of waiting years to collect my money. So, I said, "I'm not working anymore 'til somebody pays me big bucks." You see, with a small hit like *Haunting Fear*, I could make five times as much as on a work-for-hire movie like *Inner Sanctum*. But the difference is, when you're doing an *Inner Sanctum*, distribution is no longer *your* problem. You don't even have to

Dawn Wildsmith fights the mutants in *Warlords* (1989). *(Courtesy Fred Olen Ray)*

decreased so dramatically that I'd say 90 percent of all the companies that existed five years ago are no longer in business. There are only about twelve video distributors left and they only release three or four titles a month now. They don't take on a lot of product, and every title they do take on has to be a hit for them. One loser could wipe them out. So they're very picky.

Q: What film would you like to be remembered for?

FOR: I don't think I've made it yet. But I do think that some of the films I'm doing now that are looked down upon by the critics will probably justify themselves in the long run. Look back at the Roger Corman movies of the 1950s. Roger was spending a hundred thousand dollars or so on each movie, with no stars, no special effects, in black and white, and and with running times of

care whether it comes out. You get your paycheck and you get it right away. And so I wanted to work on bigger budget movies where I'd get a paycheck, and that's mostly what I've done for the past few years. I also started funding other people's movies—people who were starting out and showed some promise.

Q: How has the market changed since you got into the business?

FOR: Dramatically. There's no room for the little guys anymore. I used to say you were safe as long as you didn't spend more than $125,000 on a film—because for $125,000 you're able to take the little distributor's money and still come out ahead. But if you spend, say, four hundred thousand dollars, it's still not enough to make a better movie so that you can move to the next plateau, and who'll buy it? The video market has

David Carradine travels the wastelands in *Warlords* (1989). (Courtesy Fred Olen Ray)

about sixty minutes each. And today those movies are *beloved* by millions and even critically admired. Now, we're making movies that run eighty-five minutes or more, in color, with one or two big-name stars in them for the exact same amount of money he was spending in the '50s! Think about it. In the '50s, a hundred thousand dollars must have gone a tremendous distance, but it certainly doesn't show on the screen. Today, we couldn't get away with a sixty-minute movie, especially one where you wheel out some cheesy-looking monster in the last five minutes for a lackluster final confrontation scene. Today, we're doing better, slicker work—because we have to! That's why I think that eventually the accomplishments of all the people who are doing independent filmmaking right now will become a little more appreciated. Who in the early 1970s would ever have thought that twenty years later people like Ray Dennis Steckler or Al Adamson or Jess Franco would achieve some degree of respectability? I think Sam Arkoff summed it up perfectly when he said: "Time dignifies anything."

SELECTED FILMOGRAPHY

1978: The Brain Leeches; **1979:** The Alien Dead, The Halloween Planet; **1982:** Scalps; **1984:** Biohazard; **1985:** The Tomb, Star Slammer, Armed Response, Death Farm; **1987:** Cyclone, Bulletproof, Commando Squad, Phantom Empire, Moon in Scorpio; **1988:** Deep Space, Hollywood Chainsaw Hookers; **1989:** Evil Spawn, Warlords, Beverly Hills Vamp, Alienator; **1990:** Demon Sword, Bad Girls from Mars, Macon County War; **1991:** Sex Bomb, Empire of the Dark, Mob Boss, Spirits, The Alien Within, Little Devils, Evil Toons, Haunting Fear, Teenage Exorcist; **1992:** Inner Sanctum, Witch Academy, Angel Eyes, Demon Cop; **1993:** The Coven, Possessed by the Night, Dark Universe, Biohazard II, Step Monster, Hollywood Scream Queen Hot Tub Party; **1994:** Inner Sanctum II, Dark Is the Night, Dinosaur Island, Mind Twister, Bikini Drive-In; * Millennium Countdown, Death House, Save Me, Ghost Wars.

*Date Unknown

Mutants on fire in *Warlords* (1989).
(Courtesy Fred Olen Ray)

FRED OLEN RAY

Jim Wynorski poses with early leading lady Raven De La Croix. "The most gorgeous woman I'd ever seen," he says. *(Courtesy Bill George)*

Jim Wynorski

BY BRUCE G. HALLENBECK

Jim Wynorski has been called the Russ Meyer of the horror-fantasy exploitation film because, similar to that celebrated soft-core maestro, Wynorski has a fondness for populating his movies with pneumatic women who look as if they just stepped off a Frank Frazetta poster or comic book cover. His stock company of busty heroines includes former underage porn star Traci Lords, whom Wynorski cast in her first non-porn film, a 1988 remake of the classic Roger Corman sci-fi quickie, *Not of This Earth* (1957); Raven De La Croix, the incredibly voluptuous *Cheri* magazine centerfold who starred in his first film as a director, *The Lost Empire* (1986); and Becky Le Beau, whom Wynorski "discovered," and who went the opposite route of Traci Lords by moving on to develop her own line of soft-core videos called *Soft Bodies*.

The forty-something Wynorski collaborates most frequently with his exploitation film idol, producer Roger Corman, but he has also teamed up with other exploitation producer-directors on occasion such as Fred Olen Ray with whom Wynorski codirected *Dinosaur Island* (1994) for Corman's Concorde Pictures, and *Hollywood Scream Queen Hot Tub Party*, a 1993 video release featuring some of the genre's most eye-popping babes—Brinke Stevens, Michelle Bauer, and Kelli Maroney—cavorting in the buff. Clearly, Jim Wynorski is a director who is not in the game just for the money, but because he truly enjoys his work.

Q: Your bio says that you're a Long Island boy and that you once worked for the publishing giant Doubleday. True?

JW: Yes, on both counts. I worked at Doubleday in the fiction department when I was twenty-two years old.

Q: How did you make the transition from publishing to exploitation filmmaking?

JW: I worked at Doubleday from 1972 to 1977. Around 1977, I was asked to do the *Star Wars* book campaign. They had no idea at the time how successful that movie was going to be—this was early in 1977. I'd always been a big horror and science fiction movie fan, collected posters and stills from those films, read *Famous Monsters of Filmland* each month, and so on, so I really enjoyed working on the *Star Wars* campaign, and decided to leave Doubleday—which was a very lucrative position—pack up my belongings, and move to Los Angeles to make it big in the movies. I realized it was a long shot because a lot of people try to do the same thing, but I figured I had a chance, so I sold a lot of my movie posters and stills to finance the trip and went to L.A. That was in '78. I bummed around a couple of years, like everybody does, then I got a job at Twentieth Century–Fox as production assistant on a TV series called "Breaking Away." Unfortunately, the series got cancelled after a few episodes. Anyway, the show was filmed on location, and one day flying back from location, I met somebody who knew Julie Corman, Roger Corman's wife, and was asked if I had any scripts to show her. I had always admired Roger and loved Roger's films, so I went to meet his wife, told her a couple of script ideas I had, and she said, "I'd like you to meet my husband." Roger and I got along very well right from the start. He hired me that day to do promotion work for him, and I took the job because I figured it would give me a chance to hang around the studio—I'd be an "in" rather than an "out" person in other words. I started out shooting and cutting trailers—which to me was like a dream come true. I'd shoot these things on the sets of other films currently in production. It really didn't matter since out of necessity the trailers usually bore little or no resemblance to the films they were actually promoting—a situation that got me into a little bit of trouble at first. I was working on the trailer for this Italian pickup, a Jules Verne–type story set in the 1800s called *Island of the Fish Men* about some guys who go to an island where there's this mad professor creating fish men. Barbara Bach was the heroine of the picture, which was now called *Something Waits in the Dark;* Roger wanted to promote it as a slasher film even though the slasher genre, I felt, was inundated at the time. But he felt differently, and when the film went out, it bombed. Just bombed. So they looked at me and said, "Well, why don't *you* do a campaign on it?" This was my fourth week there. Cronenberg's *Scanners* [1981] had just come out and was making a big splash, so I started thinking, Why not change the title of the Italian film to *Screamers*? Then, taking a cue from an episode of the old Arch Oboler *Lights Out* radio series about a guy being turned inside out, I came up with a campaign and the slogan "You will actually see someone turned inside out—while he's still alive!" Roger wasn't aware of any of this. He just said, "Go ahead, make a new campaign." So, I got ahold of Rob Bottin, who was still not very famous at that point—it was pre-*The Thing* [1982]—and another FX genius, Chris Walas,

got this busty redhead to play a scientist, and we shot this trailer for *Screamers* where you see the skin on this guy's hand peel away as he starts turning inside out. The trailer looked great. It was very futuristic; a good-looking girl in a lab coat gets it ripped off and she's wearing a bra and panties, and there's this inside-out creature, which you don't entirely see, except for his hand, chasing her. We opened the film in Atlanta on a Friday night, and the next morning I got a call from Roger. He said, "Did you do the trailer for *Something Waits in the Dark*?" I told him I called the film *Screamers* now and what was in the trailer, and he said, "Is that scene in the film?" I told him no, and he said, "Well, we're gonna have to put it in the film. They rioted at the drive-ins in Atlanta last night!" They were looking for that inside-out guy, and tore the place apart because he wasn't in the film. I thought I was fired, but what Roger really was concerned about, since the film had done very respectable numbers, was somehow inserting that scene into the picture, and making the campaign not such a lie. He was very impressed that I had turned the film around from a flop to a hit, with very little money but a lot of ingenuity. So my job was kind of secure after that.

Q: So did the scene end up being in the film?

JW: We took all the footage I had shot for the trailer and cut together a sequence that lasted about two minutes where the girl gets chased by the inside-out guy and inserted it into the first fifty release prints. They were physically cut in by hand over the course of a weekend. But if you rent the video, that scene is not in there because it isn't on the negative. We didn't want to make fifty new prints because that would have been too expensive.

Q: That takes a lot of guts.

JW: Well, that was my initiation into the Roger Corman style of making movies. And from there on, he would let me do other things, until finally he let me direct one.

Q: Does Corman interfere much when you're making a film?

A ghoulish member of the lost race inhabiting *The Lost Empire* (1986), Wynorski's first film as a director. *(Courtesy Eric Caidin)*

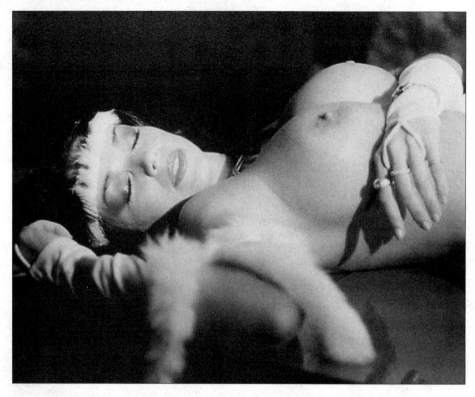

Raven De La Croix in *The Lost Empire* (1986), Wynorski's sci-fi tribute to the films of Russ Meyer. *(Courtesy Bill George)*

JW: Hardly at all. Especially with me because I've done so many pictures that have been successful for him. We've had an argument here and there, but it usually gets worked out amicably. I respect his opinion quite highly. I was a big fan of his when I was a kid. I loved his stuff.

Q: Speaking of which, tell me some other directors and films that influenced you—helped make you what you are today.

JW: Well, cartoons. I know that. Warner Brothers cartoons. I loved Howard Hawks's *The Thing* [1951] because, even as a kid, I thought this is humorous. It didn't have a great monster, but I liked the film anyway because it was suspenseful, and when it wasn't suspenseful, I was laughing because the characters are so engaging. In my movies, I also try to have characters you can like, so that even if the sets are shoddy or the monster's not as good as it could be, you can still go along for the ride. That's especially true of something like *Deathstalker 2* [1987], where the sets are so cheesy—but you like John Terlesky's Deathstalker character and you like his leading lady, Monique Gabrielle, being cute, so you can go along with that little team regardless of the film's imperfections.

Q: Yes, Terlesky's sort of a lovable "doofus" in that film.

JW: That's exactly what he is, a lovable doofus. He's short of muddling through. He's not a deathstalker at all. He's Deathstalker in name only.

Q: The first film I remember seeing your name on was *Sorceress* [1982], as a writer.

JW: The first one I wrote was *Forbidden World* [1981].

Q: That was a fun movie.

JW: It was a very fun movie.

Q: A little gross in spots, but fun.

JW: Hey, I enjoy that movie! I think it's a real hoot!

Q: Then you wrote *Sorceress*. Wasn't that shot in Argentina?

JW: No, in Mexico. That was a wild picture. I wrote *Sorceress* in four days. Roger came to me on a Wednesday and said, "You know, we missed the boat on that Schwarzenegger *Conan* picture. We shoulda been there first." And then he said, "Why don't you take the next couple of days off? Use the weekend. Come in with a script on Monday." So I rushed home and cobbled together a seventy-six-page script with large margins, which ultimately became *Sorceress*.

Q: There was a lot of humor in that film.

JW: Well, there was more but it got cut out.

Q: Why?

JW: Roger, at that time, didn't appreciate my brand of hip humor. It was only when I had actual control of a picture that I could put a lot more of that stuff in and get away with it.

Q: When he asked you to write the script for *Sorceress*, did you get paid?

JW: I think I got paid a thousand dollars extra for doing the script even though I was a full-time employee at Roger's company, which was New World Pictures at that time. Frankly, I would have paid *him* a thousand dollars just for the screen credit. But it was at that point that I realized I could make some real dough here, so I stopped doing advertising and started making movies. For my next picture, *Screwballs* [1984], a *Porkys*-type picture, I even got a piece of the action because I was the producer and brought in some money. It was a very successful picture on video. I think they're up to eighty thousand or a hundred thousand copies in distribution so far.

Q: Raven De La Croix was in that one. How did you end up working with her?

JW: Well, I met Raven somewhere around '82 and we

started dating. I thought she was the most gorgeous woman I'd ever seen, the most unbelievably built woman I'd ever seen. So I subsequently cast her in *Screwballs* in a short but happy role as "Miss Anatomical." After that, I made my first full feature as a director, *The Lost Empire*, and put her in that one, too.

Q: That brings up an interesting point—or a couple of interesting points: your predilection for casting

Roger Corman film alumnus Dick Miller goes to his death at the robotic hands of the killbots in Wynorski's *Chopping Mall* (1986). *(Courtesy Bill George)*

JIM WYNORSKI

164

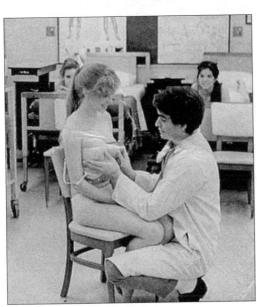

JIM WYNORSKI

165

THE SLEAZE MERCHANTS

166

very busty women in your films. Is this something you do because you know it's commercial, or is this a personal taste of yours?

JW: I would say both. It certainly is commercial—and it's very easy on the eyes when you're making a movie.

Q: It's led to your being called the Russ Meyer of fantasy-horror films.

JW: Well, *The Lost Empire* was kind of my tribute to Russ Meyer.

Q: I can see that. I don't think there's a girl in there with a flat chest.

JW: I don't think so, either. I hope not, anyway.

Q: What happened between that and your "breakthrough" movie, *Not of This Earth*?

JW: In most parts of the country, *Lost Empire* came out on a double bill with an Italian pickup called *Dawn of the Mummy*. But *Empire* won the Seattle Drive-In Movie Award—a precursor to the Joe Bob Briggs Award—two years running. It was shown there in competition with other drive-in films. It was so successful that Vestron, who released it on video, approached me with the idea of doing a film for them about a killer in a shopping mall. That's when I came up with the idea for *Chopping Mall* [1986], a film that was really a hoot and a half. We had some very pretty girls in that one—Barbara Crampton, who was in *Re-Animator* [1985], Kelli Maroney, Suzanne Slater—and Paul Bartel and Mary Woronov were in that one, too. I carried over Angela Ames from *Lost Empire* for that show too.

Q: The original title was *Killbots*, wasn't it?

JW: The original, *original* title was *R.O.B.O.T.* And then it became *Killbot* and then *Chopping Mall*. It actually went out under the title *Killbot*, but it did no business. It needed a new title, but I didn't know what else to call it. Then the guy who changes light bulbs for Corman came into the screening room, watched a few scenes from the picture, and said, "Why don't you call it *Chopping Mall*?" And I said, "That's funny, *very* funny!" So, I ended up calling it *Chopping Mall* and it was a lot more successful.

Q: Sounds like Corman's company was very democratic.

JW: Well, whoever came up with a good idea—that's the one we went with. We weren't above taking a good idea from anybody. All those great catchlines for the film's ad campaign—"Where half off is just the beginning!" or "Where shopping costs you an arm and a leg!"—grew out of that title, which was so campy that that's why I think the film did so well.

Q: Didn't you also do *Deathstalker 2* around this time?

JW: Yes, right after *Chopping Mall*, I went straight into *Deathstalker 2*. I was down for about three weeks between the two pictures. We filmed it in Argentina, in a little town about an hour out of Buenos Aires. I forget what it was called, but the studio we shot in looked like a standing set from one of those Spanish *Blind Dead* pictures. Every time I walked in there I thought of those movies, with all the Gothic columns and so on. Unfortunately, the studio was also located next to a freeway, so no matter where you went on the lot, you heard cars and trucks roaring by.

Q: Must have made it difficult doing sync sound.

JW: It made it impossible. We had to do a lot of looping—putting the dialogue in afterwards—on that show. But the picture was tremendous fun for me. I was far away from everybody. We threw out the script—totally threw it out—and every day we were writing new sequences because if the Argentinians couldn't do something that was called for in the script, we'd have to come up with something different. They were very accommodating and very nice people, but they didn't have a clue how to do a lot of the things we needed. But sets could be built cheaply and quickly, sets we couldn't afford to build here in L.A.

Q: What I enjoyed about that film was that it showed you're such an unabashed film fan. There are a lot of "quotes" from such films as *Plague of the Zombies* [1966], *Pit and the Pendulum* [1961], lines stolen from *Goldfinger* [1964] . . . .

JW: There's a whole tribute to *Goldfinger* in there! And Warner Brothers cartoons—nobody says

The alien (Arthur Roberts) mixes an out-of-this-world cocktail in Wynorksi's *Not of This Earth* (1988), a remake of the 1957 Roger Corman classic of the same name. *(Copyright © 1988 Pacific Trust/Courtesy Eric Caidin)*

"Yipe!" in a film anymore! After that, I came back to the States and did *Big Bad Mama II* [1987]. Angie Dickinson, Robert Culp, and Danielle Brisebois from "Archie Bunker's Place" were in that.

Q: Didn't Brisebois have a nude scene in that?

JW: Yes, she did.

Q: That must have helped the film's notoriety.

JW: It certainly did.

Q: *Not of This Earth* seems to have been your "breakthrough" film. It certainly got more publicity than most of your other films, largely because of the casting of Traci Lords. How did the film come about?

JW: While we were at an optical house doing some effects work for *Big Bad Mama II*, I came across an original print of the old Corman film.

Kelli Maroney was there, and Raven, and we had a big hoot watching it. So I said, "I think we could have a blast remaking this picture." And they said, "Well, who are you going to get to play the Beverly Garland part?" There were some newspapers lying around, and I saw a story in one of them about Traci Lords. So, I said, "Let's get Traci Lords!" She even looks a little bit like Beverly Garland.

Q: Fred Olen Ray has some fairly unprintable things to say about working with Lords, but I recall reading that you found the experience relatively easy.

JW: Well, at the time I think she was easy to work with. I haven't worked with her since. I wanted to use her in *The Haunting of Morella* [1989], but she didn't want to do any nude scenes, so I told her I couldn't use her. I said, "Traci, I admire you for what your goals are, but if you won't do any nude scenes, I just can't use you in the picture." However, Traci and I got to be good friends after *Not of This Earth* because my sense of humor and hers are very close. She hated her leading man. So did I. He scratched my car. That black car he drives in the movie was my car, and in the scene where he was pulling into the house we were using, he scratched the side of my car. I threw a fit. Then I realized it wasn't entirely his fault. We went so fast on that show, we got giddy. You know that black dress Traci's wearing at the end of the film? There's a zillion takes where she falls out of that dress.

Q: Must be collector's items now.

JW: They *are* collector's items. She had to run a lot in that dress, and run at top speed, so that's why she's always holding herself in.

Q: The thing I enjoyed about your *Not of This Earth* was that it was an almost scene-for-scene remake of the original. It's kind of like the nudie version.

JW: They're very close! Very close! We even shot it in twelve days, which was the same shooting schedule as the original picture.

Q: Didn't you make a bet with Corman that you could do it in the same amount of time?

JW: That's right. Because I had some money in that show, I had complete freedom in casting it and everything. With the profits, I bought a

The alien (Arthur Roberts) gets Wynorski's version of a surprise birthday present (Becky LeBeau) in *Not of This Earth* (1988). (Copyright © 1988 Pacific Trust/Courtesy Eric Caidin)

nice new house. So, you might say I'm now living in the "House of Lords."

Q: Has it been shown on TV?

JW: I don't think it has. I think they're keeping it off TV because of continual video sales. I'm very unknowledgeable in that area. But I did do a special TV version of it. It's much longer and has a lot of interesting stuff that wasn't in the video version.

Q: Didn't you do the same thing with *Transylvania Twist* [1989]?

JW: Yeah, the TV version of *Transylvania Twist* is much longer than the theatrical or tape version.

Q: Wasn't that your next film after *Not of This Earth*?

JW: No, I did *The Return of Swamp Thing* next. It starred Louis Jourdan, whom I hate.

Q: Why?

JW: Let's just say I hate him.

Q: Tough guy to work with?

JW: I hate him. That's all I can tell you. On the other hand, his co-star, Heather Locklear, was the sweetest lady I've met in a long time.

Q: I had always heard she was kind of tough to work with.

JW: Nope! Absolutely not. Heather sits there, she reads a book, I say, "Heather, over here, you say

JIM WYNORSKI

Former-teen-porn-star-turned-legit-actress Traci Lords in Jim Wynorski's *Not of This Earth* (1988). She hasn't appeared for Wynorski since as she refuses to do any more nude scenes. *(Copyright © 1988 Pacific Trust/Courtesy Eric Caidin)*

this line." She's there. She laughs. She has a good time. She's very easy to work with.

Q: But Louis is not.

JW: I hate him!

Q: *Transylvania Twist* had some interesting people in it. I'm a big fan of the old "Man from U.N.C.L.E." TV series, and you had Robert Vaughn and David McCallum—both men from U.N.C.L.E.—in that film.

JW: I'm the hugest "Man from U.N.C.L.E." fan there is.

Q: Then Robert Vaughn must have been kind of an idol of yours when you were a kid. What kind of experience was it directing one of your idols?

JW: It was great. He's a wonderful guy, although the first day or two, he didn't quite know what to

make of me. I was laughing on the set all the time. I was getting stuff done, but laughing all the while I was doing it. He was only on that film for six days, and we'd already been in production when he showed up. By that time, I was laughing my ass off on that show. There were certain moments I couldn't watch because I was laughing so hard.

Q: Is this common for you to have so much fun on the set?

JW: Most of the time, yes.

Q: There was a lot of *Young Frankenstein*–type humor in that film that really worked.

JW: Well, I didn't want to make fun of the genre, I just wanted to have a good time with it. There are so many takeoffs of different things in that film. If you don't like one scene, there's another one comin' up like two seconds or a minute down the line that will crack you up. But, again, a lot of stuff was cut out of that picture. There's a whole "Twilight Zone" bit in that film where they're flying in a plane; I did a takeoff on the famous Bill Shatner episode where he sees this creature on the wing of the plane and he tries to warn people but they don't see it. In *Transylvania Twist*, Bill pulls open the curtain and sees *himself* out there on the wing! It's a very odd scene, but it slowed down the picture so we cut it out. It's in the video release, though.

Q: You said that Robert Vaughn at first didn't know what to make of you. Did he eventually get into the spirit of things?

JW: Well, when he first came onto the set, I introduced him to everyone as Robert "The Magnificent Seven" Vaughn. Through the whole day, whenever he walked on, I would say, "Ladies and gentlemen, Robert 'Bullitt' Vaughn." And I got progressively more eclectic in the titles. Like "Teenage Caveman" Vaughn. Robert "Unwed Mother" Vaughn. I figured I was either gonna really piss him off—because he was very aloof that first day—but I figured, okay, let him get mad at me, we'll have a little argument and that'll break the ice. He'll know who I am! But he never got riled by it. Finally, toward the end of

the first day, he really got into it and we were having a blast. When he's not shooting, he's reading a book. But he's always there and he's always ad-libbing and making me laugh. McCallum has a great sense of humor, too.

Q: I talked to Lana Clarkson about working with McCallum on *The Haunting of Morella.* She thought he was very intense.

JW: I found him to be a very sweet, very nice guy who would talk to anybody. I've even had him over to my house. He was very aware that I liked "The Man from U.N.C.L.E.", as was Vaughn. But Vaughn didn't want to do any "U.N.C.L.E." parodies in *Transylvania Twist*. He said "I've done so many of those! Please!" So I purposely kept away from them until the scene in the movie where he puts this record on, where he says, "I'm going to play my dear Uncle Marius's favorite song." Well, when he put the record on, we played a tape of "The Man from U.N.C.L.E." theme, and he broke up. We didn't use that music in the actual picture, but you do see him breaking up, and that's why.

Q: I think *The Haunting of Morella* is one of your best films.

JW: I hate *Morella.*

Lana Clarkson and Maria Ford in *The Haunting of Morella* (1989), Wynorski's erotic tribute to the works of Edgar Allan Poe and Britain's Hammer Films. "I hate it. There's no laughs in it," he says.
(Courtesy Bill George)

The title character himself in Wynorski's further adventures of the superhero of the bayous, *The Return of Swamp Thing* (1989). *(Copyright © 1989 Lightyear Entertainment, L.P./Courtesy Eric Caidin)*

Q: Why?

JW: There are no laughs in it. I consciously made an effort to make a film that was oppressive. I wanted to make one that didn't have a single joke in it. It was an attempt to do something very Gothic, a Poe-Hammer kind of film.

Q: That's the reason I liked it. It was the first period Gothic film in quite some time. The atmosphere really worked.

JW: Well, I watch it and say, "I wish I could have done it better." I didn't like Nicole Eggert in the part very much. She was a nice girl, I'm not saying that; quite pleasant. But she was wrong for the role in my estimation.

Q: The film did fairly well, didn't it?

JW: Quite well, although a lot of critics panned it. But I have to tell you that reviews mean very little to me because if you believe the good ones, you have to believe the bad ones. The only opinion that counts is that of the general public. I try to please as many people as I can when I make a picture, but I'm mostly trying to please myself.

In any case, I'll still go to the bank and cash the check. But most people seemed to like *Transylvania Twist* and that was a commercial loser, while *Morella* got panned and was a success, so who can tell.

Q: Maybe the difference was that *Morella* had more nudity.

JW: Maybe. But overall, the campaign worked. The poster was a great piece of classy but edgy ad art. It suckered people into buying the picture. Bad cover art is always what nails you.

Q: The most recent film of yours I've seen is *Sorority House Massacre II* [1991].

JW: You know, I've lost track. I wrote that script in

JIM WYNORSKI

Voluptuousness and violence in *Hard to Die* (1992), Wynorski's feminist take on the mucho macho *Die Hard* films, featuring Gail Robyn Harris. *(Courtesy Bill George)*

JW: Yeah, I brought in five of what I thought to be the most luscious babes to be in that show. I directed it under a pseudonym, Arch Stanton—the name on the gravestone at the conclusion of Sergio Leone's spaghetti Western *The Good, The Bad and the Ugly* [1966]—but when it went out and started getting a lot of good reviews, I went back and put my own name on the picture. That's one time when I let reviews influence me. Every reviewer said, "This film stinks, but I loved it!" They turned it into a guilty pleasure. So I thought I was a fool to put somebody else's name on it.

Q: What films have yours have we missed talking about?

three days! I was goin' a mile a minute on that one. It was shot in seven days with a day and a half of pickup. The picture came in at around seventy-five minutes when it was finished, and, I thought, we need to pad it out more. So, we went back for a day and a half and shot the strip bar sequence as well as some other interiors and a few exteriors of the cops walking around in the rain to add the time we needed.

Q: The film certainly delivers on the T & A level.

JW: Oh, *976-EVIL* [1990]. We missed *Munchies* [1990]. That was a children's movie. And there's also *Hard to Die* [1992], which is sort of a sequel to *Sorority House Massacre II* that's in release now. This is kind of a funny story. Julie Corman had said to me, "Jim, let's do a film on the set at Concorde while Roger and I are away on vacation. Only don't tell Roger." So, I did. I wrote the script in three days, we cast it, and I made the picture in literally seven days while they were on vacation. They came back and watched the picture and they loved it. But then Roger said, "Jim, I want you to make the picture again, only this time make it even more outrageous." And I did. I literally remade the picture. It was originally titled *Tower of Terror*, a sort of female version of *Die Hard*. After that I did *Sins of Desire* [1993] with Tanya Roberts. That's out now. And *Little Miss Zillions* [1993] with Howard Hesseman and Steve Landesburg.

Q: Isn't that also called *Home for Christmas* on TV?

JW: That's right. That's the title it goes under on cable to make it sound a bit like *Home Alone*. Then there's *Dinosaur Island* (1994), Fred Ray's and my version of *Jurassic Park*. Then there's *Body Chemistry III*, a sequel to *Body Chemistry II*, which I made in 1993. The new one stars Andrew Stevens and Morgan Fairchild. Meanwhile, I'm just sitting around waiting for more "Man from U.N.C.L.E." tapes to come out on video.

SELECTED FILMOGRAPHY

1981: Forbidden World; **1982:** Sorceress; **1984:** Screwballs; **1986:** The Lost Empire, Chopping Mall; **1987:** Deathstalker 2, Big Bad Mama II; **1988:** Not of This Earth; **1989:** The Return of Swamp Thing, Transylvania Twist, The Haunting of Morella; **1990:** 976-EVIL, Munchies; **1991:** Sorority House Massacre II; **1992:** Hollywood Scream Queen Hot Tub Party, Ghoulies IV, Hard to Die; **1993:** Body Chemistry II, Little Miss Zillions, Sins of Desire; **1994:** Dinosaur Island, Body Chemistry III.

Wynorski again mixed babes, blood, and belly laughs in *Ghoulies IV* (1992), featuring Antonia Dorian. *(Courtesy Bill George)*

JIM WYNORSKI

175

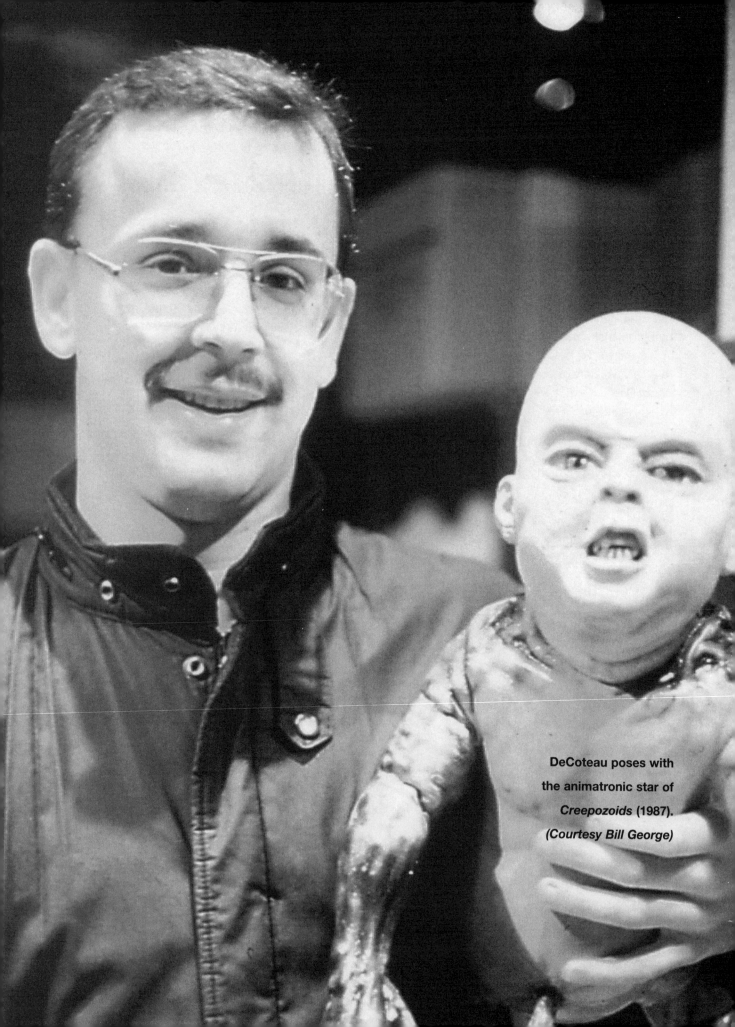

DeCoteau poses with the animatronic star of *Creepozoids* (1987). *(Courtesy Bill George)*

David DeCoteau

BY BRUCE G. HALLENBECK

David DeCoteau (pronounced Dakota) has been in the exploitation film business since he was a teenager. He started out working in a variety of capacities with such diverse talents as monster movie king Roger Corman and avant-garde German filmmaker Wim Wenders.

With the goal of becoming a director himself, DeCoteau shifted to the adult movie scene in the early 1980s to get some firsthand experience. By the age of twenty-one, he'd directed almost forty hard-core titles (none of which he'll name) and felt "burned out." It was time for him to get into a different area of cinematic exploitation, and, as luck would have it, help arrived just in time in the form of legendary horror/sf/fantasy film producer Charles Band, who agreed to put up part of the money for DeCoteau's first "legit" feature, a horror movie called *Dreamaniac* (1986). Also produced by Band, DeCoteau's next opus, *Creepozoids*, starring DeCoteau's most frequent leading lady, scream queen Linnea Quigley, followed in 1987. Thereafter, under his own name and a pseudonym (Ellen Cabot), DeCoteau produced and/or directed a slew of low-budget, high-profit features for Band and several other independents, as well as operating his own company, Cinema Home Video, which distributes the work of independent filmmakers and upcoming exploiteers just starting out.

DeCoteau's association with Band's production company, now called Full Moon Entertainment, continues to this day, although DeCoteau's career itself seems to have come full circle, shifting from sex to horror back to sex again with a series of erotic fantasy films for Full Moon's adult-oriented "Torchlight" banner. DeCoteau describes these films as "soft and lush rather than hard-core," and says that two are ready for release—with many more on the way.

Q: You've just turned thirty-one and you've already made what seems like a bazillion movies!

DD: That pretty much describes it! I've stopped counting, so I'm not sure what the exact figure is right now. But it's a lot. I have my fingers into everything. I've had regional filmmakers all over the country making them for me for release on my own video label, which I just sold. And I'm now on staff at Charles Band's Full Moon Entertainment. Awhile back I pitched Charlie an idea for a line of movies with a real erotic or hypersensual tone to them—not erotic thrillers, but sci-fi and *Beauty and the Beast*–type stuff—with lots of T & A that I'd shoot for less than half the price of a typical Full Moon movie, and we're just now gearing up. So far I've done two of them, *Virgin Hunters* [1994] with Morgan Fairchild, and *Beach Babes from Beyond* [1994] with Joe Estevez, Joey Travolta, Jackie Stallone, Burt Ward, and Linnea Quigley. I'm also doing Moonbeam titles, which is the family film division at Full Moon.

Q: From erotica to family films—that's quite a stretch.

Prolific exploitation horror/sf/fantasy film producer Charles Band gave DeCoteau (left) the opportunity to break out of adult fare by putting up the money for his first "legit" film, _Dreamaniac_ (1986). _(Courtesy Bill George)_

DD: Yeah! From G rated to unrated!

Q: I love the story about how you met Roger Corman. How old were you then—sixteen?

DD: I think I was seventeen when I met Roger. I was president of the Roger Corman Fan Club, which had no members except myself. I created a letterhead and made a big whoop-de-do about it up in Portland, Oregon, where I'm from. You see, I came from a poor family; I knew that if I was going to move to Hollywood and make it in films and didn't get a job within two months, I would end up having to go back. So I had a plan of attack, which was to charm the hell out of Roger Corman. I was a big fan of Roger's and would correspond with his company using my Roger Corman Fan Club letterhead. They'd send

me stills, posters, news about upcoming films— they were very good to me. When I went down to Los Angeles on vacation, I called them up, and they said, "Roger would love to meet with you." It turned out to be a very long meeting. I was a very energetic teenager with absolutely no social skills, and sat there making a fool of myself, listing Roger's credits to him and so on. But Roger loved every minute of it. He said, "Well, whenever you move to Los Angeles, give me a call. We'll be able to put you to work." I thought it was just a standard Hollywood line. I went back to Portland and when I graduated from high school I worked for the summer as a projectionist in a local movie theater to earn some money to finance my move to Los Angeles. When I got there, I called Roger and got his secretary, Maryann Fisher. I told her Roger had said he'd give me a job as soon as I got to Los Angeles, and she said, "How come I find that very hard to believe?" I said, "Well, that's what he told me." And she said, "I'll ask him about it next time I see him." But I insisted, and, seeing how serious I was, she said, "Well, let me check on it." She put me on hold, then three or four minutes later, she came back on the line and said, "Okay, come to work!" Sure enough, Roger had remembered, and he gave me a job working as a production assistant in the casting department, in the model-making department, and so on. I even helped making sets. I worked with Jim Cameron, who was Corman's art director at the time, and Jim Wynorski, who was the advertising manager. I learned a lot very quickly because with Roger you get your feet wet doing everything. Then,

after a few months, I left, feeling I was ready to produce and direct myself! I didn't want to be bothered doing all that production assistant shit anymore! Actually, I wasn't a very good PA at all, to tell you the truth. I'd show up late—the kind of stuff you're not supposed to do. Now that I'm directing, if a PA did stuff like that on one of my shows, he wouldn't be around much longer.

Q: What did you do then?

DD: I thought I was ready to produce and direct, but no one else did, so I got a job working as a craft service person for Wim Wenders, the German director, on a film he did here called *The State of Things* [1982] that was sort of an homage to Roger. Wenders was a big fan of

Grisly FX shots from *Murder Weapon* (1988), the story of a mad female slasher played by Linnea Quigley. DeCoteau directed under the pseudonym Ellen Cabot. (*Courtesy Dave DeCoteau*)

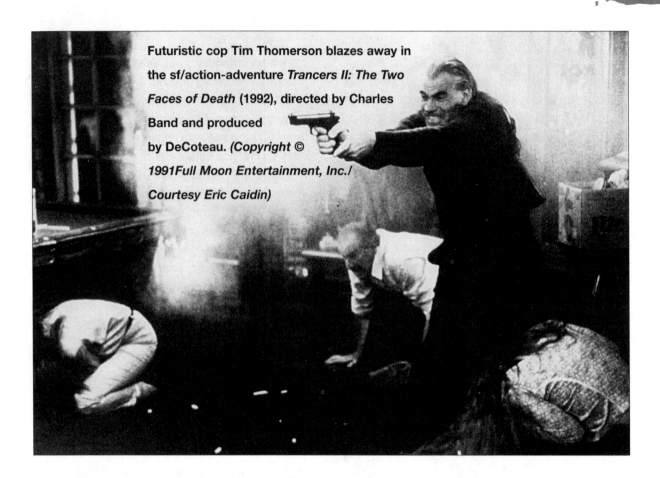

Futuristic cop Tim Thomerson blazes away in the sf/action-adventure *Trancers II: The Two Faces of Death* (1992), directed by Charles Band and produced by DeCoteau. *(Copyright © 1991Full Moon Entertainment, Inc./ Courtesy Eric Caidin)*

Roger's and of maverick American directors in general. People like Sam Fuller were in the cast, as was Roger. Half the film was shot here, and the other half in Portugal with a very, very small European crew. I left that film because being a craft service person—which amounts to supplying the donuts and coffee for the cast and crew—was even worse than being a PA, although the money is better. I had the same job on *Crimes of Passion* [1984], a Ken Russell film starring Kathleen Turner and Anthony Perkins.

Q: That must have been an interesting experience! Is Ken Russell truly insane?

DD: It was an absolute hoot! And, yes, he truly is. He's a wild man. He's not very sociable, though. I think about three weeks into shooting, I finally tapped him on the shoulder by the craft service table and said, "Ken, my name's Dave DeCoteau and I'm the craft service guy here." And he said, "Yes?" I told him I thought his film *The Devils* [1971] was way ahead of its time and a pretty brilliant movie. And he said, "It was a bit of a

romp, wasn't it?" Yeah, well, I guess you could describe it that way! That's about all the conversation I had with Ken Russell, but I was impressed by how professional and how economical a director he is. He shoots *very* fast. After that I worked on a film called *Tuff Turf* [1985] with James Spader and Robert Downey, Jr., which was a lot of fun, and an HBO special called *Summer Jobs* that was a very unpleasant experience. It made me realize I didn't want to do craft service work anymore, so I called a friend who was making adult films, and I got into the hardcore racket. I worked my way up pretty quickly and became a cameraman, soundman, and, soon after, started directing them—about forty in all over a two-year period. I was twenty-four!

Q: That couldn't have been boring work!

DD: Actually, it becomes very dull. After the first few times, it's meat-and-potatoes straight through. But I always tried to do something special with these things. I always cared about how they looked. I made sure there was plenty of dialogue and that the camera moves were slick. I wanted to make them resemble a real movie as much as possible. One thing about the adult film business that may surprise people is that it's extremely well run, very organized and professional, and well funded too. The money was incredible. I was getting paid two thousand dollars a day as a director!

Q: How did you move from hard-core to horror?

DD: The whole idea was to save up enough money and use the experience I'd gotten making adult films to direct a movie of my own. I hired a writer, a woman named Anne Hamilton [later the executive producer of TV's "thirtysomething"], who was a struggling writer at the time, and gave her five hundred dollars to write a horror movie for me to shoot. Anne completed the script and

showed it around town to some other companies as a sample of her work in order to get more jobs. One of these companies was Charles Band's Empire Pictures. A friend of Anne's, Debra Dion, worked there. Anne had gone to school with her. Debbie read it, liked it, and wanted to know what the status of it was. Anne said, "They're going to start shooting it next week." Debbie asked if there was a distribution deal on the film yet, and Anne told her to call me. Debbie called me on a Thursday. I just happened to be living down the street from Empire, and, about thirty minutes later, was sitting in her office. She said, "Why don't you wait here a minute. Charlie wants to talk to you." And I said, "Charlie?" And she said, "Charlie Band." And I said, "Oh, my God! I've been a big fan of his for years!" Which was true. So, Charlie came in, met me, and a few minutes later offered to pay for the postproduction on the film and reimburse me for all the money I'd spent so far in exchange for the distribution rights. He also offered me another picture after that, which he would fully finance. I said, "Great!" The deal was consummated on a Friday, and I started shooting on Monday. That was the beginning of my horror movie career. The picture was called *Dreamaniac*. It

DeCoteau teamed up once more with producer Charles Band to direct *Puppetmaster III: Toulon's Revenge* (1992), starring Guy Rolfe. "We had a terrific script, and it all came together very nicely," DeCoteau says. "It looked like a real movie!" (Copyright © 1991 Full Moon Entertainment, Inc./Courtesy Eric Caidin)

DAVID DeCOTEAU

wasn't a very good picture, but that wasn't as important as the fact that I'd brought it in on schedule and on budget. I'd proven that I was a man of my word. I said I could make a film for a certain price, and I did. That was, and still is, very important in the independent filmmaking arena, since independent producers like Charlie Band are more interested in the practical side of filmmaking rather than the aesthetic side. If you do what you say you can do, you work. I did six pictures for Band that year and a few others for different distributors—Film Trust, Trans World Entrtainment, South Gate Entertainment; there were a lot of independents out there at the time. At the end of 1988, I made a picture called *Dr. Alien* for Charles Band at Empire, and while I was making the movie, he sold the company and formed Full Moon Entertainment. For Full Moon I produced *Crash and Burn* [1991], *Puppetmaster II* [1991], and *Trancers II: The Two Faces of Death* [1992]. Then Charlie asked me to direct *Puppetmaster III* [1992], which I produced as well.

Q: That's a good little film; in fact, it's probably the best in the series.

DD: It did turn out to be a good movie. We shot it at Universal Studios, you know. We had an international cast and a terrific script, and it all came together very nicely. It looked like a real movie!

Charlie then offered me the chance to codirect *Trancers III* with Courtney Joyner. I would have done it except that I'd just gotten a new manager, who was also Quentin Tarantino's manager; Quentin had written a script for me to direct called *My Best Friend's Birthday*. But I hated it. I didn't understand it. So I passed on that project but kept the manager and she sent me all over the place, to Tri-Star, to all the major studios, in the hopes of getting me work at one of the majors. But making the segue from independent filmmaking to the majors is tough. It happened more frequently in the late '70s and early '80s. But because the video industry created so many feature filmmakers, there was a glut on the market, and being an independent filmmaker was no longer that special. It got to the point where even if you had two dozen independent movies under your belt, the majors would rather hire somebody who didn't have any credits because they felt you were used goods. Well, that mentality has unfortunately put the majors in the position they're in now, which is close to bankruptcy and corporate takeover. I realized that the major studios only wanted to work with the top ten guys in town. And nine of those guys are always available! For me to get a job with the majors I would have to be attached to a script that was absolutely brilliant, and, unfortunately, there aren't that many of those out there. Those that do come along are often optioned by the major studios just to get them off the market. The studios have no intention of making them—they just want to keep anyone else from making them. It's crazy. Anyway, after about a year and a half of doing the major studio shuffle, where nothing happened, I went back to Charlie with my tail between my legs and said, "Look, this is a disaster. I haven't worked in a year and a half. My video company is thriving and that's what I'm living on right now. I really, really want to get back into making movies for you." He asked me what I had in mind, and I told him my idea for a series of erotic films. I said, "I'll make 'em for three hundred thousand dollars apiece. I'll need a two-week shooting schedule for each film. I'll shoot 'em in 35 mm with name casts, using your cameras, on your existing sets, and I'll make 'em as erotic as we can get away with. Your distributor, Paramount, might like that." So, we decided to do a couple of these three-hundred-thousand-dollar erotic movies, and that's basically where I am now. I'm going to Romania next spring to do *Huntress I* and *II*. *Babes I* and *II* and *Blonde Heaven* will be done next year as well. I'm on staff, and get a paycheck every Friday whether I work or not. Charlie owns me! But I'm more than happy to be owned because I have too many friends out there who are on welfare. It's tough out there. There's very little work.

Q: Tell me a little more about Charles Band. I've heard conflicting stories about how good a guy he is to work for. Obviously, you consider him to be your savior.

DD: Yeah. Charlie is totally honest with you. He's a wonderful human being. We've had maybe two or three arguments on the twelve or thirteen films I've done for him. He expects the best. If he doesn't get it, he doesn't scream at you; he just doesn't use you again. Directing low-budget features for him or anyone else isn't easy. First of all, everybody on the set—all sixty members of the cast and crew—want to be directors, too. If they see you being uncertain or unsure or unprofessional or nonproductive, you've lost 'em. Crews are good only when the director's good. He sets the tone, the beat, the pace at this level of filmmaking. You gotta move, and you gotta move quick. You've got to get a lot of setups in the can. You've got to learn to compromise and do the best you can under those conditions and move on. You've got to realize you're not going to change the world with your flick. There's no room for that at this level.

Q: Speaking of working quickly, it sometimes seems as though you and two of your colleagues in the exploitation film field, Fred Olen Ray and Jim Wynorski, have a competition going to see who can make films faster. Is that true?

DD: Not really. Fred and Jim and I are beer-drinking buddies. We're friends. There's never really been any competition among us. First of all, I've referred Fred to jobs, and he's done the same for me. Ditto for Jim. We go back and forth. It's a really terrific relationship. Fred sometimes borrows my camera. Sometimes he'll show up on the set and hang out. He was even in a series of documentaries that I grandfathered that Brinke Stevens produced. We're always talking about working together on a feature, though. We just haven't found the right project or the time to do it.

Q: Let's move on to another of your associates: Linnea Quigley. While you didn't actually discover Linnea—*Return of the Living Dead* [1985] was her breakthrough—it seems as though *Creepozoids* and the many other movies she's made with you are really what turned her into a B movie queen for a while.

DD: There's something about Linnea. She's just a really terrific package. If I had a nickel for every gorgeous blonde who comes through this office, I could finance my next nine movies. But for some reason, she just really clicked. I met her back in 1981. She'd just done a horror flick called *Graduation Day*, directed by Herb Reed. I told her I wanted to make horror movies too, so I kept her number and we kept in touch. When *Creepozoids* came up, I asked her if she wanted to be in it. At the time she wasn't working much, so she said, "Sure." We became pretty good friends, and I put her in every movie I did. Or

Dave DeCoteau's spectral beauties, Michelle Bauer, Linnea Quigley, and Brinke Stevens, in *Nightmare Sisters* (1987). (Courtesy Dave DeCoteau)

You'll end up working for me, which you like doing, and it will also start upping your price. Because of your contract with me, other people will be forced to pay you thirty thousand dollars or more." She said, "Great idea!" But her man-

tried to, at least. After *Creepozoids* she got real busy. But she always seemed to find time for me, which was good. We did *Sorority Babes in the Slimeball Bowl-a-Rama* [1987], *Nightmare Sisters* [1987], and *Linnea Quigley's Horror Workout* [1990]. A lot of stuff. But then things turned weird. She was very hot, but, like most of us, she got tied in with some really bad managers. I was with a top agency for about a year, and they did nothing for me. They'd tell me not to do B movies. That's pretty much what agents and managers do. They don't realize that's how we make a living! A lot of agents and managers are very inexperienced. They're more schmoozers and fortune-tellers and liars than they are career-molding entrepreneurs. They seem to have your best interests in mind, but basically they feel that if you do B movies it tarnishes their reputation. They'd rather you not work at all. I asked Linnea if I could put her on exclusive. I said, "You're telling me you want to make more money, so this is what I'll do. I'll put you on a monthly fee. You'll get paid every month whether you work or not. You'll work for me. If you get any offers, you'll have to pass on them, with the exception of offers totaling thirty thousand dollars or more.

ager said, "Linnea, you're crazy to do this. You're taking yourself off the market." She said, "Well, no, I'm not, I'm getting paid every month. I'm doing films and if anybody else wants to use me, they have to pay me thirty thousand dollars or more." But he convinced her not to take my offer. Frankly, I think he was hot after her or something and felt there was something going on between Linnea and me, that we were romantically involved. But we weren't and never have been. Anyway, he and I got together over lunch, and he completely belittled me. He treated me like shit in this restaurant, telling me that I was half a director—and here I had three or four films in various stages of production all over the country! I wasn't some small-time operation. I had a full staff of people, and I had money coming in. I was operating very well, and very reputably. And he basically destroyed the relationship between Linnea and me. Linnea was crushed, I was furious, and it took years before we worked together again.

Q: What type of films do you enjoy seeing?

DD: Foreign films, mostly. Films by Bertolucci, Fellini, and those guys. The classic directors who have done so much with so very little because their filmmaking priorities are completely different. They're in it for their art. In this country, it's tough to do that. Believe it or not, I'm not into most current filmmakers, although I appreciate the efforts of the Renny Harlins and the Jim Camerons. I appreciate the work and I know the effort they put into making their big blockbuster special-effects-heavy movies. But they're not the kind of films I want to make. They're movies that I watch once—maybe. I like quirky stuff— the kind of independent American dramas made by people like Jim Jarmusch and John Jost, that sort of thing. Basically, I'm looking for something different. Something that's completely unpredictable. And I've found that the major studio films are just big-budget versions of the type of B movies me and many other guys are making. In the studio development departments, when a script comes in, the phrase is "dumb it down." They're panderers. The studios are not here to change the culture of America. The number-one export business in America is entertainment, and you'd think the big studios would have a greater sense of responsibility because of that. But they don't because it's not their job to be responsible. It's their job to make money.

Q: Maybe they've learned something from the failure of films like *The Last Action Hero* [1993].

DD: I hope they did. They pandered too much with that one, and I think the audience felt like they were being laughed at. They felt ripped off, and nobody bought into it. Another example is

John Woo, who did great things in his native country of Hong Kong. But I don't think his first American film, *Hard Target* [1993], is much of a movie. It's flashy and all that, but empty. His stuff in Hong Kong was very unpredictable, strange, and offbeat. But with *Hard Target*, he just wanted to satisfy his American studio, and the result was like an episode of the TV series "Hunter." We've seen it all before. I want to see something *different*. It doesn't even have to be great—as long as it's offbeat.

SELECTED FILMOGRAPHY

1986: Dreamaniac; **1987:** Creepozoids, Sorority Babes in the Slimeball Bowl-a-Rama, Lady Avenger, Nightmare Sisters, Assault of the Killer Bimbos, Deadly Embrace; **1988:** American Rampage, Dr. Alien (a.k.a. I Was a Teenage Sex Mutant), Murder Weapon, Assault of the Party Nerds, Ghettoblaster, Ghostwriter; **1990:** Linnea Quigley's Horror Workout, Robot Ninja, Skinned Alive; **1991:** Ghoul School, Crash and Burn, Shock Cinema Volume One, Steel and Lace, Puppetmaster II; **1992:** Puppetmaster III: Toulon's Revenge, Shock Cinema Volume Two, Trancers II: The Two Faces of Death, Beasties; **1994:** Virgin Hunters, Beach Babes from Beyond.

DeCoteau has also directed more than forty adult films, but won't reveal their titles.

A candid shot of Bret McCormick snapped by director of photography D. P. Nunn early one morning during the production of *Blood on the Badge* (1992). *(Courtesy Bret McCormick)*

Bret McCormick

BY JOHN McCARTY

"People will watch anything," says Bret McCormick, commenting not on the degree of craft in his films but the video generation's insatiable appetite for images that move—any image—no matter how awkward the movement may be. "I'm here to fill that need."

The Dallas-based up-and-comer has been filling this need for almost a decade now, often on budgets that make many of his sleaze merchant brethren in this book seem like Hollywood high rollers. "My first film cost too much, which made it that much harder to recoup my investment," he says. "I was determined never to make the same mistake again."

For commercial reasons, McCormick has turned to making low-budget action movies in recent years. But his heart belongs to the poverty-row horror/sci-fi trash "with an edge" that he revelled in as a kid and sought to emulate—and outdo—in his debut work as a filmmaker. The film was called *Tabloid* (1985), an outrageous spoof of the magazines we see at the check-out counter of every grocery store. A cross between *The Rocky Horror Picture Show* (1975) and the perverse early works of John Waters ("Without the sex," McCormick hastens to add), the film earned the endorsement of no less a personage than pop culture guru Andy Warhol, who termed it "Americana. [The work of] the Norman Rockwells of today." ("Warhol was in town at a book signing," McCormick says. "We took *Tabloid* down to him, and he agreed to look at it. It amused him enough that he gave us a blurb.")

Tabloid art for McCormick's debut feature, *Tabloid* (1985). *(Courtesy Bret McCormick)*

Tackling Americana of another kind, McCormick satirically—and metaphorically—probed the dark side of TV evangelism in his next film, *The Abomination* (1986), the story of a woman who is convinced by a TV preacher that tumorous parasitic beasts are nesting in her bowels—beasts that hatch and spread to other victims like a cancerous form of fundamentalism. "We didn't have enough money to do it right," McCormick says. "But it still has its moments. After the old woman throws the tumor in a garbage can, it crawls out in the middle of the night and pulsates its way up the stairs to her son's room, inches over and across the bed onto

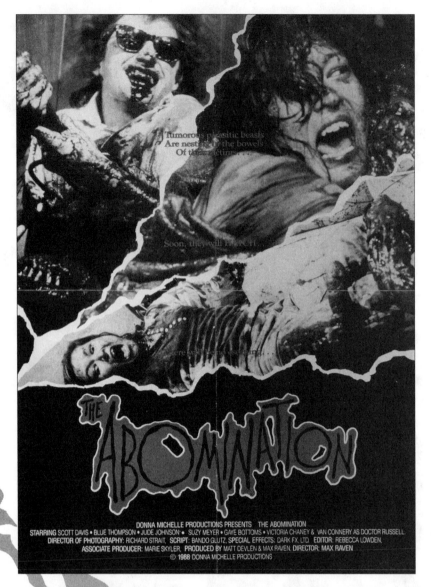

Poster for Bret McCormick's (a.k.a. Max Raven) satiric probe of the dark side of TV evangelism, *The Abomination* (1986). *(Courtesy Bret McCormick)*

BM: Oh, I was corrupted *very* early on. One day when I was about twelve, I was reading a magazine called *Famous Monsters of Filmland*, and in the pen pals section there was this little article about a group of boys in New York who had done their own *Frankenstein* film. I'd always been interested in home movies—my uncle shot pictures of the family picnics and so on, and I was always helping him out. When I read this article, I said, "Hey, we've got a movie camera in the family. If these guys are doing it, I can too." So, I got some friends together, we pooled our allowances, and one weekend we did a little thing called *Crypt of the Werewolf.*

the boy's face. The tumor drops in his mouth, he swallows it, and it takes over his mind."

In addition to his own writing, producing, and directing duties, McCormick has also penned a sequel to the legendary S. F. Brownrigg exploitation film *Don't Look in the Basement* (1973), which he and the elder Brownrigg, a close pal, hope to get onto the video shelves "someday." So, even though Bret McCormick does more action these days, he remains a filmmaker clearly committed to his roots—not only in Dallas, but in the trash epics of the past he loves so well.

Q: What corruptive influences led to your becoming an exploitation filmmaker?

Q: You were primarily interested in horror films?

BM: Yes. From a very early age. And my parents used to encourage me because they thought it was unusual for a four-year-old to have such a passion. By the time I was five or six, they would be waking me up in the middle of the night when they ran across *The Beast from 20,000 Fathoms* [1953] or something on TV, and they would call me into the bedroom to watch it with them. I would get *TV Guide*, scour it for horror films, and plan my week around what horror films were on TV. I got to the point where I'd seen so many that I realized that most of them were done on just pathetically low budgets, and that if I was really interested in making them it was probably a pretty accessible career. All through junior and senior high school, I made three- to six-minute shorts with my friends. When I was seventeen I got the opportunity to work as assistant cameraman on a low-budget dinosaur picture called *The Crater Lake Monster* [1977] with effects by the great David Allen, and that experience *convinced* me that I wanted to make movies. So, I opted to go to the University of Texas at Arlington, where I took some filmmaking courses under a guy named Andy Anderson, who later went on to make *Positive ID*, a popular and very well-received independent film shot here in Texas. After a year, I took some time off to travel around the world. I spent some time in Iran, where I met my wife. When we came back, I went to the Brooks Institute of Photography in Santa Barbara, California, and completed their associates program in motion picture production. Rather than trying to make it in Hollywood, however, I decided to come back to Dallas-Fort Worth, and I've been trying to make it happen here ever since.

Q: Why Dallas and not Hollywood?

BM: Because the Dallas Film Commission was aggressively trying to court the motion picture industry here in Texas. They'd built a very large complex with state-of-the-art equipment and soundstages to draw in feature film and commercial production companies from all over. And it became a very popular, reasonably priced, high-tech center for production. Oliver Stone shot two or three of his films here, including *JFK* [1991]. I worked in postproduction for a company called Allied Film and Video headquartered there. Then I opened up my own office in the complex, and was there until very recently when I joined some friends with a company called Open Door Productions that has a nice little studio of its own.

Q: Tell me about the genesis of your first film, *Tabloid*. How did that come about?

BM: I ran into a man named Max Devlen, who had done a little film called *Invisible Maniac*. We had similar interests and decided to get together and raise some money to make an anthology film I'd dreamed up called *Tabloid*, which I envisioned as a sort of midnight movie, nutty John Waters type of thing for people who were offended by John Waters. It consisted of a series of short films inspired by the type of off-the-wall tabloid newspaper headlines you see in the supermarkets. I wrote and directed a story called *Barbecue of the Dead*, a guy named Glen Coburn who'd previously done a film called *Blood Circus from Outer Space* came in and wrote and directed an episode called *Baby Born with Full Beard*. Another episode was called *Killer Vacuum Destroys Town*. And Matt and I wrote a wraparound that tied the whole thing together. When we finished it, Troma was interested in distributing it, but we would have ended up having to pay for the 35 mm blowup (we shot the film on 16 mm), and the deal wasn't good enough in other respects as well, so we wound up making a deal instead with JVC to release the film in Japan, and I released it on home video myself in the United States through an L.A. company called Tapeworm that distributes films to the home video market for people who need help getting their tapes out there.

Q: Why was JVC interested in a film that was essentially a satire on the tabloid newspaper, which, as far as I know, is mostly a Western phenomenon?

BM: There's an insatiable appetite for product no matter what in the Far East, but excluding Japan and a few other territories, they don't pay much. They import a lot of product from here because the mind-set over there—and it's changing now—is that American films are the best, and so people marketing grade B and C movies have played on that and found ready sales. Fortunes have been made on films that couldn't be given away over here. But that's winding down now.

Q: Did you make any money on it?

BM: No, that's the one film I've never made my money back on. The film sold about a thousand copies here—not remarkable, but Tapeworm

A promotional flyer for *Armed for Action* (1992),
starring Joe Estevez, Martin Sheen's younger brother.
(Courtesy Bret McCormick)

THE SLEAZE MERCHANTS

told us we were lucky to move that many copies of a film with a title like that. But as a result of that experience, we learned something. Most buyers didn't want the film because it wasn't classifiable as either a horror film, an action film, or a comedy. It was a bit of all three. So we talked to people like Charles Band and others about what type of picture would move, and at the time they told us horror. So in 1987, I shot a couple of back-to-back horror movies, *The Abomination* and *Ozone: Attack of the Redneck Mutants* [1987]. I shot them on Super 8, crammed them full of as many gross-out special effects as our meager budgets would allow, and transferred them directly to tape.

Q: You used the pseudonym of Max Raven on those films, why?

BM: Since we were shooting them on Super 8, we didn't know how they would look, if they would come off or how successful they would be—would they be damaging to our reputations in the long run? So, all of us connected with them decided to use pseudonyms. I took the name Max Raven, and I've used it and several other pseudonyms like Bando Glutz and B. A. Jenkins occasionally since then when I've felt like it.

Q: How did these films fare in the marketplace?

BM: They got good reviews, and we made our money back since the budgets were so low, but they went nowhere because all the distributors who told us to go out and make horror movies didn't want them by that time. So, I decided to change my game plan entirely. Rather than make a film and *then* try to interest a distributor, I contacted a variety of distributors to find out what type of pictures they were seeking and were willing to finance themselves to get them done. That's the approach I've taken ever since, and it's been working out a lot better for me financially.

Q: What kind of films were they asking for?

BM: Primarily action. I linked up with a company called Reel Movies to make *Highway to Hell* [1989] with Richard Harrison, then Action International Pictures for whom I wrote and directed *Armed for Action* [1992] and *Blood on the Badge* [1992], both starring Martin Sheen's younger brother, Joe Estevez. And for Fred Olen

The freely illustrated flyer for *Highway to Hell* (1989), which made the film look like a promo for a Mexican or Filipino movie.
(Courtesy Bret McCormick)

Ray's company, I did a picture called *Macon County War* [1990], starring Grizzly Adams himself, Dan Haggerty.

Q: Whom you didn't much like, I gather?

BM: He was a jerk from the word go. Belligerent, rude. I'd been warned about this from the start.

bit easier for me to get backing. Distributors know that if I say I can do this many car crashes for the bucks they're giving me, I can do it.

Q: When you say "these things" you mean, of course, exploitation films. What's your definition of an exploitation film?

BM: It's a film that derives its main impetus or drawing appeal from whatever sensational elements it has—sex, violence, action, or whatever. The exploitable element in my films is action, which I define as the destruction of inanimate objects as opposed to the destruction of people.

Q: Whom do you see when you envision the audience for your films?

BM: When I got into this business, I wanted to make films for people who were like me—people who loved watching the whole gamut of bizarre, low-budget, schlocky horror/science-fiction stuff. But after I'd done a few projects in that category, I found that fewer and fewer distributors were even willing to look at a low-budget horror film because there was such a glut on the video market—my primary outlet. So, I shifted to low-budget action films because that's what the distributors I was working with were willing and able to finance. The audience for my most recent films are people who love to watch action for the sake of action—the people who've seen all the

Even Fred had warned me. But we needed some kind of a name, and Haggerty filled the bill. I'd never work with him again, though. Joe, on the other hand, was just a sweetheart. Very pleasant, accommodating, eager to do whatever was needed to get the shot—and a good actor, too, by the way.

Q: So you're no longer having difficulties getting financing for your films.

BM: It's *always* difficult. Let's just say it's not getting *increasingly* difficult for me, as it is for so many other people, especially if they're depending upon the private sector for funding. If I was going to the private sector, not directly to the distributors themselves, it would be a lot more difficult because of the sorry state our economy is in, especially Dallas, which is no longer a boom town. But I've done a number of these things now, the résumé's a little more impressive, and so it's a big-budget stuff and will gravitate to action films, even if they're made on a low budget, because they love to see action. The distributor gives me a wish list—we need this many car crashes, this many explosions, we want to see this many guns, et cetera—and a budget, and I tell them what I can do for that budget. Then I either throw a script together or modify one they already have and do what's basically a programmer to fill their distribution pipeline.

Q: Who are your heroes in the exploitation film arena?

BM: Sam Raimi, Frank Henenlotter, Ted Mikels, Herschell Gordon Lewis, Roger Corman—Corman especially because he's the guy who was able to make it work better than anybody else. He was able to take these little pictures with these low budgets and be very successful with them.

Q: Why do you think exploitation films have caught on with so many people in recent years?

BM: A lot of us grew up watching these films at the drive-in. We saw films there that just weren't available anywhere else. There was a kind of forbidden intrigue, underground or otherworld feel to the whole experience. Today, home video is kind of like the way the drive-in used to be for us. B movies go straight to video instead of straight to

the drive-in. In fact, there aren't many drive-ins left, which is a shame. When I grew up and became a filmmaker, I was interested in developing relationships with the people who made these films, seeing what else they'd done, and how. I think this is the case with a lot of kids. They see one of these films that was not made under a major studio banner, that's obviously not an A budget picture, that's so cheap the filmmakers didn't have enough money to do it the right way, but which breaks all the rules, and they say, "I could do that!" It's the same reason people liked Bob Dylan. He couldn't sing, but he had something to say and people thought it was kind of audacious that he kept singing even though he

Sometimes you have to cross the line.

DAN HAGGERTY
MACON COUNTY WAR

AMERICAN-INDEPENDENT Presents A M.A.R.S. Production DAN HAGGERTY in "MACON COUNTY WAR"
Starring BENTON JENNINGS ROCKY PATTERSON MALINDA BRYANT DORA INGRHAM CHARLIE ROGERS
RICHARD PERRIN and TIM BUCHANAN   Director of Photography SHAWN FREEBURG
Associate Producer TOM ALEXANDER   Executive Producer PETER STEWART
Written, Produced and Directed by BRET McCORMICK
©MCMXC AMERICAN-INDEPENDENT PRODUCTIONS, INC.

Promotional materials for
Macon County War **(1990).**
The female model is not
actually in the film! *(Courtesy*
Bret McCormick)

BRET McCORMICK

195

Josh McCormick (Bret's son, right) and Colin Moore take a break from playing aliens in *Invasion of the Space Varmints* (1991). *(Courtesy Bret McCormick)*

couldn't carry a note. People listened to him at first saying, "Gosh, I could do that," and then they got hooked. And I think that happens to people with regard to exploitation films. At first you may feel ripped off—the film promises more than it delivers—but then you're struck by the audaciousness of it all, and you get hooked. It's trash, but you get intrigued by the handling of the exploitation elements—and the fact that the guy had the guts to do the film in the first place and the guts to play it in a theater or release it to home video without fear of being stoned to death. It's showmanship. You pull the wool over

their eyes—and since people pay their money when they come in, you don't have to worry if they're disappointed. Though it's kind of an unspoken thing, a lot of filmmakers working in this low-budget arena feel exactly that way.

Q: What about your films? Do they promise and then fail to deliver?

BM: All of the films I've made delivered what they promised in the sense that the people who financed them knew exactly what we were going to do, what we were shooting for. As far as the way they're marketed, well, that's a different story. They may be sold in a way that promises something that isn't delivered. By that time, I'm gone; I have nothing to do with how they're marketed, and I've often been disappointed in the fact that the distributors will sometimes market a picture of mine in a way that's totally misleading. The atrocious marketing campaign for *Highway* to Hell is an example of just how absurd the low-budget production/distribution world can be in this regard. The film was delivered to Tom Moore at Reel Movies International for foreign distribution. Since the film had a budget of $12,500 and Tom's a penny-pincher anyway, he was reluctant to spend any more than absolutely necessary to market it. A Swedish distributor owed him a favor, and the Swedish distributor, in turn, was owed a favor by a famous Spanish illustrator named FABA. So, Tom collected his favor by having FABA do an illustration for the film's flyer for free. Since the art was needed in a rush and there was no time to send photos of the actual cast members, Tom had to describe what he wanted over the phone. Through that round-about path, information became muddled and we ended up with a flyer that looks like a promo for a Mexican or Filipino movie. The villain looks nothing like the villain [Benton Jennings] in the film. But at least Tom Moore got his artwork without spending a penny. And the film made more than one hundred thousand dollars in foreign video sales. With *Macon County War*, Fred Olen Ray prepared a flyer with a busty female model posing next to Dan Haggerty, and she's not even in the film! Fred says people don't notice. In any case, it's out of my hands by then.

Q: What's the ultimate exploitation film?

BM: The ultimate exploitation film has yet to be made. The field is constantly evolving. Lately, the John Woo pictures and Asian supernatural stuff like *A Chinese Ghost Story* have been gaining a lot of popularity. I think it will be made because there's a resurgence of interest in low-budget independent filmmaking going on, the likes of which we haven't seen since the early '70s. It's ridiculous to keep making one-hundred-million-dollar-plus pictures. It doesn't make financial sense. It's not conducive to any real artistic vision, so a lot of people are out there doing things on very small budgets—and this time exploitation is included as a bona fide outlet, it's not looked down upon. You don't have to emulate Truffaut or Godard to be considered avant-garde or credible. You can emulate Herschell Gordon Lewis.

SELECTED FILMOGRAPHY

1977: The Crater Lake Monster; **1985:** Tabloid; **1986:** The Abomination; **1987:** Ozone: Attack of the Redneck Mutants; **1989:** Highway to Hell; **1990:** Macon County War; **1991:** Steele's Law, 3 Days to a Kill, Invasion of the Space Varmints; **1992:** Fatal Justice, Armed for Action, Blood on the Badge, Mardi Gras for the Devil; **1993:** Angry Blue Planet, Striking Point; **1994:** Children of Dracula: Interviews with Real Vampires. **1995:** The Fearmakers (TV series), Cyberstalker, Take Down, Timechasers.

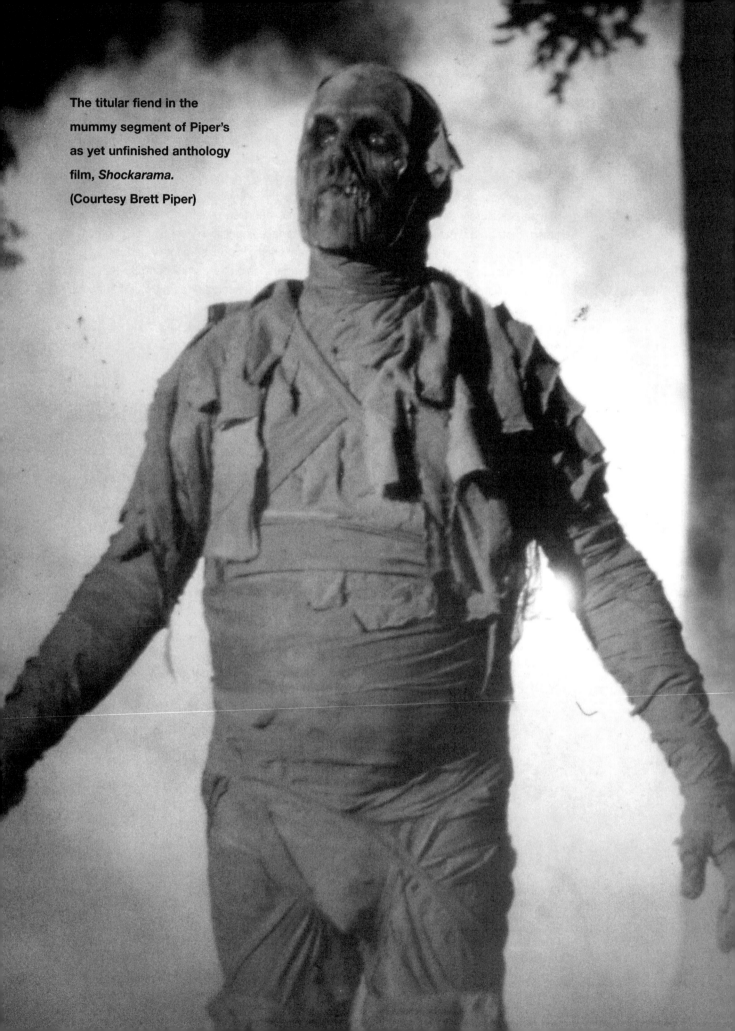

The titular fiend in the
mummy segment of Piper's
as yet unfinished anthology
film, *Shockarama.*
(Courtesy Brett Piper)

Brett Piper

BY BRUCE G. HALLENBECK

A cross between Raymond Chandler and George A. Romero, *Dying Day* (1989) recounts the film-noirish story of a man on the run from zombies and their evil master. In *Dark Fortress* (1990), a teenage cave girl battles for survival against all manner of prehistoric beasts in a burned-out, postapocalyptic world of the future. And in *The Return of Captain Sinbad* (1993), the titular Arabian Nights hero encounters two-headed giants and monstrous flying reptiles in his pursuit of a precious diamond secreted on a remote, forbidding isle.

If you've never heard of any of these films, you needn't feel ignorant nor uninformed. *Dying Day* was picked up for distribution by schlockmeister Sam Sherman's Independent-International Pictures, new scenes were added, and was released under the title *Raiders of the Living Dead.* The infamous Troma Team acquired *Dark Fortress*, tacked on a typical "Tromaville" prologue, and issued it as *A Nymphoid Barbarian in Dinosaur Hell*. And *Sinbad*, a forty-minute children's film narrated by Roddy McDowell, has yet to find a distributor under any title.

In addition to their unfortunate distribution histories, what all these films have in common is that they were written, produced, and directed by Brett Piper, one of the best-kept secrets in the exploitation film business. The closest thing to a one-man band in today's committee-run film world, the multitalented Piper even handles his own special effects; his FX company is called Cheap Tricks, a perfect moniker considering that the budgets of Piper's elaborately mounted films would scarcely provide for the catering on an average Hollywood production.

For those who want to break into the exploitation film business, Brett Piper is one of the most inspirational figures since Fred Olen Ray—but as writer, producer, director, animator, and all-around FX ace, he's even more of a maverick. Piper has lensed all of his features in his home state of New Hampshire with the exception of *They Bite* (1993), which was shot in Florida. And he has no intention of "going Hollywood."

Filmmaking has been in Piper's blood all his life. "I made my first films when I was eleven years old," the quadruple-threat filmmaker recalls. "I bought a Kodak Brownie regular 8-mm camera for fifteen dollars. There's never been any other serious consideration about what I wanted to do with my life since."

Of course, like all struggling filmmakers, Piper has had to undertake a variety of other jobs not only to make ends meet but to support his filmmaking ambitions. He's worked construction, been a newspaper pasteup artist, and has worked on and off at an amusement park for the past nine years doing everything from painting signs to designing buildings. Meanwhile, he's kept busy writing scripts and making animated films in his spare time.

The now forty-year-old Piper made his first feature in 1982. It was called *Mysterious Planet*.

"Not exactly a classic," says Piper of his most famous film, *Dark Fortress,* which was released by Troma as *A Nymphoid Barbarian in Dinosaur Hell* (1990). *(Courtesy Brett Piper)*

Although never released in the United States, it has found distribution on video abroad. "In fact, we had fairly decent distribution on that one overseas," Piper says. "It's had pretty wide exposure in Korea, South Africa, Australia, and Europe. But it was done so cheaply and so crudely that you couldn't really release it domestically."

The film, Piper's answer to *Star Wars* (1977)—albeit on a somewhat smaller scale—came together as a result of his determination to launch his filmmaking career in his own home state and avoid the pitfalls of Hollywood. "I walked into the office of an investment broker here in New Hampshire, threw some sketches down on his desk, and said, 'I want to make a movie and I need to raise money,'" Piper relates. "He turned out to be a kind of frustrated artist type, so we sat down and talked about the project for about an hour, and he got ten of his buddies to put up five hundred dollars apiece to make the film. And that's how I got started."

The actual production cost of *Mysterious Planet* may have been five thousand dollars, but deferred actors' salaries amounted to another five

thousand dollars, Piper says. "But it was still so cheap that I ended up making some money on it. Not a lot, but everybody ended up making something. Even the actors were all paid off." The film was shot silent in 16 mm. "We postdubbed all the audio on my brother's cassette recorder! It's really a horrendous movie," Piper says. "Everybody has a skeleton in the closet. Mine's out there walking around."

Despite the film's virtually nonexistent budget, it boasts some elaborate and convincing special effects that are a tribute to Piper's resourcefulness and ingenuity. "They're not as good as some of the stuff in my later films," he admits, "but we were able to pull them off because we did 'em ourselves. It's all labor, and you're not charging anything to the production."

If you ask Piper what he has against Hollywood, his response is quick and forthright: "Have you ever *been* to Hollywood? Have you ever *talked* to the people out there? That should answer your question. Hollywood people have absolutely no use for a person like me, who makes movies for under a hundred thousand dollars. They really don't. The other thing is, most of what goes on in Hollywood isn't about making movies anyway. It's about meeting people and getting your name in the paper and being famous and making a lot of money—which is not a bad thing in itself, but the actual making of the movie, I don't think, is a particular concern out there."

Although Piper would eventually like to achieve a position where he can finance his movies for "a quarter to a half million dollars," he claims no aspirations beyond that point. "It's not necessary," he says. "The important thing is to get the films *made*, no matter what it takes.

"My second film, *Dying Day*, was made before *Mysterious Planet* had earned back a dime. I went to the same people and said, 'Look, we're still talking nickels and dimes here. You guys haven't really lost any money, and I don't think I had a fair shot—not with five thousand dollars.' And they said, 'Okay.'" And so *Dying Day* was backed to the princely tune of $17,500. "I sat down and wrote scripts for six movies in about a week," he says. "The fastest one was a werewolf movie that I still kind of like. I wrote it in one night. The idea was to try and raise money for the package of all

six. I figured I'd go out and raise a couple hundred thousand dollars and I'd make all six movies, and have a package to sell instead of just one movie at a time.

"It didn't work out that way. *Dying Day* was part of the package and it was the only one that got made. The idea was that these were going to be basic genre films, almost like a generic brand, like in a white box on the video shelf. One box would say *Werewolf* on it. Another would say *Vampire*, another *Sea Monster*, and another *Zombie*—that's what *Dying Day* was, my generic zombie movie. The plot concerns a vendetta, a family curse. It turns out that members of this guy's family are all being bumped off by zombies because of something that took place a hundred years ago between his ancestor and somebody else."

When the film was completed, Piper sent a copy of it to Sam Sherman, the "mini-mogul" behind Independent-International Pictures, who picked it up for distribution for thirty-five thousand dollars, putting the production immediately in the black.

"The problem," Piper laments, "was that Sherman kept 'improving' the film for me until it turned into *Raiders of the Living Dead* and became a total piece of garbage. He invested another hundred thousand dollars in it and basically made another movie, using my original as if it were stock footage. He'd bring his story up to a graveyard scene and then cut to the

Low budget or not, *Battle for the Lost Planet* (1987) contains some of Piper's most impressive special effects and model work. *(Courtesy Brett Piper)*

BRETT PIPER

Mutant War (1988), starring legendary Hollywood B movie tough guy Cameron Mitchell, followed almost immediately. "Mitchell doesn't even remember it!" Piper laughs. "He just couldn't care less. It was actually a sequel to *Battle for the Lost Planet*, with more aliens and mutants. I wrote it in a weekend."

one from my movie. And then he'd bring his stuff up to a scene of a guy fighting off zombies and cut in a shot from my film of zombies being blown up. That's why we share credit on the film as director in the version that went into release. What amuses me—and I say this in all objectivity—is that his hundred-thousand-dollar movie isn't really up to the standard of my $17,500 movie. My sister called me up after seeing *Raiders of the Living Dead* on the USA cable network and said, "'You showed me that a couple of years ago, didn't you?' And I said, 'Yeah.' And she said, 'But didn't the film you made have a plot?'"

Although *Dying Day* was actually filmed in 1983, it wasn't released until 1989. During that time, however, Piper had turned out several other projects. *Battle for the Lost Planet*, filmed in 1987, was another ultra-low-budget sci-fi film, which, like *Mysterious Planet*, features some very imaginative special effects and model work. The film's accomplished animation and matte paintings make it look far more expensive than it actually is. Piper sold it for overseas distribution shortly after completing it for the stratospheric sum of sixty thousand dollars, making it his most successful film up to that time.

Mutant War also marked Piper's debut in 35 mm. "Never again," he remarks of the experience. "Thirty-five is awkward as hell, and if you're not doing a movie intended for release to theaters, you don't need the extra trouble, not to mention the extra expense," he says. "That whole film was a grinding experience. The guy handling the business end of things was a complete screwup. I kept waiting for a contract and some money in the bank to start shooting, but they never came. By the time winter rolled around we had to make a decision whether to shoot or not to shoot, so I started shooting it with money out of my own pocket. It was hand to mouth every day. It got so cold, the camera froze. I ended up never being paid for that one."

Piper followed up with *Dying Day* and then *Dark Fortress*, which would mutate into what has become Piper's "most famous" film, *A Nymphoid Barbarian in Dinosaur Hell*. Shot in New Hampshire as well, with some location footage shot in neighboring Massachusetts, the film was made for fifty thousand dollars, much of that cost covered by one of the actors who'd been in Piper's *Mutant War*.

"Anything that's wrong about *Nymphoid Barbarian* is totally my fault," the self-critical Piper

Piper's seagoing monster flick
They Bite (1993) may soon eclipse
Nymphoid Barbarian as his best-
known work. *(Courtesy Brett Piper)*

Piper's yet-to-be-released children's film, *The Return of Captain Sinbad,* is far and away his most professional-looking venture into model animation. *(Courtesy Brett Piper)*

admits. "I've got no one else to blame. The shoot went very smoothly. We hired local people from community theater and basically took an entire summer to make the film. We'd shoot for two days, knock off and regroup, then shoot for two more days. There were really no problems at all—except that I wasn't up to the job. I spread myself a little too thin.

"As for Troma's acquiring the picture, retitling it, and adding a short prologue, that was fine," he says. "It wasn't like it was a classic movie and they ruined it. If anything, it's no worse a movie now that it ever was."

While *Nymphoid Barbarian* may not be a classic, it was bolstered by the best effects work Piper

had yet pulled off. "Considering what the film cost—which was about fifty thousand dollars—I really shouldn't feel that embarrassed by it. But the sound mix was not good, and the answer print was below par, and those two things can just clobber you. But the effects *are* good, although I'm working on a dinosaur project right now in which the effects are far better. The basic trouble with that film was that I did the writing, directing, producing, the photography, and the special effects. I simply took on too much for my own good."

Piper's most recent feature, *They Bite,* may soon eclipse *Nymphoid Barbarian* as his best known work. A takeoff of such grade B monster-from-the-deep classics as *Horror of Party Beach* (1964) and *Humanoids from the Deep* (1980), it's Piper's best-written, most entertaining, and slickest live-action film to date. And some of the film's special effects, particularly in the finale where a flying saucer emerges from the sea, are first-rate given the film's budget of $140,000, which, while astronomical for Piper, is hardly *Jurassic Park*–sized. (He has also completed a mummy tale for a proposed anthology tentatively titled *Shockarama*, featuring Christina Veronica and Ron Jeremy, two veterans of the cast of *They Bite*.)

If *They Bite* is Piper's most accomplished live-action film, his yet-to-be-released children's film, *The Return of Captain Sinbad,* is far and away his most professional-looking venture into model animation. Chock-full of visual references to to such classics of the genre as *King Kong* (1933), *The 7th Voyage of Sinbad* (1958), and *Jack the Giant Killer* (1962), the film is every bit as charming as those films, and its animation every bit as slick as one of Rankin-Bass's animated puppet films for television (as in 1964's *Rudolph the Red-Nosed Reindeer*). Piper himself classifies the film as "Rankin and Bass meet Ray Harryhausen," and terms it "the one film I'm actually happy with."

"It took over a year to make," he says. "Roddy McDowell was my number-one choice to narrate, and I figured, what the hell, I might as well just call him and ask. I got his address out of *Who's Who* and sent him a synopsis and some stills of the puppets. He must have called me back as soon as

For Troma's Class of *Nuke 'Em High Part III* (1994), Piper created this flying piranha/baby and other amazing creatures. (Courtesy Brett Piper)

he got the material. We talked a little bit, we worked it all out—and that's how Roddy McDowell came to narrate it!"

As far as future projects are concerned, Piper says he's entertaining at least three possibilities. "One is finishing my anthology film, *Shockarama*," he remarks. "I've got another movie that I wrote a couple of years ago called *Spaceman*, which is a comedy. It could be done dirt cheap for about sixty or seventy thousand dollars; if I can raise the money, I definitely plan to make that one. And I've got another dinosaur movie in mind, but that would cost at least a half million to do properly, so we'll have to wait and see."

In addition, Piper has also found time to do FX work for a number of Troma releases, including *Class of Nuke 'Em High Part III* and *Psycho-Backo*, the heartwarming tale of a backhoe operator who merges with his machine and goes on a psychokinetic killing spree.

Only at Troma . . .

SELECTED FILMOGRAPHY

1982: Mysterious Planet; **1987:** Battle for the Lost Planet; **1988:** Mutant War; **1989:** Raiders of the Living Dead (a.k.a. Dying Day); **1990:** A Nymphoid Barbarian in Dinosaur Hell (a.k.a. Dark Fortress); **1993:** They Bite, The Return of Captain Sinbad.

Cast of Characters

ERIC J. CAIDIN is the owner and operator of the Hollywood Book and Poster Company, one of the most popular outlets for movie and TV memorabilia on the West Coast. With partner Johnny Legend, Eric has also been involved in arranging retrospectives of the work of such varied cult figures in sleaze merchantry as Herschell Gordon Lewis and Ted V. Mikels at horror/sci-fi conventions and grindhouses throughout the United States. In addition, he has proudly made appearances in several low-budget sleazefests himself, notably Gary Levinson's *Hellroller*, *The Aftermath*, and *Rock 'n' Roll Wrestling*.

WALTER L. GAY is a lifelong horror enthusiast. His main fields of interest are British horror films, European terror and "trash" cinema, and domestic drive-in and grindhouse horrors of days gone by. Walt's reviews have appeared in Chas. Balun's *Deep Red* magazine, and in John McCarty's *Official Splatter Movie Guide,* Vol. II (St. Martin's Press). He currently publishes a no-frills fanzine called *The Ghastly Ones*.

BRUCE G. HALLENBECK is an author, screenwriter, and filmmaker. An expert on Hammer horror, Bruce has contributed articles and reviews to such genre magazines as *Fangoria*, *Femmes Fatales*, *Little Shoppe of Horrors* (for which he does all the cover stories), *Black Oracle*, and *Monsterland*, as well as the books *The Modern Horror Film* (Citadel Press), *John McCarty's Official Splatter Movie Guide,* Vol. II (St. Martin's Press), and *Dark Zones* (Warner Books). *Monster of the Northwoods*, his study of Sasquatch, upstate New York's version of Bigfoot, was published by North Country Books. Bruce also wrote and directed the feature film *Vampyre* (1991), and *Fangs* (1992), a documentary on the vampire film hosted by Veronica Carlson, which is now in domestic release through Bruce's own label, Pagan Video, and internationally through Meridian Films.

KEN HANKE is a Florida-based freelance writer and independent filmmaker. His books include the critically acclaimed *Ken Russell's Films* (Scarecrow Press), *Charlie Chan at the Movies* (McFarland Publishing), and *A Critical Guide to Horror Film Series* (Garland Publishing). Ken is also a frequent contributor to *Films in Review* and *Filmfax*, and served as a "contributing splatterologist" for *John McCarty's Official Splatter Movie Guide*, Vols. I and II (St. Martin's Press). Ken's most recent film, *A Dream Unbound*, is currently making the film festival circuit, and he is now at work on a new film, as well as two books, *Early Sound Features from Hollywood* (McFarland Publishing) and *Bob Hope: A Bio-Bibliography* (Greenwood Press).

About the Editor

JOHN McCARTY was born in Albany, New York, in 1944. He has been a movie fan since he was five and started making his own films in his early teens. After graduating from high school in 1962, he attended Boston University, where he majored in film and began writing seriously on the subject. Following a stint in the Peace Corps, where he worked in educational television in Bogotá, Colombia, John returned to the States and pursued a career as a broadcaster and advertising copywriter. His affection for the horror film genre (and concern with what was happening to it) led to the writing of *Splatter Movies: Breaking the Last Taboo of the Screen* (St. Martin's Press). It has become a cult classic. He has written more than a dozen books on films and filmmakers in and out of the horror genre, including: *John McCarty's Official Splatter Movie Guide,* Vols. I and II, *Thrillers: Seven Decades of Classic Film Suspense* (Citadel Press), and *Hollywood Gangland: The Movies' Love Affair with the Mob* (St. Martin's Press). He lives in upstate New York with his wife, Cheryl, four crazy cats, and a neurotic dog.

Index

Page numbers of illustrations are in italics. Titles of films are in italics.